THE BOLSHEVIKS AND

THE BOLSHEVIKS AND THE OCTOBER REVOLUTION

Minutes of the Central Committee
of the Russian Social-Democratic Labour Party
(bolsheviks)
August 1917–February 1918

Translated from the Russian by
Ann Bone

Pluto  Press

English translation
first published 1974 by Pluto Press Limited
Unit 10 . Spencer Court . 7 Chalcot Road . London NW1 8LH

Copyright © Pluto Press 1974

ISBN 0 902818 54 6 paperback
ISBN 0 902818 55 4 hardback

Printed by the Compton Press Limited,
Compton Chamberlayne . Salisbury . Wiltshire

Cover photograph David King Collection

Designed by Richard Hollis, GTR

Contents

Part Two:
The CC fighting for the success of the October
armed rising and to consolidate
Soviet power

Part Three:
The CC during the struggle to withdraw from the imperialist war and the conclusion of the Brest peace

Publisher's Introduction

These minutes span the period from August 1917, when the Bolsheviks began preparing for insurrection, to their decision the following February to accept the 'peace' imposed by Imperial Germany. The period includes the October revolution and the first crises of the Soviet regime.

The minutes are working documents. They were meant to remind the Central Committee of their decisions and of the main reasons for making them. They were written down hurriedly, often in pencil, on scraps of paper; occasionally they were illegible. They were never meant to present a balanced assessment of current events. Nor were they meant for people other than the participants themselves. Posterity was about to inherit a new society, not a scrapbook.

The minutes present therefore a very distorted and indistinct picture of the upheavals wrenching Russian society at the time. They obscure even the workings of the Central Committee itself. But where they do throw light, that light is amazingly direct and intense.

The minutes show the Central Committee deeply split on almost every major issue of the day : on the need for insurrection, on the retention of sole power, on the need to retreat before superior force. They show an even deeper division between the revolutionaries on the Central Committee, impatient to dare, terrified in case they miss the rare opportunity to change the pace of history, and the routinists who rev hard but in the old gear. At no time do the minutes present a picture of monolithism in the Central Committee.

*   *   *

The minutes are translated from the second Russian edition, prepared by the Institute of Marxism-Leninism, and published in Moscow in 1958. They are accompanied by the notes to that edition and explanatory documents selected by the Institute.

While the Institute's additions provide a useful historical

context for the minutes, they constitute an independent and unjustified source of distortion. Some of the notes are simply untrue (as can be seen from this edition's comment on note 198, p. 311). More often they contain a grain of truth, but so submerged under sophistry, false interpretation and innuendo as to make it inaccessible to any but the most expert reader.

The distortions introduced by the Institute are of two kinds. One attempts to build Lenin's stature at the cost of diminishing all his comrades', and Trotsky's in particular. This is done explicitly in the notes and, more subtly, by including many of Lenin's letters and speeches of the time as supporting documents, while excluding all but the most damaging documents written by other members of the Central Committee.

The second distortion inflicted on the Russian edition is the impression that conflict, deeply-felt disagreements and intense personal animosities were aberrations amongst the Bolshevik leaders, not the stuff of normal existence.

We have tried to correct the worst deceptions practised in the second Russian edition by adding notes specially prepared for this edition by Tony Cliff. These are easily distinguished from the Institute's notes, which are translated without amendment.

For the most part, the layout of the minutes in the Russian edition has been followed ; elsewhere, minor changes of presentation have been made for the sake of clarity.

Translator's Note and Glossary

The minutes were written in haste and much use was made of initials and abbreviations. Apart from a few shorter titles or organisations which I have written out in full for the translation (e.g. MK : Moscow Committee), I have followed the original, giving the expanded form and a translation in the glossary below.

Where an English version of Russian names, words or initials is already familiar (e.g. CC, Trotsky, Zinoviev), it has been used. Otherwise, the Russian is transliterated strictly.

Black Hundreds
	The extreme monarchist and nationalist 'Union of the Russian People'.
CC	Central Committee
Duma	The State Duma was the Russian parliament granted by the Tsars. City dumas were elective municipal councils.
IML	Institute of Marxism-Leninism under the CC
Junkers	Officer cadets in the military schools
Kadets	Constitutional Democrats (KDs)
Kulak	A rich peasant
Muzhik	*The* Russian peasant
Orgburo	Organisational Bureau of the CC
Peter	St. Petersburg or Petrograd, later Leningrad
Pood	36lb in weight
Rada	Ukrainian parliament
RKP (b)	*Rossiiskaia kommunisticheskaia partiia (bol'shevikov)* Russian Communist Party (bolsheviks)
RSDLP (b)	Russian Social-Democratic Labour Party (bolsheviks)
Seim	Polish parliament
Sovnarkom	*Sovet narodnykh komissarov* Council of People's Commissars
SRs	Socialist-Revolutionaries
TsIK	*Tsentral'nyi ispolnitel'nyi komitet* Central Executive Committee (of the Soviets)

Vikzhel'	*Vserossiiskii ispolnitel'nyi komitet zheleznodoro-zhnogo soiuza* All-Russian Executive Committee of the Railway Union
VKP (b)	*Vsesoiuznaia kommunisticheskaia partiia (bol'-shevikov)* All-Union Communist Party (bolsheviks)
Voenka	*Tsentral'nyi biuro voennykh organizatsii pri TsK RSDRP(b)* Central Bureau of the Military Organisations under the CC RSDLP(b)
Volost	Township
VTsIK	*Vserossiiskii tsentral'nyi ispolnitel'nyi komitet* All-Russian Central Executive Committee (of the Soviets)
Zemstvo	Local government assembly

The dates in the minutes observe the Julian calendar while it was in force in Russia; dates in square brackets give the equivalent date on the Western calendar, 13 days on, which the Russians themselves adopted in February 1918.

Apart from Tony Cliff's supplementary notes, a new introduction and an amended index, nothing has been added to or taken away from the Russian edition of 1958. Not having access to the original manuscripts, I have preserved what might in fact be errors on the part of the Russian editors and printers.

The materials on which the book is based are first-hand notes taken at meetings between October 10 [23] 1917 and February 24 1918 by one of the Central Committee members (*f.*17, *op.*1, *ed. khr.*33-43; 403-412) and the CC secretariat's minute book with fair copies of minutes, often transcribed by E.D.Stasova, for the time between August 4 [17] 1917 and February 24 1918 (*f.*17, *op.*1, *ed.khr.*59). The references given by the Russian editors to the Central Party Archives in the Institute of Marxism-Leninism have been transliterated directly.

Other Russian references only transliterated in the text are :

KPSS v rezoliutsiiakh i resheniiakh s'ezdov, konferentsii i plenumov TsK 'The Communist Party of the Soviet Union in resolutions and decisions of congresses, conferences and CC plenums' (Moscow 1954).

Listovki petrogradskikh bol'shevikov. 1917-1920. 'Leaflets by the Petrograd Bolsheviks. 1917-1920' (1957)

Oktiabr'skoe vooruzhennoe vosstanie v Petrograde 'The October armed insurrection in Petrograd' (Moscow 1957)

Perepiska sekretariata TsK RSDRP(b) s mestnymi partiinymi organizatsiiami 'Correspondence of the secretariat of the CC RSDLP(b) with local party organisations' (Moscow 1957)

Pervyi legal'nyi Peterburgskii komitet bol'shevikov v 1917 godu 'The first legal Petersburg Committee of Bolsheviks in 1917' (1927)

Protokoly zasedanii VTsIK Sovetov rabochikh, soldatskikh, krest-'ianskikh i kazach'ikh deputatov 11 sozyva 'Minutes of the sessions of the All-Russian Central Executive Committee of the Soviets of Workers', Soldiers', Peasants' and Cossack Deputies of the Second Convocation' (Moscow 1918)

Sochineniia 'Collected Works'
The extracts from Lenin's collected works, newly translated for this edition, are from the fourth Russian edition, which is available in English with the same volume numbers.
The Russian edition of Stalin's collected works up to 1934 is also available in an English translation.
Engels' 'Revolution and Counter-revolution in Germany' is to be found in the standard two-volume *Selected Works* of Marx and Engels, prepared by the Institute of Marxism-Leninism, Moscow.

These titles of newspapers and journals appear in transliterated Russian in the text because this is the custom elsewhere and makes cross-reference easier and because many titles are so similar that translation could lead to confusion :

Birzhevye vedomosti	Market Gazette
Gorod i zemstvo	Town and Zemstvo
Izvestiia TsIK i	Proceedings of the Central Executive
Petrogradskogo Soveta	Committee and the Petrograd Soviet
Kommunist	Communist
Krasnaia gazeta	Red Newspaper
Leningradskaia pravda	Leningrad Truth
Molot	Hammer
Nash vek	Our Times

Nashe slovo	Our Word
Novaia zhizn'	New Life
Petrogradskaia pravda	Petrograd Truth
Pravda	Truth
Priboi	The Tide
Proletarii	Proletarian
Proletarskoe delo	Proletarian Cause
Proletarskaia revoliutsiia	Proletarian Revolution
Prosveshchenie	Enlightenment
Rabochii	Worker
Rabochii put'	Worker's Path
Rabochii i soldat	Worker and Soldier
Rabotnitsa	Woman Worker
Rech'	Speech
Sbornik sotsial-demokrata	Collection for the Social Democrat
Soldat	Soldier
Soldatskaia pravda	Soldiers' Truth
Sotsial-demokrat	Social Democrat
Vpered	Forward

PART ONE
The Central Committee during the preparation for the armed rising

Minutes No.1
Session of the CC plenum
August 4 [17] 1917

Present :
Stalin, Smilga, Bukharin, Dzerzhinsky, Rykov, Ioffe, Dzhaparidze [Alesha], Bubnov, Sokolnikov, Oppokov [Lomov], Muranov, Sverdlov, Sergeev [Artem], Miliutin, Nogin, Stasova, Kiselev.

Agenda :
1. General plan of the CC's work with reference to the report of the previous CC.
2. Its formation.
3. Editorial board and literature.
4. Stockholm Conference.
5. Conference on Defence.
6. Moscow Conference[1].

At the beginning of the session, the members of the previous (pre-Congress) CC[2] made a report on its work.

Comrade N[ogin] announced that there were rumours that K[amenev] was involved in provocation and that the *TsIK* knew of these rumours.

The CC decided to instruct comrade N[ogin] to ask the *TsIK* what they had done to investigate the rumours about K[amenev] since K[amenev] is a member of the *TsIK*. When the CC has received a reply, it will make up its mind[3].

After this, the list of CC members elected at the Congress was announced, and also the candidates and the procedure for admitting them to membership[4].

Those present recognised that they now constituted the CC and set to work.

The question of an Inner Committee was raised next and it was approved unanimously.

It was proposed that it should consist of either 11 or 9 people. 9 voted for the first proposal, 5 for the second.

It is decided that the Inner CC is to consist of 11 people[5].

It is resolved that the Inner Committee should organise its work on the principle of a strict division of functions (Stalin's suggestion).

The Inner Committee and the regions are to keep in very close contact by reporting in writing to each other at regular intervals.

The CC plenum meets once a month.

All members present in St. Petersburg take part in sessions with the right to vote.

A decision is made to organise a group of travelling agents to carry on particular campaigns.

Setting up this group is referred to the Inner Committee.

CC members are allotted to regions by decision of the CC (passed unanimously).

The next question was that of the newspaper and journal.

It is resolved unanimously that *Rabochii i soldat* is to be the CC organ[6].

It is decided that the editorial board is to consist of three members plus a representative of the Military Organisation[7] plus a representative of the Petersburg Committee.

It is resolved that for the time being neither the Petersburg Committee nor the Military Organisation will have a separate organ.

Comrade B.* proposes that the editorial board should follow the CC line *unswervingly* (passed unanimously).

It is decided that *Vpered*[8] will remain as the weekly Party organ and the Inner Committee is charged with opening talks with the *Vpered* group on this subject.

It is decided that all funds and expenses for *Rabochii i soldat* are to be concentrated in the CC.

Rabotnitsa[9] remains the central women's journal.

It is decided that the 'press office' is to be disbanded but the cuttings office kept – its relationship with the central organ is to be settled by the Inner Committee.

A collegium of contributors is organised under the editorial board. Elected to the editorial board :

> Ko – 15 [votes]
> Kov – 12 [votes]
> Min – 12 [votes][10]

---

* Like this in the text of the minute notes. Bukharin or Bubnov.

In the event of his release, T[rotsky] will go on the editorial board (against – 11, for – 10).

Adding to the editorial board and replacing members if comrades leave is delegated to the Inner Committee.

The question of the attitude to take to the Stockholm Conference is not discussed since the April Conference passed a resolution which was confirmed by the Congress[11].

The subject is raised of the CC's attitude to the Conference on Defence[12].

After a debate the following proposals are put to the vote :

1. Party groups not to go to the Conference but to send a reasoned refusal (rejected).

2. The groups who are invited to go to the Conference and organise themselves there (4 in favour).

3. Party groups to do everything they can to dissuade people from going but if non-Party groups go all the same, then the Bolsheviks get themselves organised at the Conference and stage a walk-out (for – 8, against – 6).

4. The CC instructs its members in Moscow to organise all the Bolsheviks so that they can make a demonstration of walking out (since it is assumed that the Defence Conference will be in Moscow).

In conclusion, comrade Bukharin is commissioned to write a manifesto for the Party in accordance with the Congress decision that the CC should do this[13].

Minutes No.2
Session of the CC plenum
August 5 [18] 1917

Present :
Oppokov [Lomov], Dzerzhinsky, Smilga, Sokolnikov, Stalin, Sergeev [Artem], Muranov, Ioffe, Dzhaparidze [Alesha], Bukharin, Nogin, Miliutin, Bubnov, Sverdlov, Kiselev, Rykov, Stasova.

Agenda :
1. Inner Committee.
2. Manifesto.

3.   Moscow Conference.
4.   Deployment of manpower.
5.   Campaign on denunciation.
6.   Campaign on the Constituent Assembly.
7.   Implementation of Congress decisions.
8.   Work in the Petersburg Committee.
9.   Leave.

Comrade N[ogin] reports that Gots has answered officially about K[amenev], that they have elected a commission to investigate the rumours and that the commission has so far found nothing.

The CC resolves to demand the inclusion of a CC member in the commission of inquiry and elects comrade D[zhaparidze – Alesha].

It also resolves to tell K[amenev] about all this and to suggest to him that he should stop work temporarily.

An Inner Committee is elected :

Stalin, Sokolnikov, Dzerzhinsky, Miliutin, Uritsky, Ioffe, Sverdlov, Muranov, Bubnov, Stasova, Shaumian (and until the latter's arrival, Smilga).

Functions are allocated by regions.

For the Moscow region – four CC members (Nogin, Oppokov [Lomov], Bukharin, Rykov).

For the Urals – one (Krestinsky. It is resolved to send him a letter telling him about his election and the decision to entrust the region to him.)

For the Donets basin – one : Sergeev [Artem].

For the Caucasus – two in turn : Dzhaparidze [Alesha] and Shaumian.

For Finland – one : Smilga.

The Inner Committee is charged with servicing and organising the remaining regions (Volga, South, North-West, Siberia).[14]

The manifesto[15]. Not approved; referred back for revision.

The Moscow Conference.

After a discussion, a vote is taken :

1.   To boycott – 4 in favour.
2.   Not to appeal for a boycott – 7 in favour.
3.   To go in and organise a group which would draw up a declaration and then walk out when the Conference has just opened

and they have chosen a praesidium (before the Conference starts work)[16] – Unanimous.

For the purposes of the campaign, the CC decides to issue :

1.   A leaflet*[17].
2.   A resolution[18].
3.   To publish a series of articles in *Rabochii i soldat*[19].

Where organisations are concerned, action in the form of meetings, demonstrations and strikes is considered necessary – each organisation decides the mode of action according to local conditions[20].

Comrade D[zhaparidze] raised the question of supporting the Moslem organisation[21]. It is resolved that the CC promise to give 5000 roubles to support this organisation but because of the poor state of its finances at the moment, it is assigning 1000 roubles straight away and the rest when it can.

It is decided – taking account of the wishes of the Kazan organisation, methods of communication and so on – to attach the Kazan organisation to the Moscow region[22].

Maintenance for CC members in St. Petersburg is set at 500 roubles for those with a family and 400 roubles for those without; extra maintenance for extra functions is not allowed; where possible, maintenance is received from local organisations; shortage of funds will be made up by the CC.

Document 1
Declaration by the Bolshevik members of the delegation at the Moscow Conference

Deadly danger threatens the cause of the revolution : the landowners and bourgeois parties are getting ready for bloody reprisals against the workers, soldiers and poor peasants, they are planning to restore unlimited oppression and coercion over the masses of the people, to take back power over them completely.

At this hour, this government, which calls itself a government for the 'preservation of the revolution' fails to act against counter-revolution, against parties which want the landowner-bourgeois yoke

*   See p.16.

restored and demand the continuation of the predatory war. On the contrary, it summons hardened counter-revolutionaries to a state conference in Moscow, ensures an overwhelming majority for them there and intends to come to a final agreement with them and to rely on them openly in its future work. The Provisional Government publicly recognises branded enemies of the people as saviours of the country, declares the gravediggers of the revolution to be its live forces. For the Provisional Government, this is the culmination of its whole policy, aimed at struggle with the workers, whose newspapers and organisations it crushes, at struggle with the soldiers, to whom it made a present of the restoration of the death penalty, at struggle with the peasants, to whom it does not give land.

The Provisional Government itself has become a tool of the counter-revolution and international reaction. It called the Moscow Conference so that it could draw new strength here for a fresh campaign against everything the revolution has gained.

Encouraged by this friendly policy, the enemies of the people — landowners, bankers, factory-owners — have rallied round the Kadet Party to save their war profits, estates and capital. For the counter-revolutionary executioners, the Moscow Conference is a very convenient opportunity to come to an understanding, a very convenient cloak for organising a Russia-wide counter-revolutionary conspiracy. The Kadets' preliminary conference has already set up a permanent political centre for the counter-revolution, relying on armed support from the army high command and the reactionary section of the cossacks.

The Moscow Conference is a gross deception and a distortion of the people's will. At the very time when it is being called, the convocation of the Constituent Assembly, which really represents the people, is being postponed yet again for two months thanks to the intrigues of the bourgeoisie, who are implacably following their aim — total sabotage of the Constituent Assembly and its replacement by a body in which it can be assured of a majority.

While it undermines the Constituent Assembly, the bourgeois counter-revolution openly puts up the Moscow Conference in opposition to the Soviets of Workers' and Soldiers' Deputies. With its help, it hopes to deal a decisive blow to these organs, which have been entrusted by the working class with the duty of protecting the interests of the revolution, the duty of fighting for peace, for land, for bread. The Social-Revolutionary and Menshevik parties, however, who are now in a majority in the Central Executive Committee of the Soviets, did not oppose the calling of the Moscow Conference, did not try to fight against this enterprise which is clearly to the advantage of the counter-revolution, and they could not fight for they themselves favour an agreement, favour joint work with the bourgeois-landowner coalition, they themselves were always ready to make concessions, rejected the transfer of all authority to the workers, soldiers and peasants, and proposed that power be shared with the bourgeois counter-revolution.

The Moscow Conference demonstrates to wide strata of the urban and peasant poor that a vigorous struggle is needed against counter-revolution; the working class, dependable guardian and bulwark of the revolution, was the first to protest openly against the Moscow parade of counter-revolutionary forces organised by the Provisional Government.

The general strike held by the Moscow proletariat expresses the thinking and the will of the politically-conscious proletariat of all Russia, which is wise to the game of the counter-revolution. The working class raises its own slogan of proletarian and peasant revolution against the war cry of the mobilised bourgeoisie.

We, members of the revolutionary party of the proletariat, did not come here to enter into negotiations with enemies of the revolution, but to protest on behalf of the workers and the poor peasants against the convocation of a counter-revolutionary assembly, to expose its true nature to the whole country. But they decided to shut us up and the SRs and Mensheviks in the Soviet majority cooperated in this decision. However, we are convinced that our voice and our protest will reach the masses of the people who are rallying round us more and more, round the revolutionary party of the proletariat. On their behalf, we declare: the proletariat will not allow the bourgeois oppressors to triumph.

The proletariat will continue the revolution to the end, get land for the peasants, peace, bread and freedom for the people.

The Russian proletariat and the international proletariat together will put an end to the rule of capital over enslaved mankind.

Bolshevik delegates from the city government
Bolshevik delegates from the trade unions
Bolshevik members of the delegation from the workers' cooperatives
Bolshevik representatives of committees of public organisations
Bolshevik delegates of the union of urban employees
Bolshevik delegates of the army and navy committees
Bolshevik members of the delegation from the *TsIK* of the Soviets not admitted to the Conference

Proletarii No.4, August 30 [17] 1917.

Document 2
Appeal by the CC RSDLP (b) on the State Conference
August 12 [25] 1917

THE MOSCOW CONFERENCE IS TODAY

The counter-revolution is entering a new phase of development. It is going over from destruction and devastation to the consolidation of the positions it has taken. From violence and outrages, it is moving to 'legal channels' and 'constitutional arrangements'.

The revolution can and must be conquered, say the counter-revolutionaries. But this is not enough. Approval is needed for it, too. For this, matters must be arranged so that the 'people' themselves, the 'nation' gives approval and not in Peter or on the front alone but in all Russia. Then the victory will be secure. Then the conquests gained can serve as a basis for the counter-revolution to make new conquests in the future.

But how can this be arranged?

It would have been possible to speed up the convocation of the Constituent Assembly, the only body representative of the whole Russian people, and ask it for approval of the policy of war and destruction, ravages and arrests, massacres and executions.

But the bourgeoisie will not do that. It knows that it will not get either recognition or approval of the counter-revolution's policy from the Constituent Assembly, where the peasants are in the majority.

So it is trying to get (has got already!) the Constituent Assembly postponed. It will very probably postpone it even further so as to manage to block it completely in the end.

But what then is the 'way out'?

The 'way out' is the substitution of the Moscow Conference for the Constituent Assembly.

Assembling a conference of merchants and industrialists, landowners and bankers, members of the Tsarist Duma and Mensheviks and SRs tamed in advance, and declaring this conference a 'national assembly' in order to get approval from it for a policy of imperialism and counter-revolution and to transfer the onus of the war on to the shoulders of the workers and peasants – this is the 'way out' for the counter-revolution.

The counter-revolution needs its own parliament, its own centre and it is making one.

The counter-revolution needs the vote of confidence of 'public opinion' and it is making it.

This is the essence of it.

In this respect, the counter-revolution is taking the very same path as the revolution. It is learning from the revolution.

The revolution had its parliament, its effective centre and it felt that it was organised.

Now the counter-revolution is trying to create one in the very heart of Russia, in Moscow, using – the irony of fate! – the SRs and Mensheviks.

And this at a time when the revolution's parliament has been reduced to a simple appendage of the bourgeois-imperialist counter-revolution, when war to the death has been declared on the Soviets and committees of the workers, peasants and soldiers!

It is not hard to understand that in these circumstances the Conference called in Moscow for today is bound to be transformed into an organ of the counter-revolution's conspiracy against the workers, who are threatened with lock-outs and unemployment, against the peasants, to whom they 'do not give' land, against the soldiers, who are deprived of the freedom achieved in the days of the revolution, a conspiracy cloaked in the 'socialist phrases' of the SRs and Mensheviks who support this Conference.

For this reason, it is the task of the vanguard workers to:

1. Tear the mask of popular representation from the Conference, revealing its counter-revolutionary anti-popular nature.

2. Expose the Mensheviks and SRs who are cloaking this Conference in the flag of 'preservation of the revolution' and leading the masses into deception.

3. Organise mass meetings to protest against this counter-revolutionary machination of those who 'preserve' . . . the gains of the landowners and capitalists.

Comrades! Call meetings and pass resolutions protesting against the Moscow Conference!

Ally yourselves with the Putilov workers and organise collections today in aid of the persecuted and victimised Party press as a symbol of protest against the 'conference'.

Do not be tempted to provocation and do not demonstrate in the streets today!

Central Committee of the RSDLP

Newspaper *Proletarskoe delo* (Kronstadt)
No.26, August 25 [12] 1917.

Minutes No.3
Session of the Inner Committee [of the CC]
August 6 [19] 1917

Present :
Stalin, Smilga, Dzerzhinsky, Sokolnikov, Muranov, Miliutin, Sverdlov, Stasova, Uritsky.

Agenda[23] :
1. Petersburg Committee.
2. Conference of Factory Committees.
3. Insurance Conference.
4. Conference on Defence.
5. Moscow Conference.
6. The prisoners.
8. The allocation of functions.
9. Helsingfors.

It is resolved that the Petersburg Committee should be informed about our attitude to the Moscow Conference since the Committee passed a resolution at its session the previous day boycotting the Conference in the belief that it was following the CC line[24].

Miliutin is assigned to the Conference of Factory Committees which opens on August 7[25] to direct all the work and deliver the report on the current situation.

Smilga is delegated to the Insurance Conference (opening 10.8)[26].

Bearing in mind that the Conference on Defence will be held in St. Petersburg, comrade Glebov [Avilov] (Central Bureau of Trade Unions) is charged with organising a campaign following the line laid down by the CC and Sverdlov is to have talks with him.

Next there is a discussion on the division of functions between Inner Committee members.

The editorial board has already been set up.[27]

The question of the journal[28].

The financial side is entrusted to comrade Savel'ev, and the editorial board is to set up the collegium.

Uritsky and Smilga are delegated to the Petersburg Committee (until the arrival of Bubnov). A telegram is being sent to the latter to come immediately.

The organisational side of the work is entrusted to the Secretariat, to consist of five CC members.

Muranov is unanimously elected treasurer.

Members of the secretariat are : Dzerzhinsky, Ioffe, Sverdlov, Muranov, Stasova.

A group is formed under the CC to take charge of work in the trade union movement, and the CC is to invite one member from the movement with a consultative vote. Sverdlov is to organise the group[29].

Several members of the CC (3) are charged with organising an electoral commission for the Constituent Assembly. Representatives from the Bolshevik group in the *TsIK,* the trade unions and representatives from the national sections of our Party should be included in its membership.

Uritsky, Sokolnikov and Stalin[30] are elected to this commission from the CC.

Stalin is to have talks with Gots about the commission on the K[amenev] affair.

A resolution is passed on the Moscow Conference.

It is decided to transfer all management business to the Orgburo, which will decide which of its comrades is to be in charge of this work (Ioffe is selected).

About Helsingfors – it is decided to ask Smilga to exert every effort to make a journey to Helsingfors possible. When he receives a permit from headquarters – he must go[31].

The remaining business was carried over to the next meeting.

Document
Resolution by the CC RSDLP(b) on the Moscow Conference of August 12
August 6 [19] 1917

At this moment, state power in Russia is moving wholly into the control of the counter-revolutionary imperialist bourgeoisie, with the obvious support of the petty-bourgeois SR and Menshevik Parties. A policy aimed at inflaming and prolonging the war, the refusal to give land to the peasants, soldiers being deprived of their rights, the restoration of the death penalty, the use of force against Finland and the Ukraine, and finally the fierce attack on the most revolutionary element in the proletariat – the social-democrat internationalists – these are very clear signs that a counter-revolutionary policy is in force. To strengthen its influence and position, the counter-revolutionary bourgeoisie is trying to create a strong all-Russian centre, to gather its forces together to move, fully armed, against the proletariat, against the democracy. This is the purpose the Moscow Conference called for August 12 is intended to serve.

Representatives of institutions belonging to the very state structure which was overthrown by the revolution such as the Tsarist State Duma, a nest of counter-revolution, and representatives of countless organisations of the upper bourgeoisie make up the dominant majority of the Moscow Conference, and its task is to fabricate popular opinion and in this way to deceive the broad masses of the people. Just at the time when a centre is being organised for the counter-revolutionary bourgeoisie through calling the Moscow Conference, the Soviets and soldiers' and peasants' committees are being systematically reduced to the role of simple appendages to the imperialist mechanism. While the Moscow Conference is being convened, the Constituent Assembly is put off for longer and longer. The bourgeoisie is cautiously but steadily moving towards its goal – the sabotage of the Constituent Assembly and its replacement with organs where it is sure of a majority.

It is, therefore, the task of the Moscow Conference to endorse a counter-revolutionary policy, to support the continuation of the imperialist war, to defend the interests of the bourgeoisie and landowners, to lend its authority to the persecution of the revolutionary workers and peasants. This is why the Moscow Conference, which the petty-bourgeois parties – the SRs and Mensheviks – have given cover and support, is in reality a conspiracy against the revolution, against the people.

In view of what has been said, the CC RSDLP suggests to Party organisations that they: 1. reveal the truth about the Conference called in Moscow, a body designed to serve the counter-revolutionary bourgeois conspiracy against the revolution; 2. denounce the counter-revolutionary policy of the SRs and Mensheviks supporting this Conference; 3. organise mass protests by workers, peasants and soldiers against the Conference.

Rabochii i soldat No.14, August 8 1917.

Minutes No.4
Session of the Inner Committee [of the CC]
August 8 [21] 1917

Present :
Bukharin, Ioffe, Smilga, Dzerzhinsky, Miliutin, Sverdlov, Uritsky, Stalin, Stasova, Muranov.

Agenda :
1. Conference on Defence.
2. The journal.
3. Leave.
5. Petersburg Committee.
6. Hunger strike in Kresty.
7. K[amene]v.

First a decision is reached on a Bolshevik declaration to be made at the Conference on Defence.* Sverdlov is charged with implementing the decision.

It is decided that the journal is to be called *Prosveshchenie*. The suggestion that it should be called *Kommunist*[32] received one vote less.

The allocation of departments, the estimates and the list of contributors are approved.

There is a report on *Vpered*. It is transferred completely to the CC. It is decided that the editorial board should consist of the same CC three plus Uritsky and Bezrabotnyi (Manuilsky).

The question of leave of absense.

It is decided to give Stasova leave straight away until 1 September and to put off considering Miliutin's leave until Bubnov arrives.

Uritsky and Smilga report on the work of the Petersburg Committee :

1. The municipal campaign : a list of 60 members has been compiled for the Central City Duma[33]; three appeals (to workers, soldiers and women)[34] have been written ; it is decided that municipal meetings should be arranged in all parts of the town on Sunday the 13th [August];

---

* See p.23.

2.   The Petersburg Committee will draw up its accounts at the first opportunity ; the difficulty is that the material has been seized by the security services[35] ;

3.   Volodarsky has been elected to the editorial board[36].

4.   The Petersburg Committee resolved to set up a joint-stock company to acquire a printing press and intends to publish an organ of its own ;

5.   The Petersburg Committee asks the permission of the CC to investigate the B[agdat'e]v affair[37] ;

6.   The Petersburg Committee is going to be reorganised – a general city conference is being called in the near future[38].

The plan for the municipal campaign is approved by the CC as well as the list of candidates put forward by the Petersburg Committee with the exception of one member, T-v*.

The Petersburg Committee's request regarding the B[agdat'e]v affair is granted but it is added that a parallel investigation of B[agdat'ev]a and S-a* is desirable.

The resolution of the CC (plenum) that *temporarily* only one organ – *Rabochii i soldat* – should come out is confirmed.

It is reported that a hunger strike is planned in Kresty and that Trotsky is against it. A decision is made to find out whether the hunger strike has begun and if it has, to enlist the help of the Petersburg Committee in getting protest resolutions passed in works and factories against the authorities' behaviour towards the detainees (with a corresponding appeal in the newspaper)[39].

If it has not yet begun, however, then the newspaper should print an appeal not to hunger-strike, but a protest campaign should be organised in any case.

It is decided to set up a commission of lawyers to mount the case for the defence at the forthcoming political trials[40].

The K[amene]v affair.

He is suspended from work. It is decided at his request not to investigate his conduct in making the *TsIK* speech[41] until his explanation has been received.

Our attitude to the conference in Stockholm will be clear

---

*   Indecipherable.

from the article which is to appear tomorrow, the 9th, in *Rabochii i soldat*[42].

Attention was drawn during the debate to K[amene]v's behaviour with regard to L[enin] and Z[inoviev] (about non-appearance)[43].

Document
The Bolshevik declaration read out at a session of the Conference on Defence
August 8 [21] 1917

1.   Capitalist governments, trying to justify the predatory war they are waging, consistently describe it to the people everywhere as a just, 'defensive' war. In reality, millions of workers and peasants in every country (both those supporting Germany and those allied with England) are sent to fight so that other people's land can be seized, so that other nations can be oppressed.

2.   Russia's Provisional Government recognised and continues to recognise the secret treaties concluded by the Tsar; the Russian bourgeoisie allied itself with the English, French and American bourgeoisie and it receives millions from these capitalists in exchange for waging a struggle against the revolutionary workers and soldiers. Bound by secret treaties, the Provisional Government has not taken a single definite step towards halting the war but, on the contrary, it is dragging it out in every way it can; on the orders of Anglo-American capital, it sent an unprepared army into the attack to ruin the revolution and now it is trying to put the responsibility for the failure of this military adventure on to the revolutionary social-democrats, who were the only ones to give an open and positive warning of the inevitable consequences of this adventure. The present government of 'preservation of the revolution', which brought back the death penalty, firing squads, the Tsarist secret political police, administrative punishment and so on and is in reality the government of the preservation of the propertied classes from the revolution, firmly took the path of international imperialist reaction and eliminated even the idea of a democratic peace between peoples from its policy.

3.   Now the governments of England, France, Italy and America have come out openly against the Stockholm peace conference even though it is called by governmental, 'ministerial' socialists and not by revolutionary socialists. 'War until final victory' – that is Miliuk-

ov's slogan – 'War without end' has gained undisputed mastery and the programme for peace without annexations has been openly rejected by all the bourgeois governments, whose demands for annexation grow and grow.

4. Because of the destructive tactics of the SR and Menshevik Parties directing the Soviets, in spite of their promise to struggle for peace, the Soviets of Workers' and Soldiers' Deputies positively supported the offensive demanded by the annexationists and did not take definite steps towards peace. Instead of giving all questions of war and peace to the soldiers, workers and peasants to decide, the majority in the Soviets left complete power in the hands of the bourgeoisie who were inflaming the war.

5. By renouncing any power in favour of a counter-revolutionary government with 'unlimited authorisation', the majority in the Soviets gave free rein to the chief promoters of an imperialist policy. It assigned itself the role of a powerless accomplice to the bourgeoisie in the prolongation of a war which is threatening the masses of the people with famine and ruin and which is destroying the work of the revolution. The organisation of assistance in the 'defence of the country' which was undertaken by the Soviet majority does not in the least serve the interests of the country or the interests of the people, but the interests of the bourgeoisie, who are getting rich from the war as never before and get the opportunity to use the working class for their imperialist purposes.

6. Throughout the period of the revolution, the bourgeoisie made every effort to achieve, and with the help of the Provisional Government has achieved, the complete protection of the profits and privileges of property-owners where financial and economic policy is concerned. In these areas, the policy of robbing the workers, plundering the country's resources and preserving the scandalous profits of the capitalists has remained completely intact. And the Provisional Government's latest declaration shows that in the future, too, the protection of the interests of the bourgeoisie in the economic sphere remains a precondition for the Provisional Government's practical policy as a whole.

7. The use of the working class for imperialist ends is expressed in efforts to involve proletarian organisations in the general mechanism of the imperialist state which maintains the war. In these circumstances, even the organisation of production takes on a character of capitalist servitude, labour conscription becomes the enslavement of the worker by the state*, the regulation of production

---

* In the document: *of the state.*

is turned into an auxiliary apparatus for military headquarters. The inevitable result of this situation is the complete absence of rights for the working class, its deprivation of the right to strike, etc. The working class must counter this plan with workers' control over production, regulating it not in the interests of financial capital but in the interests of the working masses and the rural poor, not in the interests of an imperialist war but in the interests of peace, not in the interests of aid for foreign bankers but in the interests of aid to the international proletariat.

8. Only when they have taken power completely into their own hands will the revolutionary workers, peasants and soldiers be able to put an end to the secret annexationist treaties, to break all agreements with native and foreign capitalists, to propose to peoples everywhere that the war be halted by a just peace, only then will they be able to support peoples in their struggle against capitalist oppressors and to organise the effective defence of a country in which the revolutionary proletariat has triumphed against any encroachment by imperialism.

9. On the strength of this, we, revolutionary social-democrats, declare: so long as power remains in the hands of the bourgeoisie, we refuse to give it the means to continue the imperialist war. We refuse to contribute even indirectly to the imperialist policy of the present government of counter-revolutionary dictatorship. We will go on working in solidarity with the international proletariat to establish universal peace among peoples through general proletarian revolution.

CC RSDLP
CC of Polish and Lithuanian Social-Democrats
CC of Latvian Social-Democrats
Bolshevik group in the *TsIK*
Bolshevik group in the Petrograd Soviet of Workers' and Soldiers' Deputies
Bolshevik group in the Moscow Soviet of Workers' Deputies
Bolshevik group in the Moscow Soviet of Soldiers' Deputies
Bolshevik group in the Moscow Regional Bureau [of Soviets] of Workers', Soldiers' and Peasants' Deputies
Bolshevik group in the Moscow City Duma

Rabochii i soldat No.15, August 9 1917

Minutes No.5
Session of the Inner Committee [of the C C]
August 13 [26] 1917

[No list of those present in the original.]

Agenda :
1. Transfer of the printing press.
2. The newspaper *Soldat*.
3. Winding up the affairs of *Rabochii i soldat*.

It is decided that the printing press as well as *Priboi*[44] should be moved into new hands because they might be confiscated. It would be as well to transfer the printing press to the unions. Sverdlov is charged with putting this into effect.

On the newspaper *Soldat*, a decision is passed to rename it *Proletarii* and to transfer it to the C C for conversion into its central organ[45]. This decision is made because there are doubts over whether it is possible to publish *Proletarii* on the *Trud* press, for technical considerations, that is. Stalin is charged with putting this into effect.

On the question of winding up the affairs of *Rabochii i soldat*, a decision is made to require a detailed account of all revenues and expenditures and to transfer the balance to the C C account[46].

Minutes No.6
Session of the Inner Committee [of the C C]
August 14 [27] 1917

[No list of those present in the original.]

Agenda :
Information from Moscow.

Comrade Iurovsky arrived from Moscow and announced that there had been a report at a Moscow Committee meeting about the formation of a Provisional Revolutionary Committee in Moscow consisting of 7 people : 2 Bolsheviks, 2 Mensheviks, 2 SRs and 1 from military headquarters. He reported on the intention to put the plans of the counter-revolutionary military bureau headed by Kornilov, Gruzinov and others[47] into practice, on the possibility that the bureau chiefs might be arrested, on halting the movement of cossacks to Moscow through the railwaymen, etc.

In view of all this, the CC resolved to enter into communication with the SRs and the remains of the *TsIK*[48] for information purposes, pointing out in advance that creating an information bureau does not bind any of its participants to anything.

At the same time, it was decided to send comrade Bubnov to Moscow to get precise information on what has happened and is happening there.

Sverdlov and Dzerzhinsky are assigned to the information bureau.

Minutes No.7
Session of the Inner Committee [of the CC]
August 16 [29 1917]

[No list of those present in the original.]

Agenda :
1. Stockholm Conference.
2. Zimmerwald.
3. Insurance Conference.
4. Military Organisation.
5. *Soldat.*

With regard to the Stockholm Conference, the earlier decision against going there is confirmed. Our attitude continues to be negative. On the *TsIK* plan to organise a campaign of meetings on the subject of the Stockholm Conference – a resolution is to be worked out to serve as a basis for the speeches of our agitators. Stalin, Sokolnikov and Uritsky are charged with composing a resolution[49].

A decision is made not to send a special delegate to the Zimmerwald Conference[50] because it is not technically feasible. It is decided that Radek and Orlovsky [Vorovsky] should be charged with representing the CC, making it strictly mandatory on them to leave Zimmerwald in the event of a majority decision to go to the Stockholm Conference.

A resolution is passed to commission Skrypnik with organising the whole Insurance Conference[51], providing a speaker from the CC to report on the current situation.

Two statements were heard from the Central Bureau of the Military Organisations (the statements were put into the CC archives) : 1. concerning *Soldat* and 2. a protest against Smilga's and Stalin's treatment of the Bureau*.

With regard to the Bureau, a decision is passed that the Military Bureau is the organisation in charge of work among soldiers. In this connection it is resolved that : according to Party rules, no self-contained directing Party organisation can exist in parallel with another Party organisation. This refers both to local organisations and to all-Russian ones. So the All-Russian Bureau of the Military Organisations cannot be an independent political centre either.

It is recognised that the publication of a newspaper for soldiers is desirable. *Soldat* will remain such a newspaper. The CC entrusts the publication of this newspaper to the present editorial board and is including a CC member on it with the right of veto. The editorial board is appointed by the CC. The Military Bureau can make proposals on its membership for CC confirmation. Sverdlov and Dzerzhinsky are assigned to hold talks with the Military Bureau and to establish the right relationship between it and the CC. They are also charged with temporarily keeping an eye on the editing of *Soldat*[52].

Document 1
Statement from the Central Bureau of the Military Organisations to the CC RSDLP(b)

The Central Bureau of the Military Organisations, having considered the CC's decision about the publication of the newspaper, has resolved to bring the following to the notice of the CC: according to our Party rules, the Military Organisation, in the same way as any Party organisation generally, has autonomy in publishing its organ

---

*   See Documents 1 and 2 below.

and no Party body can be deprived of this right. The CC could only close a newspaper in the event of the newspaper in question pursuing a distinctive line of principle and refusing to adhere to the decisions of Party congresses in its articles. In passing the resolution closing the newspaper *Soldat* as an organ of the Military Organisation in the present circumstances without any serious justification, the CC is directly exceeding its powers.

The Central Bureau of the Military Organisations draws the attention of the CC to the fact that the first newspaper to appear after the events of July 3-5 was put out by the Military Organisation after enormous effort and that even though political reality and the interests of agitation among the soldiers required the existence of a special popular newspaper to serve these masses, the Military Organisation gave up its whole apparatus, ready for action, to the CC and submitted to its decision to create one common organ and to include only one member of the Military Organisation on the editorial board of this organ. Now that the newspaper *Rabochii i soldat* has been closed and the CC has created its own new central organ, the Military Organisation has found it necessary and opportune to issue its own newspaper *Soldat*, for during the time that a shared newspaper existed, the Organisation became convinced that a mixed type of newspaper completely fails to serve its purposes and does not provide for the masses among whom the Military Organisation organises propaganda and agitation work.

The Central Bureau of the Military Organisations points out to the CC that the material and technical circumstances cited by the CC in its resolution do not exist to justify such a suppression and that furthermore, the CC declared officially through comrade Stalin that it was only temporarily and for purely technical reasons that the CC plenum decided to limit itself to one newspaper and that at the first opportunity, as soon as the Military Organisation found it necessary (literally Stalin's expression) to publish its own organ, the CC was obliged to provide it with *corresponding* sums of money.

Acting in the spirit of the decision of the CC plenum referred to above, the Central Bureau of the Military Organisations suggests to the CC that it establish close links with the editorial board of the Military Organisation's central organ to avoid possible faults in its work, either by including one of the CC members in its membership or in some other form which the Central Committee finds convenient.

Archives of the IML, *f*.17, *op*.1, *ed. khr.* 18, *ll*.8-9.
Printed for the first time

Document 2
Statement to the CC RSDLP

Members of the Central Bureau of the Military Organisations protest in the strongest possible way against the conduct of CC members Stalin and Smilga at the joint session of these organisations on August 13th.

At the suggestion of members of the Military Organisation, it was decided to discuss at this session the question of the Military Organisation's organ, the newspaper *Soldat*, with reference to the latest CC resolution to abolish it as an organ of the Military Organisation. Comrade Stalin, who had been charged with putting this CC resolution into effect, declared that there was nothing to discuss with representatives of the Central Bureau of the Military Organisations and that once a CC resolution had been constituted, it must be put into effect without any discussion whatsoever. Comrade Smilga, too, made a similar declaration on the subject of the newspaper's financial resources.

The Central Bureau of the Military Organisations considers this kind of behaviour by CC comrades completely unacceptable, both from a formal point of view and from the point of view of the elementary principles of party democracy. Unfortunately, the Military Organisation must state that *unacceptable* measures and actions such as these are no accident but, *from the moment* the previous CC membership changed, they have been made a direct system of persecution and repression of a very strange character, applying to the whole, large organisation. The Central Bureau of the Military Organisations demands of the CC that the formal relationship between these two organisations be settled immediately in a normal way, taking into account the fact that the present state of things hinders the Central Bureau of the Military Organisations in the work entrusted to it by the All-Russian Conference of the Military Organisations.

August 15 1917

Archives of the IML, *f*.17, *op*.1, *ed. khr*.18, *ll*.5 - 7.
Printed for the first time

Minutes No.8
Session of the Inner Committee [of the C C]
August 20 [September 2] 1917

[No list of those present in the original.]

Agenda :
1. Literature.
2. Resolution about the Moscow Conference for the Petersburg Soviet of Workers' and Soldiers' Deputies.
3. Collaboration in *Novaia zhizn'*.
4. *TsIK* collections on August 28 and 29*.
5. Riazanov's statement.
6. Congress of Workers' Sections of the Soviets.
7. Manifesto to the workers of all countries.
8. Commission for the Constituent Assembly.
9. The Military Organisation.

I.   a. *Proletarii.*
Expanded collegium of contributors.
The decision is taken to divide up the newspaper into sections and put comrades in charge of them who would also be included in the collegium.
The following sections are planned :
1. Trade union – under comrade Glebov.
2. Food supply – comrade Vladimirov.
3. Literature – comrade Lunacharsky.
4. Municipal – comrade Uritsky.
5. Section of political comment – comrade Bezrabotnyi [Manuilsky].
6. News reporting – comrade Karakhan.
7. Party life – comrade Sverdlov.
8. Round Russia – comrade Ioffe.
9. Soldiers' section – comrade Menzhinsky or Nevsky.
10. Peasants' section – comrade Nevsky.
11. Factory and insurance sections – comrade Skrypnik.
12. Foreign section – comrade Uritsky.

---

* A slip in the text of the minutes notes. It should read : 27-28. See p.36.

In addition, it is decided to include a representative from the Petersburg Committee on the editorial board with the right to vote.

b. *Soldat*.

The decision is made to assign comrade Bubnov to the editorial board of *Soldat* with the right of *veto*.

c. *Vpered*.

The editorial board consists of 5 people (comrades Stalin, Sokolnikov, Miliutin, Bezrabotnyi [Manuilsky] and Uritsky).

Vpered is the CC's organ for popular propaganda; there is not to be discussion.

d. *Prosveshchenie*.

Comrades Stalin, Sokolnikov, Miliutin, Lunacharsky, Savel-'ev and Riazanov are elected to the editorial board and it ought to be pointed out to the last of these that the journal will promote the line of the Zimmerwald Left[53].

e. *Priboi*.

Priboi is edited by the *Vpered* editorial board but *everyone* does not have to consider the booklet in detail unless *two* people who have made themselves familiar with the booklet disagree in their assessment of it.

Not on the agenda – the printing press[54].

Comrade Ioffe is instructed to bring order into the state of affairs at the printing works and dispatch and to make a report to the next CC meeting.

II.   *Resolution about the Moscow Conference for the Petersburg Soviet of Workers' and Soldiers' Deputies.*

A draft resolution for the group is read out; Sokolnikov, Stalin and Dzerzhinsky are charged with reworking the draft and presenting it to the group in its final form*[55].

III.   *Collaboration in Novaia zhizn'*[56]

It is decided to oblige Party members to send the editorial board a refusal to contribute.

IV.   *TsIK collections on the 28th and 29th to mark the first six months of the revolution.*

Comrade Dzerzhinsky's announcement is heard.

A decision is made to refuse to take an active part in the col-

---

*   See p.33.

lections, citing the *TsIK's* attitude to the Bolsheviks and the violation of decisions passed by the Congress of Soviets[57].

V.   *Riazanov's statement that Lenin and Zinoviev will appear
in court*[58].

Comrade Uritsky is instructed to bring it to comrade
Riazanov's notice that he had no authority to make such a statement.

VI.   *Manifesto to the workers of all countries*[59].

It was heard and given back to the author for revision.

The remaining questions were taken off the agenda.

Document
Draft of the resolution on the Moscow Conference moved by the Bolshevik group in the Petrograd Soviet
[August 21 (September 3) 1917]

1.   The Provisional Government called the Moscow Conference for
the purpose of reaching agreement with the landowners, bankers
and factory-owners on the positive promotion of a programme of
bourgeois counter-revolution. At the Conference, the Provisional
Government declared openly that it rejected any kind of social
and land reform, any 'encroachment on the private property of
particular groups or sections of society' whatsoever. At the same
time, the Provisional Government abandoned all hypocritical
phrases about 'peace without annexations' and unceremoniously
took its stand on continuing the predatory war.

2.   The counter-revolution, skilfully working to get the convocation
of the Constituent Assembly put off again and again, took advantage of the rigged 'popular' conference in Moscow which the Provisional Government obligingly organised to put forward their next
demands, the complete destruction of the mass organisations belonging to the workers, soldiers and peasants, the conversion of the
army into a meek tool of the counter-revolutionary high command,
the introduction of the death penalty behind the front lines. The
Provisional Government, obediently following the counter-revolutionary policy of a struggle 'by blood and iron' against the masses
of workers and peasants, gave in straight away and will go on
giving in to the orders of the Kornilovs, the Riabushinskys, the
Miliukovs and other examples of the 'live forces' in the bourgeois-
landowner coalition.

3. The platform of the so-called 'revolutionary democracy' presented by Chkheidze at the Moscow Conference revealed its complete political bankruptcy. It is even a direct rejection of the All-Russian Congress of Soviets' platform setting out the demand for a peace without annexations or reparations. The so-called 'revolutionary democracy' went so far as to make shameful concessions dictated by the desire to conclude an 'honest alliance' with implacable enemies of the workers and peasants. On its behalf, Tsereteli held out his hand to the bourgeois-landowner parties, made a new deal with them and entered into the commitment to fight against the 'danger from the left'.

With this in mind, the Petrograd Soviet of Workers' and Soldiers' Deputies resolves:

1. To categorically condemn the policy of deals and alliances with enemies of the proletarian and peasant revolution adopted by the *TsIK* and its delegation at the Moscow Conference.

2. To recognise that the revolution can only be saved by eradicating the dictatorship of the counter-revolutionary bourgeoisie and achieving a concentration of power in the hands of the workers and the poor peasants.

3. To protest against the fact that the Central Executive Committee took part in the Moscow Conference without raising the issue in advance for the Petrograd Workers' and Soldiers' Soviet to consider and, grossly breaching the rights of the Bolshevik group as representatives of the revolutionary proletariat, excluded it from the delegation.

Proletarii No.8, September 4 [August 22] 1917.

Minutes No.9
Session of the Inner Committee of the CC
August 23 [September 5] 1917

[No list of those present in the original.]

Agenda :
I. Participation in the Bureau organising collections.
II. Suit for libel against *Rech'*.
III. Military Organisation.
IV. Peasants' associations.

V. All-Russian Congress of Workers' Sections of the Soviets.
VI. CC plenum.
VII. Comrade Kamenev.

I. *Participation in the Organisational Bureau in charge of marking the first six months of the revolution and arranging collections*.*

With reference to the collections, the last meeting's decision[60] is confirmed ; it is decided that a delegate (comrade Sverdlov) is to be sent to the Bureau to uphold there the Party's freedom to choose its own slogans and speeches.

II. *A decision is made not to sue Rech' for libel[61].*

III. *Military Organisation.*

Voenka's financial report is presented ; comrade Sverdlov's report is heard.

The earlier CC decision concerning *Voenka*[62] is confirmed.

IV. *Peasants' associations.*

The plan of organisation is passed to the Military Bureau under the CC to be worked out in detail and a circular letter about the importance of work among the peasants is to be addressed to the local organisations.

V. *All-Russian Congress of Workers' Sections.*

Adjourned to the next session.

VI. *CC plenum.*

It is decided to convene it on September 3[63].

VII. *Comrade Kamenev.*

It is decided that an official statement should be made to the *TsIK* that if the commission of inquiry under the *TsIK* has not rehabilitated comrade Kamenev by August 29, the CC RSDLP will be forced to suggest to comrade Kamenev that he should disregard his statement about withdrawing from public activity.

---

* See p.36.

Document
Resolution by the CC RSDLP(b) on marking the first six months of the revolution

On August 22, our Party's Central Committee received a suggestion that it should take part in a committee to organise a $TsIK$ collection to mark the first six months of the revolution. After considering this suggestion and noting:

1. that the $TsIK$ sanctioned the arrest of Bolshevik members of the $TsIK$ and thus handed them over to the counter-revolution;

2. that the $TsIK$, violating the rights of the representatives of the proletariat, excluded Bolshevik members of the $TsIK$ from the delegation to the Moscow Conference in an open attempt to gag the representatives of the revolutionary party of the proletariat and prevent them protesting against the counter-revolutionary assembly in Moscow;

3. that the $TsIK$ acted regardless of the will and against the will of the progressive proletariat by taking part in the Moscow deal with the bourgeoisie without consulting the Petrograd proletariat at all and in spite of an active protest by the whole Moscow proletariat;

4. that the $TsIK$ tacitly connived in the introduction of the death penalty, putting soldiers' lives at the mercy of the counter-revolutionary oppressors, while the Petrograd, Moscow and a number of provincial Soviets rebelled against the counter-revolutionary terror —

the Central Committee of the RSDLP (bolsheviks) emphatically protests both against these latest actions and against the $TsIK$'s whole policy which has forced the progressive proletariat to turn away from it and, in view of the fact that the inclusion of its representatives in the commission organising the collection would signify a vote of confidence in the present majority and the present policy of the $TsIK$, it resolves to refuse to send representatives to the commission for the organisation of a collection for the $TsIK$ on August 27-28.

Proletarii No.10, September 6 [August 24] 1917.

Minutes No.10
Session of the Central Committee
August 30 [September 12] 1917

Present :
Miliutin, Rykov, Ioffe, Sverdlov, Bubnov, Dzerzhinsky, Sokolnikov, Stalin, Kamenev, Muranov and Stasova.

Comrade G. Z[inoviev]'s proposal is heard raising the question [before] the CC of his return and work.

A decision is made to mount a campaign of meetings in all
three areas to pass resolutions* demanding the release of those
arrested after the events of July 3-5 and the return to their posts
of the leaders of the working class being prosecuted – Lenin,
Zinoviev, etc. Furthermore, it was made the duty of CC members
of the 'Committee for the People's Struggle against Counter-revolution'[64] to raise there, too, the question of those being prosecuted
for July 3-5. The question of withdrawing from the Committee
of Struggle was brought up in connection with these last issues.
But no decision was taken to leave it. This decision can only be
taken in its wider connection with the questions* of arming the
workers and of power. Comrade G. Z[inoviev] is to be told that
the CC will exert every effort to enable him to be as close to Party
and newspaper work as possible.

Agenda :
1. Political situation.
2. Duma group.
3. Riazanov.
4. *Novaia zhizn'*
5. The Lithuanians.

The first question is adjourned to the next session[65].
On the subject of the Central Duma in Petrograd, a decision
is taken to present a declaration** which must include, apart from
a stand on principles, a concrete proposal – the demand for the

---

*   *demanding the release ... in its wider connection with the questions*
        is written at the end of the minutes as an insertion.
**   See p.38.

release of those arrested and the return to their posts of those being prosecuted [for] July 3-5[66].

It is decided to impose a boycott on the Kadets, that is, not to allow them into any executive organs[67].

As far as the Duma group in general is concerned, it is decided to grant it autonomy, leaving its general leadership to the CC members of the group[68].

3.   There is a report on Comrade Riazanov's unacceptable behaviour at the joint session of the trade unions and factory committees[69] and his conduct, which is doing an appreciable amount of harm to the Party, is assessed generally.

A decision is adopted to tell Riazanov that he is censured for his behaviour at the joint session and bring it to his notice that speeches against the Party cannot be tolerated from Party members. It is decided to send him a warning to this effect through comrade Miliutin.

4.   The subject of collaboration in *Novaia zhizn'* is raised once again in view of a statement by several contributors*.

It is decided that because of the special situation a meeting of contributors is to be arranged, with comrades Uritsky and Miliutin taking part, where it will be explained how things stand and a new proposal made to contributors to *withdraw their signatures* from the newspaper.

Document 1
Declaration by the Bolshevik group read out at a session of the Petrograd Central City Duma
September 1 [14] 1917

We, city councillors, revolutionary social-democrats, representatives of 183,000 Petrograd voters, find it necessary today, at the first day's session of the new Petrograd Duma, to make the following statement:

The City Duma is beginning its work in troubled days when the reaction is mobilising its forces and attacking the outposts of the revolution, stopping at nothing. Democracy's every resource must now be organised and exerted for the struggle with the counter-revolution.

---

*   See p.41.

Our Party represents the workers and soldiers. It has always energetically defended the interests of the proletariat against oppressors of every sort and defended them with special consistency and determination in the present revolutionary epoch.

This has made it an object of hatred for the privileged classes and their hangers-on. The social-democratic Bolshevik Party has always been a target for the slanders of the bourgeois and the yellow press.

When the masses of workers and soldiers, moved by a grave disquiet for the fate of the revolution, came out into the streets of Petrograd on July 3-5 at a critical moment to demand that all power be transferred into the control of organs of the revolutionary democracy with full authority, our Party decided, after vigorous attempts to stop the demonstration, to intervene in this elemental movement to give it the maximum amount of organisation possible in the circumstances. Provocative firing, planned in advance, produced confusion and cast a shadow of bloodshed over the demonstration. The Government did not take the trouble to reconstruct a picture of the troubles through a complete investigation or even to calculate the number of dead by categories. If this had been done, it would have become manifestly clear that there was no question of an armed rising on July 3-5 and that the number of casualties among the demonstrators themselves was higher than the number of those who fell victim to criminal provocateurs from the other side and the casual passers-by. Instead of making such inquiries, the coalition Government preferred to accuse a large workers' party of conspiracy and mass murder, but that was not enough. With the unscrupulous touch of the revived secret political police department, an absurd, completely inflated trial was organised, charging high treason and collusion between our Party leaders – those merciless front-line fighters against any kind of imperialism – and the reactionary, predatory German government. This trial was conducted by officials inherited from the old regime, relied on Tsarist laws and violated even these laws to the prejudice of the accused.

Even now these persecutions have not yet stopped. Even now the newspapers *Rech'* and *Birzhevye vedomosti* disseminate provocative rumours about a 'Bolshevik conspiracy', and many of our noted Party figures are still in prison.

None the less, the dense atmosphere of lies has already dispersed. Morally, the monstrous trial is rotten to the core. After the tragic Kornilov days, it has become clear to the whole democracy that it has in our Party its most advanced and reliable contingent and that its victimisation was part of the systematic preparation of an open reactionary movement. Now it is plain that our imprisoned and hounded comrades were the victims of the counter-revolution.

That is why we express our confidence that the first Petrograd City Duma elected on the basis of universal and direct suffrage will regard it as its duty to say what it thinks about the fact that our Party, whose representatives now make up a third of its membership, has been defamed and will demand as a result, not an amnesty – no, we do not want that for we know the court will put our enemies to shame – but release in advance of trial.

Citizen councillors !

The voters sent us here not only to criticise and not to oppose but to work fruitfully and creatively; to gradually carry out that wide municipal programme which was the banner under which we fought our electoral campaign.

We believe that it is quite possible for us to collaborate effectively with socialist and sincerely democratic elements in the City Duma on this course. We believe that the socialists will justify with honour the faith put in them by the population, which voted for them with such an overwhelming majority.

But, citizen councillors, the counter-revolutionary conspiracy, long and skilfully prepared, has finally broken out into the Kornilov mutiny. The forces which gave it birth remain even now a terrible threat to the great Russian revolution. Not least among them is the so-called Party of the 'People's Freedom'. We declared before, in the previous Duma, that this counter-revolutionary Party would not get a single vote of ours. What was then obvious only to us is now clear to all socialists and democrats. The Petrograd Soviet of Workers' and Soldiers' Deputies, in its entirety, without distinction of party or group, protests now that this Party, hostile as it is to the people, must not have any share in power.

Citizen councillors ! We, revolutionary Bolshevik social-democrats, consider any form of collaboration with patent enemies of the revolution in executive organs of the city government unacceptable to us and presume that all socialists in this Duma will take the same view. Let only the genuine revolutionary democracy take the management of the great revolutionary Petrograd into its hands and we, too, will take our place in its ranks to work intensively and selflessly for the benefit of the capital of the world revolution, in accordance with the faith shown in us by the proletariat and garrison of Petrograd.

Rabochii put' No.1, September 16 [3] 1917.

Document 2
Statement to the CC RSDLP

Dear comrades !

We, Bolshevik contributors to the newspaper *Novaia zhizn'*, learning of the decision passed by the CC RSDLP requiring us to withdraw from the circle of contributors, ask you to take the following circumstances into consideration:

1. First of all, we consider it inappropriate that the CC should take decisions determining the political conduct of this or that group of Party members in matters directly concerning them and on which they are better informed without consulting such Party members in advance.

2. We in no way seek to justify the statements of the editorial board of *Novaia zhizn'* (to which none of us belong) during the last electoral campaign, but at the same time we consider that the sharp polemic between *Novaia zhizn'* and *Proletarii* may turn out to have been a passing and insubstantial episode. If the present 'unification' congress ends in a split, then the chances of unifying all the internationalists on which our Party Congress justifiably put so much store will be strengthened once again. In this event, the presence of a group of our Party members in *Novaia zhizn'* could play a serious and positive role.

If, however, with the preponderance of defensists at the congress which has already been established, there is no split and *Novaia zhizn'* adheres once and for all to the right wing of the social democracy – then naturally there can be no place for us on that newspaper.

In the light of these observations, we ask that our group be allowed to decide this question on its own.

If the CC does not consider these arguments of ours convincing enough, we ask them to discuss this question once again, with us, before taking the final decision.

A. Lozovsky.	On behalf of Arsky *M. Smit.*
F. Drabkina.	*Zamvy.*
M. Smit.	*Lunacharsky.*

Archives of the IML, *f*.17, *op*.1 *ed. khr.*, 21, *l*.5.
Printed for the first time.

Minutes No.11
Expanded session of the Central Committee
August 31 [September 13] 1917

Present:
Representatives of the Bolshevik groups in the *TsIK*, the Peters-
burg Soviet of Workers' and Soldiers' Deputies and the Political
Bureau and Uritsky, Dzerzhinsky, Sverdlov, Stalin, Bubnov,
Oppokov [Lomov], Muranov, Miliutin, Rykov, Sokolnikov,
Ioffe, Kamenev and Stasova.

Agenda:
1.   Discussion of the declaration on power.
After comrade Kamenev had read the draft resolution, a
general discussion opened and everyone present took part. The
following resolution-declaration[70] was adopted (see *Rabochii*[71]).

Document
On power
Resolution read out by the Bolshevik group at the session of the TsIK *on
August 31 [September 13] 1917.*

In the face of General Kornilov's counter-revolutionary mutiny, prepared
and supported by parties and groups represented in the Provisional
Government (headed by the Kadet Party), the *TsIK* considers it
its duty to declare that from now on a decisive end must be put to
all hesitation where the organisation of power is concerned. Not
only must representatives of the Kadet Party which was openly involved in the mutiny be barred from power, along with representatives of property-owning elements in general, but the whole policy
of conciliation and non-accountability which first made it possible
to turn the high command and the apparatus of state power into a
lever and tool of the conspiracy against the revolution must also
be radically changed.
The exclusive authority of the Provisional Government and its lack of
accountability are no longer tolerable. The only way out is to form
a government from representatives of the revolutionary proletariat
and peasantry, which must take the following as a basis for action:
1.   A democratic republic to be decreed.
2.   Private ownership of landed estates to be abolished immediately

without compensation and the land put under the control of peasants' committees until a decision by the Constituent Assembly, poor peasants being provided with working stocks.

3. Workers' control over production and distribution to be introduced on a state-wide scale. The most important branches of industry, such as oil, coal-mining and metallurgy, to be nationalised; large-scale capital and property to be ruthlessly taxed and war profits confiscated in order to save the country from economic ruin.

4. Secret treaties to be declared inoperative and a universal, democratic peace offered immediately to all the peoples of the belligerent states.

Immediate measures to be decreed:

1. An end to all repression directed against the working class and its organisations. The immediate abolition of the death penalty at the front and complete freedom to be restored for agitation and for all democratic organisations in the army. The army to be purged of counter-revolutionary commanding officers.

2. Election of commissars and other officials by local organisations.

3. The right to self-determination of nations living in Russia to be made a reality, the demands of Finland and the Ukraine to be satisfied first.

4. The dissolution of the State Council and the State Duma. Immediate convocation of the Constituent Assembly.

5. The elimination of all class privileges (of the nobility and others), equal rights for all citizens.

The newspaper *Rabochii* No.10, September 14 [1] 1917.

Minutes No.12
Session of the CC
August 31 [September 13 1917], evening

Present:
Muranov, Dzerzhinsky Bubnov, Rykov, Zinoviev, Miliutin, Sverdlov, Oppokov [Lomov], Uritsky, Stasova.

Agenda:
1. Preparation for the plenum.
2. Report of the Organisational Bureau.
3. Zimmerwald Conference.

4. Commission for the Constituent Assembly.
5. Municipal Commission.
6. The Lithuanians.
7. Policy.
8. The Muscovites.

I. On the first question, the following agenda is planned[72] :
1. Assessment of the current situation (speakers Kamenev and Stalin).
2. The municipal campaign (speaker Ioffe).
3. The Constituent Assembly (speaker Miliutin).
4. Reports : a. Organisational Bureau (Sverdlov) ; b. literature group (Sokolnikov).
5. Allocation of manpower (Uritsky).
6. Organisational questions, regions, etc. (Oppokov).
II. The Organisational Bureau made a report from which it emerged that CC funds are in a very weak state (about 30,000 in hand) and that particular enterprises do their accounts badly so that it is very difficult to determine how much the CC has. At present the Military Organisation is not a self-contained political organisation but a military commission under the CC. In these circumstances, *Voenka*'s work is gradually being brought into close liaison with Party work in general. All work in the Military Organisation is done under CC direction. Comrade Bubnov works on *Soldat* and comrades Dzerzhinsky and Sverdlov guide the work overall. *Rabochii* is published in 50,000 copies, and *Soldat* in 15-18,000.

The CC was instructed to organise a group to unify all the work in the trade unions and a start was made in this direction; a group has already been formed but its constitution is not yet final. A municipal group[73] has been formed, and steps are being taken to set up an insurance group. Comrade Smilga made a report at the Insurance Congress on behalf of the CC and all the work at the Conference of Factory Committees was done under the direction of the CC, represented by comrade Miliutin. Efforts have been made to extend and strengthen relations with Russia as a whole but the work is hampered because the post is so bad.

There was a debate on this report and it was pointed out that the work of the CC must be widened to cover the whole of Russia because up to now the CC's work, for purely technical reasons, has been concentrated chiefly in Petersburg. To further this policy, a group of travelling agents must be formed and this is especially necessary in order to organise the North-West and Southern regions and the Volga area, where solidarity is weak[74].

It is decided to instruct the Organisational Bureau to set up a group of travelling agents and report to the CC on the results of this work.

Minutes No.13
Session of the CC
September 3 [16] 1917

Present :
Muranov, Kamenev, Sverdlov, Ioffe, Uritsky, Bubnov, Miliutin and Stasova.

Agenda :
1. Democratic* Conference.
2. City Duma.
3. Material from the Shluesselburg factory.

On the subject of the Democratic Conference called for September 12[75], a decision is made to send the following telegram to the large organisations :

Since we consider it important that the mood of the workers, soldiers and peasants should be reflected as fully as possible at the Conference called by the Central Executive Committee on September 12, we suggest to our Party organisations that they ensure the fullest representation for us[76].

Apart from that, it is decided that a letter setting out our attitude to the Conference in greater detail be circulated to all organisations.**

About the City Duma, there was a discussion on the question of candidates for deputies to the Mayor and for members of the

---

*   In the text of the minute notes it is written here by mistake : *Moscow*.
** See p.46.

city administration[77]. Lunacharsky and Ioffe are designated by us and it is decided to support Nikitsky's candidature.

It is also agreed that the praesidium seats (5 seats counting the city Mayor) will be divided proportionately between the socialist groups, this whole matter being left to the group. It is decided to suggest to the group the following as members of the city administration : 1. Ioffe, 2. Teodorovich, 3. Shlichter, 4. Aksel'rod, 5. Piliavsky, 6. Manuil'sky, 7. Tovbina, 8. Kobozev and 9. Khanin.

Regarding the Schluesselburg factory, it is decided to pass everything over to the Military Commission[78].

In conclusion, a letter from Lenin is read.*

Document 1
Letter from the CC about the Democratic Conference
September 4 [17] 1917

Dear comrades !

You will have already received our telegram about the Conference called in Petrograd for September 12 by the Central Executive Committee.

The Central Committee of our Party passed a decision that every effort should be exerted to make the members of our Party taking part in the Conference into as large and as unified a group as possible.

On the basis of this decision, we suggest, comrades, that once you know the exact composition of the Conference, you put comrades forward wherever possible. We ask everyone you send to apply to us directly for more precise and detailed information about our tasks at the Conference.

If comrades come to us, it will give us a better opportunity to implement our decision to organise a united group at the Conference.

Because of the extraordinary importance of the Conference, we ask comrades to show the maximum amount of energy in promoting their candidates.

At the same time, we propose to pass resolutions at meetings and gatherings, in workers' districts and barracks about the Conference and its tasks, taking a lead from the resolution 'On power' which our group read out at the session of the *TsIK* of the Soviets on August 31. (Printed in No.10 of *Rabochii,* September 1).

---

* See p.47.

The address to call at: Smolny Institute, 1st floor, Room 18, Bolshevik
group.
All information can be obtained from the group member on duty.

Secretary of the CC *Elena Stasova*

P.S. The Moscow Regional Bureau is specially charged with spreading
all information about the Conference round the region because,
with the exception of the biggest towns (Kazan', Kostroma, Kana-
vino), we have not done this. The telegram will probably arrive
after this letter.

Regards *Elena Stasova*

Archives of the I M L, *f.*60, *op.* 2, *ed. khr.* 14, *l.* 16.

Document 2
To the Central Committee of the RSDLP

Maybe these lines will come too late for events are moving at a speed that
at times makes your head spin. I am writing this on Wednesday,
August 30; those to whom it is addressed will not read it before
Friday, September 2. But still, taking that risk, I consider it my
duty to write the following.
Kornilov's revolt is a most unexpected (unexpected at this moment and
in this form) and incredibly abrupt turn of events.
As with any sharp turn, it requires tactics to be revised and changed.
And, as in any revision, great care is needed to avoid falling into a
neglect of principles.
It is my conviction that those who are sliding into defensism (like
Volodarsky) or towards a *bloc* with the SRs, towards *support* of
the Provisional Government (like some other Bolsheviks) are for-
getting principles. This is very wrong, it is unprincipled. We will
become defensists *only after* power has passed to the proletariat,
after a peace offer, *after* the secret treaties and the ties with the
banks have been scrapped, *only after*. Neither the capture of Riga,
nor the capture of Peter will make us defensists. (I would very
much like Volodarsky to read this.) Until then, we are for the proletarian revolution and against the war, we are *not* defensists.
And *even now* we must not support Kerensky's government. That is unprincipled. It will be asked: is one really not to fight against Kornilov? Of course, we must. But this is not one and the same thing;

there is a dividing line; some Bolsheviks who slip into 'conciliation' go beyond it, letting themselves be *carried away* by the train of events.

We will fight and are fighting Kornilov, *just as* Kerensky's *troops* are, but we are not supporting Kerensky but exposing his weakness. That is the difference.

It is rather a fine distinction but quintessential and it must not be forgotten.

What then is the change in our tactics after Kornilov's insurgency? It lies in the fact that we are modifying the *form* of our struggle with Kerensky. Without relaxing our enmity towards him by one iota, without taking back a single word said against him, without renouncing the task of overthrowing Kerensky, we say: we must *take stock* of the situation, we are not going to overthrow Kerensky now, we are going to approach the task of struggling against him *in a new way*, namely: to reveal to the people (who are fighting against Kornilov) Kerensky's *weakness* and *vacillation*. We did this before, too, but now it has become the *main thing*: that is what has changed.

In addition, there is a change in that now the *most important thing* has become: to intensify agitation for some kind of 'partial demands' on Kerensky – tell him to arrest Miliukov, arm the Peter workers, summon the Kronstadt, Vyborg and Helsingfors troops to Peter, dissolve the State Duma, arrest Rodzianko, legalise the transfer of landed estates to the peasants, introduce workers' control over grain and in factories, etc., etc. And we must make these demands not only to Kerensky, *not so much* to Kerensky as to the workers, soldiers and peasants, *carried away* by enthusiasm as the struggle against Kornilov goes on. *Arouse their enthusiasm* further, encourage them to attack the generals and officers who have declared for Kornilov, persist until *they* demand the immediate transfer of land to the peasants, give *them* the idea that Rodzianko and Miliukov need to be arrested, the State Duma dissolved, *Rech'* and other bourgeois newspapers closed and investigated. 'Left' SRs in particular must be pushed in this direction.

It would be wrong to think that we have moved *away* from the objective of a proletarian conquest of power. No. We have come very close to it, *not head on*, however, but from the side. And agitation is needed *this minute* not so much directly against Kerensky as *indirectly*, still against him but obliquely, that is: by demanding a more and more active and genuinely revolutionary war against Kornilov. Only the development of this war can bring *us* to power but we must *speak* about this as little as possible in agitation (remembering very well that even tomorrow events may put us in power and then we will not let it go). In my view, this should be passed on in a letter (not in the press) to groups of agitators and propagandists, and to Party members in general. A ruthless fight is needed against phrases about the defence of the country, a united front of revolutionary democracy, support for the Provisional Government etc., etc., precisely as *phrases*. Now is the time for *action*: you, comrade SRs and Mensheviks, wore out these phrases long ago. Now is the time for *action*, the war against Kornilov must be fought like a revolution, bringing in the masses, arousing them, setting them on fire (Kerensky *fears* the masses, *fears* the people). Now is the moment when *action* is needed in the war against the Germans: *offer peace, immediately* and *unconditionally*, on *precise* terms. If this is done, *it is possible* either to get an early peace or to turn the war into a revolutionary one; otherwise all the Mensheviks and SRs will remain the lackeys of imperialism.

P.S. Having read through six numbers of *Rabochii, after* this was written, I must say that we turned out to be in complete agreement. I welcome wholeheartedly the superb editorials, the survey of the press and the articles of V.M-n and Vol-y. About Volodarsky's speech, I read his letter to the editors, which also 'cancels' my reproaches. Once again, best wishes and greetings!

Lenin

Written August 30 [September 12] 1917.
V.I.Lenin, *Sochineniia*, 4th ed., vol.25, pp.263-267.

Minutes No.14
Session of the CC
September 6 [19] 1917

Present
[No list of those present in the original.]

Literature group.
The editorial board of the central organ[79]: 1. Stalin, 2. Sokolnikov, 3. Trotsky, 4. Kamenev and 5. a representative of the Petersburg Committee.
Passed:
It is decided to *close Vpered*[80].

Prosveshchenie. An editorial board of six people agreed : Miliutin, Lunacharsky, Uritsky, Trotsky, Kamenev and Vetrov [Savel'ev][81].

Soldat – comrade Bubnov stays.

Priboi is edited by the editorial board of *Prosveshchenie*. If two members of the editorial board read it through and there is no disagreement between them, it is considered approved.

Comrade Sokolnikov suggests putting the management side of the printers in order, entrusting the responsibility for management to one person.

Comrades Dzerzhinsky and Kamenev are commissioned to have talks with Bonch and Kedrov.

The [Democratic] Conference.

It is decided that Lenin and Zinoviev are to be nominated as candidates at the Petrograd Soviet[82] if that is the sooner but if the *TsIK* is first, then there ; then Bubnov, Sokolnikov and Sadovsky in the Petrograd Soviet.

From the *TsIK* (Lenin and Zinoviev), Kamenev, Trotsky, Lunacharsky, Stalin, Dzerzhinsky, Miliutin(?)*, Sverdlov, Kollontai, Krylenko, Krasikov, Lashevich, Pozern, Volodarsky, Teodorovich, Nogin, Iurenev, Grinberg, Kuraev, Karakhan, Zof, Zalutsky.

Zinoviev and Lenin.

a.   Put the question of the immunity of Conference delegates to the *TsIK*.

b.   Make contact with Lenin and Zinoviev and if they agree, raise [in] the *TsIK* the question of their release on bail.

c.   The matter only to be brought up about the two together, no separation is acceptable.

The CC plenum.

It is decided to call it for the 12th[83].

The current situation.

The central organ's editorial board is charged with drawing up : 1. a resolution on the current situation and 2. a declaration to be passed at meetings[84].

Comrade Ioffe.

---

*   Like this in the text of the minute notes.

On delegating to the *TsIK*. Comrade Kamenev is charged with organising this.

The organisation of delegations to the Conference from works and regiments.

A letter is read from the Moscow Regional Bureau making this suggestion.

It is decided to organise similar agitation in Peter and the largest Russian centres[85].

The organ to be published by the Inter-District Conference[86].

It is proposed to hold up publication until the question of the Petrograd Soviet is finally decided, but to continue work on making it technically ready for publication. Comrade Ioffe is commissioned to join the Inter-District Conference.

The praesidium of the Soviets of Workers' and Soldiers' Deputies[87].

Passed : The CC resolves that the praesidium should consist of a coalition on a proportional basis, so that another 7 representing the Bolsheviks should be brought into the new praesidium along with the 7 put up by the Mensheviks and SRs.

This resolution is to be given to the Press Bureau.

Novaia zhizn'.

The earlier decision[88] is confirmed, but efforts are to be made beforehand to come to an arrangement with the editorial board of *Novaia zhizn'* through contributors who are members of our Party for the newspaper to support our list exclusively in the elections to the Constituent Assembly and not put up any other.

Comrades Uritsky and Miliutin are instructed to gather the contributors of *Novaia zhizn'* together and talk things over with them.

Larin.

The CC, on hearing the news from comrade Trotsky that comrade Larin has joined our Party, decided to bring him into : 1. the municipal group under the CC, 2. invite him on to the editorial board of the municipal organ now being started up.

The situation which has arisen in the City Duma[89].

A list of 8 people having been put up for membership of the city administration, a proposal to be made to the group to withdraw – both those who get in and comrade Lunacharsky of the Deputy Mayors – if the SRs vote to object to even one of the 8.

Minutes No.15
Session of the CC
September 13 [26] 1917

Present :
Trotsky, Kamenev, Stalin, Sverdlov, Bubnov, Oppokov [Lomov], Kollontai, Uritsky, Ioffe, Shaumian, Sokolnikov, Miliutin, Krestinsky.

Agenda :
The report of the Electoral Commission for the Constituent Assembly.

The list of members is not confirmed and the decision is postponed until a fuller meeting of the CC[90]. The Commission is charged with presenting a report showing exactly how many go to the Constituent Assembly from where and what our Party's chances are in different electoral districts.

It is decided to arrange a Party conference after the Democratic Conference for the people who have come from the localities and members of the CC[91].

A commission of 5 people – Trotsky, Kamenev, Stalin, Miliutin and Rykov – is elected to draw up declarations and resolutions for the Democratic Conference.

Document
Declaration by the Bolshevik group read out at the All-Russian Democratic Conference
September 18 [October 1] 1917

The revolution has reached its most critical point. After this, there will either be a new upsurge or a disastrous slump. The people are exhausted by war but almost more they are worn out by the indecisiveness and worried to death by the vacillations in the policy of the ruling political parties. Just over six months after Tsarism was brought down, following a number of attempts to organise revolutionary rule on the basis of a coalition between representatives of the democracy and representatives of the property-owning bourgeoisie, after the pathetic actions of a personal regime which led directly to the Kornilov plot, the motive forces behind the revolution are once again confronted by the question of power.

Each new governmental combination has begun by announcing a programme of measures to be taken by the state, and after a few weeks has shown its complete incapacity to take even one serious step forward. Once the coalition has been plainly revealed as a disaster, ever new deals with the property-owners inspire the greatest confusion, anxiety and upset in the minds of the workers and the oppressed classes of the country. Not just the urban workers, not just the soldier who has been suffering in the trenches for three years, but the peasant, too, in the most remote and backward village cannot fail to understand that the land problem cannot be solved through compromise with the Lvovs and Rodziankos. The democratisation of the army cannot be entrusted to those who were both generals and landlords speaking for serfdom in the old regime – to the Kornilovs and Alekseevs; control over industry cannot be brought about by means of Ministers who are industrialists or financial reforms by means of bankers and military marauders and their direct henchmen – the Konovalovs, Pal'chinskys, Tret'iakovs or Buryshkins. Finally, not a single serious measure to regulate food and transport, not a single reform in the area of the courts, the schools, etc., can be put into effect while there remains, in an epoch of the greatest upheavals, the old official apparatus and membership of governing bodies in the localities and at the centre, with their anti-popular spirit and obtuse bureaucratism.

In spite of all the efforts the authorities have made to subdue and weaken the Soviets, in spite of the suicidal policy pursued by the Soviets' defensist official leadership, the Soviets demonstrated to everyone the invincibility of that revolutionary power and initiative the people expressed through them at the time when Kornilov's insurgency was suppressed and the Provisional Government discredited itself for ever before the tribunal of the people and of history – by direct complicity in the Kornilov plot, on the one hand; by its readiness to hand over to Kornilov what the revolution had won, on the other. After this latest experience, which nothing will ever erase from the minds of the workers, soldiers and peasants, our Party's call at the very beginning of the revolution: 'All power to the Soviets – at the centre and in the localities' has become the cry of the whole revolutionary country.

Only a power resting directly on the proletariat and the poor peasantry, which controls all the country's material wealth and economic capability, whose measures do not stop as soon as they touch the selfish interests of property-owning groups, which mobilises all the scientific and technically-valuable resources to social and economic ends is capable of bringing as much order as can be attained now into a disintegrating economy, of helping the peasantry and rural workers to use the available means of agricultural production to the greatest effect, of limiting profit, of fixing wages and of securing true work discipline in a context of regulated production based on self-administration by the workers and their centralised control over industry; only this kind of authority can ensure the demobilisation of the whole economy with the least amount of stress.

Because the counter-revolutionary Kadet Party, fearing more than anything that power will pass to the Soviets, constantly frightens the less politically-conscious elements in the democracy with the spectre of a Bolshevik armed rising, we consider it necessary to declare once again, here in the hearing of the whole country, that in fighting for power so that its programme can be carried out, our Party has never sought and is not seeking to take power against the organised will of the majority of the working masses of the country. If all power passed to the Soviets, neither the class struggle nor the struggle between parties within the democratic camp would be abolished. But *under conditions of full and unlimited freedom of agitation* and with the Soviets constantly renewed from below, the struggle for influence and power would take place within the boundaries of Soviet organisations. By contrast, the continuation of the present policy of coercion and repression towards the working class, the army's revolutionary elements and the peasantry, aimed at stopping the revolution developing further, must inevitably, quite independently of the will of the revolutionary organisations, lead to a mighty clash such as there has seldom been in history.

Under these conditions, a coalition government is inevitably a government of coercion and repression by the top ranks over the people below. Only someone who wants to provoke civil war whatever the consequences so that the working masses and our Party can be made to take the responsibility for it afterwards can, after all the experience of the past, suggest that the democracy concludes a new alliance with the counter-revolutionary bourgeoisie.

The people crave peace. Coalition government means that the imperialist war will go on. To this day, the members of the Provisional Government have fallen in with the demands made by the allied imperialists, deadly enemies of Russian revolutionary democracy. The disastrous offensive on June 18, which our Party so persistently warned against, Kornilov's methods of getting control of the army, carried out with the direct assistance of Ministers who favoured conciliation – directly or indirectly, the allied imperialists instigated all this. The Russian revolution has already managed to squander an enormous part of its moral authority on this path without increasing its physical power at all. It is becoming ever clearer that once they have sapped the internal strength of the Russian revolution, the allied imperialists will not hesitate to conclude a peace at the Russian people's expense. Meanwhile, to go on spinelessly dragging out the war without the people believing in the aims of the war or in the Provisional Government which is waging it is to hand a major trump-card to the counter-revolution, so that it can play for a separate peace with Germany's rapacious imperialism. The creation of Soviet power means before anything else that a direct, open, positive offer of an immediate, honest and just democratic peace will be made to all peoples. The revolutionary army could only acknowledge that war was unavoidable if such a peace were rejected. But everything indicates that the revolutionary government's offer would meet such a powerful echo from the working masses in all the belligerent countries, worn out as they are by suffering, that it would become impossible to continue the war. Soviet power means peace.

Enough dithering! Enough of the policy of spinelessness and cowardice! It is impossible with impunity to keep the peasantry in suspense and torment them for half a year, to promise them land and liberty and then refuse in practice to abolish private ownership of landed estates immediately without compensation and transfer them straight away into the control of local peasants' committees until the Constituent Assembly.

Enough hesitation! Enough of that policy of ambiguity pursued up to now by the SR and Menshevik leaders. Enough delay! Enough talk! The deadline for decision has come.

A revolutionary government must act on the basis of the following measures put forward by many influential revolutionary organisations, headed by the Petrograd and Moscow Soviets of Workers' and Soldiers' Deputies.

1. The abolition of private ownership of landed estates without compensation, the land being put under the control of peasants' committees until a decision by the Constituent Assembly, poor peasants being provided with working stocks.

2. The introduction of workers' control over production and distribution on a state-wide scale, the centralisation of banking, control over the banks and the nationalisation of the most important branches of industry such as: oil, coal-mining and metallurgy; universal labour conscription; immediate measures to demobilise industry and arrange for the villages to be supplied with industrial products at stable prices. Ruthless taxation of large-scale capital

and property and the confiscation of war profits in order to save the country from economic ruin.

3. Secret treaties to be declared inoperative and a universal, democratic peace offered immediately to all the peoples of the belligerent states.

4. The right to self-determination of nations living in Russia to be ensured. All repressive measures against Finland and the Ukraine to be cancelled immediately.

Immediate measures to be decreed:

1. An end to all repression directed against the working class and its organisations. The abolition of the death penalty at the front and complete freedom to be restored for agitation and for all democratic organisations in the army. The army to be purged of counter-revolutionary cadres.

2. Election of commissars and other officials by local organisations.

3. General arming of the workers and the organisation of a Red Guard.

4. The dissolution of the State Council and the State Duma. Immediate convocation of the Constituent Assembly.

5. The elimination of all class (nobility, etc.) privileges, equal rights for all citizens.

6. An 8-hour working day to be established and comprehensive social insurance introduced.

As a special measure needed to cleanse the political atmosphere and bring the sores festering in the justice department into the open, we demand that a commission of inquiry regarded as authoritative by the democracy be appointed immediately to make a full investigation into the events of July 3-5 and check on the actions of all the legal authorities who are agents of the old regime and in whose control the inquiries against the proletariat are now concentrated.

All arrested revolutionaries to be released immediately and a speedy public tribunal appointed to deal with all the matters on which a start has been made.

*   *   *

We consider it necessary to say that completely arbitrary criteria of representation were used as a basis for calling this conference. Taken together, they allotted a place to the least revolutionary, conciliating elements of the democracy of a size which their real political role gives them absolutely no right to claim. Army organisations are quite inadequately represented and then only by their leaders who are far removed from the masses of the soldiers and who have not been re-elected for six months. Dumas and *zemstva* are only half-reformed and in any case, because of their special purpose, reflect the revolutionary and political experience of the democracy and its views very imperfectly indeed, and this applies to an even greater extent to the cooperatives, where the selection of the leading officials in charge has only a very distant connection with the political views of the democratic masses and the evolution of their attitudes. By comparison with the dumas, *zemstva* and cooperatives, Soviet representation is very restricted. Yet it is precisely these organisations which most accurately reflect the political will of the workers, soldiers and peasants. It was precisely the Soviets which took charge of the whole situation and in many places took over power, too, in the critical days of the Kornilov insurgency. That is why we consider that only those decisions and proposals of this Conference aimed at completely doing away with Kerensky's personal regime, which are also recognised by an All-Russian Congress of Workers', Peasants' and Soldiers' Deputies, can find their way clear for implementation. It is a most important task now to call such a Congress without delay.

Rabochii put' No.15, October 3 [September 20] 1917.

Minutes No.16
Session of the CC
September 15 [28] 1917

Present :
Trotsky, Kamenev, Rykov, Nogin, Stalin, Sverdlov, Bubnov, Bukharin, Oppokov [Lomov], Kollontai, Dzerzhinsky, Uritsky, Ioffe, Shaumian, Sokolnikov, Miliutin.

Agenda :
Lenin's letters*.

It is decided to fix a CC meeting to be devoted to consideration of tactical questions very soon.

---

*   See pp. 58 and 60.

Comrade Stalin proposes sending the letters out to the most important organisations with the suggestion that they be discussed. It is decided to adjourn this until the next CC session[92].

A vote is taken to see who is in favour of keeping only one copy of the letters. For – 6, against – 4, abstentions – 6.

Comrade Kamenev moved the adoption of the following resolution : After considering Lenin's letters, the CC rejects the practical proposals they contain, calls on all organisations to follow CC instructions alone and affirms once again that the CC regards any kind of demonstration in the streets as quite impermissible at the present moment. At the same time, the CC makes a request to comrade Lenin to elaborate in a special brochure on the question he raised in his letters of a new assessment of the current situation and the Party's policy.

The resolution is rejected.

In conclusion, this decision is adopted :

CC members in charge of work in the Military Organisation and the Petersburg Committee are instructed to take measures to prevent demonstrations of any kind in barracks and factories.

Document 1
The Bolsheviks must take power
Letter to the Central Committee and the Petrograd and Moscow Committees of the RSDLP.

Now the Bolsheviks have a majority in the Soviets of Workers' and Soldiers' Deputies in both capitals, they can and *must* take state power into their own hands.

They can, because the active majority of the revolutionary elements among the people in both the main cities is enough to fire the masses, to overcome the resistance of the opposition and to smash it, to win power and to hold it. For, by offering a democratic peace straight away, by giving land to the peasants straight away, by restoring the democratic institutions and freedoms trampled on and crushed by Kerensky, the Bolsheviks will form a government that *no one* will overthrow.

The majority of the people *support* us. The long and difficult journey from May 6 to August 31 and on to September 12 proved it: the majority in the Soviets of the two main cities is the result of the people moving *in our direction*. The wavering among the S Rs and Mensheviks and the increases in the number of internationalists among them prove the same thing.

The Democratic Conference does *not* represent the majority of the revolutionary people but *only the conciliating petty-bourgeois upper strata*. One cannot let oneself be deceived by the election figures; elections are not the point. Compare the elections to the City Dumas of Peter and Moscow and the elections to the Soviets. Compare the Moscow election and the August 12 Moscow strike: these are the objective facts about whether the revolutionary elements leading the masses are in a majority.

The Democratic Conference is deceiving the peasants by giving them neither peace nor land.

Only a Bolshevik government will satisfy the demands of the peasants.

*　　　*　　　*

Why is it now that the Bolsheviks must take power?

Because the impending surrender of Peter will make our chances a hundred times worse.

And while Kerensky and Co. head the army, it is not in our power to prevent Peter's surrender.

And we cannot 'wait for' the Constituent Assembly because Kerensky and Co., precisely by surrendering Peter, can always *block* it. Only our Party, once it has taken power, can ensure that the Constituent Assembly is called and once it has taken power, it will blame the other parties for putting it off and prove that accusation.

A separate peace between the British and German imperialists must and can be prevented, but only by acting quickly.

The people are tired of the dithering by the Mensheviks and S Rs. Our victory in the capitals is the only way to carry the peasants with us.

*　　　*　　　*

It is not a question of the 'day' of the rising or the 'moment' for it in a narrow sense. The general opinion of the people in contact with workers and soldiers, with the *masses*, is what will decide that.

The point is that our Party now has in effect at the Democratic Conference *its own congress,* and this congress *must* decide (must, whether it wants to or not) the *fate of the revolution*.

The point is to make the *objective* clear to the Party: an armed rising in Peter and Moscow (with its region), the conquest of power and the overthrow of the government must go on the agenda. Thought must be given to *how* to agitate for it without putting it like this in the press.

We must remember and reflect on Marx's words about insurrection: *'insurrection is an art'*[93], etc.

* * *

It would be naive to wait for a 'formal' Bolshevik majority: no revolution waits for *that*. Kerensky and Co. are not waiting either but are getting ready to surrender Peter. The patience of the Peter and Moscow workers is bound to be and will be exhausted by the pathetic wavering of the 'Democratic Conference'! History will not forgive us if we do not take power now.

No apparatus? An apparatus exists: the Soviets and the democratic organisations. The international position *just* now, on the verge of a separate peace between the British and the Germans, is *in our favour*. To offer peace to nations just now means to *win*.

By taking power both in Moscow and Peter *at once* (it doesn't matter who begins; Moscow may possibly begin), we will win absolutely and *indisputably*.

N. Lenin.

Written on September 12-14 [25-27] 1917.
V.I.Lenin, *Sochineniia*, 4th ed., vol.26, pp.1-3.

Document 2
Marxism and insurrection
Letter to the Central Committee of the RSDLP.

Among the most malicious distortions of Marxism by the dominant 'socialist' parties and probably the most widespread is the opportunist lie that it is 'Blanquism' to prepare for a rising and in general to regard insurrection as an art.

Bernstein, the leader of opportunism, has already earned a sorry reputation for himself by accusing Marxism of Blanquism and when the current opportunists cry Blanquism they do not improve on or 'enrich' Bernstein's meagre 'ideas' one little bit.

To accuse Marxists of Blanquism for regarding insurrection as an art! Can there be a more flagrant perversion of the truth when no Marxist will deny that Marx himself gave his views on the matter in the most definite, precise and categorical manner and called insurrection just that – an *art,* saying that a rising must be treated as an art, that the initial success must be won and then success added to success with no let-up in the *attack* on the enemy, taking advantage of its confusion, etc., etc.

To be successful, insurrection must depend on the vanguard class, not on a conspiracy or a party. That is the first point. Insurrection must depend on a *revolutionary upsurge of the people.* That is the second point. Insurrection must depend on that *turning point* in the history of the mounting revolution when the advanced ranks of the people are at their most active and when the *vacillations* in the ranks of the enemy and *among the revolution's weak, half-hearted and irresolute friends* are at their most pronounced. That is the third point. These three conditions for raising the question of insurrection distinguish *Marxism* from *Blanquism.* But once these conditions are present, it is a betrayal of Marxism and a betrayal of the revolution to refuse to treat insurrection as *an art.*

To prove why the particular time we are going through now must be seen as a moment when it is the Party's *duty* to recognise that the course of events has objectively put *insurrection* on the agenda and that it must treat insurrection as an art – to prove this, it is best, perhaps, to use the method of comparison and set July 3-4 against the September days.

On July 3-4, without offending the truth, the question could have been put like this: the right thing to do is to take power because even if we don't, our enemies will still accuse us of insurrection and deal with us as rebels. But no conclusion could be drawn from this in favour of taking power then because the objective conditions for a victorious insurrection did not then exist.

1. We did not yet have the support of the class which is the vanguard of the revolution. We did not yet have a majority among the workers and soldiers in the capitals. Now there is a majority in both Soviets. It was *only* the history of July and August, the experience of the 'reprisals' against the Bolsheviks and the experience of the Kornilov plot which brought it about.

2. Then there was no nationwide revolutionary upsurge. Now, after the Kornilov plot, it exists. This is proved by the provinces and the fact that Soviets have taken power in many places.

3. Then there was no *vacillation* on any serious political scale among our enemies and the undecided petty-bougeoisie. Now the vacillation is enormous: our chief enemy, allied and world imperialism – for world imperialism is headed by the 'allies' – *has begun to waver* between war until victory and a separate peace against Russia. Our petty-bourgeois democrats, having clearly lost the majority

among the people, have begun to waver enormously and have refused an alliance, that is a coalition, with the Kadets.

4. So an insurrection on July 3-4 would have been a mistake: we would not have held on to power, either physically or politically. Physically, because in spite of the fact that at times Peter was in our hands, our workers and soldiers were not then ready to *fight*, to *die* for the sake of Peter: There was not such 'savageness', such seething hatred against *both* the Kerenskys *and* the Tseretelis and Chernovs, our people had not yet been tempered by the experience of the persecution of the Bolsheviks in which the SRs and Mensheviks joined.

Politically, we would not have held on to power on July 3-4 because *until the Kornilov plot,* the army and the provinces could and would have marched on Peter.

Now the picture is completely different.

We have the support of the majority of the *class* which is the vanguard of the revolution and the vanguard of the people, capable of arousing the masses.

We have the support of the majority of the people, for Chernov's resignation is a very striking and obvious sign, and far from the only one, that the peasants *will not get land* from the SR bloc (or from the SRs themselves). And this is the chief reason for the popular character of the revolution.

We have the advantage of being a party which knows very well where it is going at a time when *imperialism as a whole* and the entire Menshevik and SR bloc are wavering in an unprecedented way.

We have the advantage of *certain victory,* for the people are already near to exhaustion and after showing them the importance of our leadership in the 'Kornilov days' and then *offering* the bloc members a compromise and *having it refused by them* amidst vacillation on their part which has continued ever since, we are giving the whole people a sure way out.

It would be a great mistake to think that our offer of a compromise has not yet been rejected and that the Democratic Conference may *still* accept it. The compromise was offered by a *party* to *parties;* it could not have been otherwise. *Parties* rejected it. The Democratic Conference is a *conference,* nothing more. One thing must not be forgotten: the *majority* of the revolutionary people, the poor and embittered peasants, are not represented in it. It is a conference of the *minority of the people* – this plain truth cannot be forgotten. It would be a great mistake, the height of parliamentary cretinism on our part, to regard the Democratic Conference as a parliament, for even *if it were* to declare that it was a parliament and the sovereign parliament of the revolution, it would still *decide noth-*

ing: the decision lies *elsewhere,* in the working-class areas of Peter and Moscow.

We have all the objective conditions for a successful insurrection here before us. We have the exceptional advantage of a position where our victory in an insurrection is the *only* way to end the most tormenting thing on earth, the vacillation which has worn out the people; where *only our* victory in insurrection will *foil* the game for a separate peace against the revolution, foil it by the open offer of a fuller, fairer, earlier peace and a peace that will *benefit* the revolution.

Finally, only our Party, after victory in a rising, *can* save Peter because if our peace offer is rejected and we do not even get an armistice, then *we* will become 'defensists', we will *head the war parties,* we will be *the* 'war' party, we will wage a truly revolutionary war. We will take all the bread and the boots away from the capitalists. We will leave them crusts and fit them out with bast shoes. We will send all the bread and footwear to the front.

And then we will save Peter.

The resources, both material and spiritual, for a real revolutionary war in Russia are still immense; the chances are a hundred to one that the Germans will at least give us an armistice. And to get an armistice now would in itself mean to win the *whole world.*

*   *   *

Once we have recognised that an insurrection by the Peter and Moscow workers is absolutely necessary to save the revolution and to save Russia from a 'separate' partition by the imperialists of both coalitions, the first thing to do is to orient our political tactics at the Conference to conditions of mounting insurrection; second, we must show that it is not only in words that we acknowledge Marx's ideas that insurrection must be treated as an art.

At the Conference, we must immediately weld together the Bolshevik group, without chasing after numbers and not being afraid to leave waverers in the waverers' camp: for the purposes of the revolution, they are more useful there than among the determined and devoted fighters.

We must compose a brief declaration from the Bolsheviks, stressing with great incisiveness that long speeches are irrelevant, that 'speeches' in general are irrelevant, that there has to be immediate action to save the revolution, that there is an absolute need for a complete break with the bourgeoisie, the wholesale removal of the present government, a complete break with the Anglo-French imperialists who are working on a 'separate' partition of Russia, that all power must be transferred immediately to the *revolutionary democrats, headed by the revolutionary proletariat.*

Our declaration must put this conclusion concisely and clearly, linking it with the programme proposals: peace for the peoples, land for the peasants, confiscation of scandalous profits and a curb on the outrageous sabotage of production by the capitalists.

The shorter and sharper the declaration the better. Only two other highly important points must be clearly made in it: the people are worn out by vacillation, the people are fed up with the indecisiveness of the S Rs and Mensheviks; we are breaking with these *parties* once and for all, for they have betrayed the revolution.

And another thing: by proposing peace without annexations straight away, by breaking with the allied imperialists and all imperialists straight away, we will immediately get either an armistice or a switch by the whole revolutionary proletariat to the cause of defence and under its leadership the revolutionary democrats will wage a really just and really revolutionary war.

When we have read this declaration, having called for *decision* and not for talk, for *action* and not for resolution-writing, we must move our whole group *into the factories and barracks*: its place is there, the pulse of life beats there, there is the source for the revolution's salvation, there the motive force of the Democratic Conference.

It is there that we must explain our programme in fiery, passionate speeches and put it like this: either the Conference adopts it *in full,* or insurrection. There is no middle way. There can be no waiting. The revolution is dying.

By putting the question like this, and with the whole group concentrated in the factories and barracks, *we will be able to gauge the right moment for the insurrection to start.*

And so as to treat the insurrection in a Marxist way, that is as an art, we must at the same time, without losing a minute, organise a *headquarters* for the insurgent detachments, deploy our forces, move reliable regiments to the most important points, surround the Alexandrinskii theatre, occupy the Peter and Paul fortress, arrest the General Staff and the government and send against the junkers and the Savage Division detachments which would rather die than let the enemy reach the city's vital centres; we must mobilise the armed workers and summon them to a desperate and final fight, occupy the telegraph and telephone exchange immediately, move *our* insurrection headquarters into the central telephone exchange and connect it by telephone with all the factories, all the regiments, all the places where the armed struggle is focused, etc.

All this is by way of example, of course, only to *illustrate* the fact that at the present moment it is impossible to stay true to Marxism, to stay true to the revolution, without treating insurrection as an *art*.

N. Lenin.

Written on September 13 - 14 [26 - 27] 1917.
V.I.Lenin, *Sochineniia* 4th ed., vol.26, pp.4 - 9.

Minutes No.17
Session [of the CC]
September 20 [October 3 1917]

Present :
Trotsky, Uritsky, Bubnov, Bukharin, Dzerzhinsky, Sverdlov, Smilga, Kollontai, Ioffe, Sokolnikov, Rykov, Muranov, Sergeev [Artem], Krestinsky, Shaumian.

Agenda :
1. Enlisting the services of comrade Larin.
2. The Unionists and Steklov.
3. Municipal work.
4. Abroad.
5. Party Conference.
6. Special Party Congress.

1. A proposal coming from comrade Larin is heard, suggesting that he be given the opportunity to make a report to the CC or its elected commission about the work comrade Larin is doing in the departments of the Ministry of Labour.

A decision is taken to invite comrade Larin to one of the CC sessions to hear his report. After that, it is decided to bring comrade Larin into the municipal work which the CC is organising across Russia.

2. It is announced that the Unionists are asking for one seat to be given to them on the Executive Committee of the Petrograd Soviet of Workers' and Soldiers' Deputies – to Steklov, as the Unionists' representative. The idea of putting up anyone who is not a member of our Party through our list is rejected[94].

3.   Comrade Sverdlov gave information about the municipal group organised under the CC, the discussions with members of the municipal council attached to the Moscow Regional Bureau[95], the municipal journal and the municipal congress. A list of ten people is confirmed for the municipal group : Ioffe, Krupskaia, Larin, Lunacharsky, Sverdlov, Smit, Manuilsky, Fradkin, Podbel'sky, Solov'ev. It is decided that a municipal organ should be published[96]. At Rykov's suggestion, the decision on whether to make it weekly or fortnightly is referred to the municipal group. The membership of the organ's editorial board is confirmed as the following : Ioffe, Uritsky, Larin, Lunacharsky, Manuilsky. On the subject of the congress, it is decided to make it coincide with the towns' congress expected in Moscow, but if the towns' congress is put off for a long time, it should be held no later than October 10. The municipal group is instructed to prepare for the congress in cooperation with the people in Moscow[97].

4.   Abroad. It is decided to hear a report by Aleksandrov [Semashko], who was at the Zimmerwald Conference [98]. A decision is made to form a group to keep in touch with other countries, to include comrade Kollontai and comrade Larin. Comrade Kollontai is entrusted with setting up the group and organising channels of communication with foreign countries. She is to present a report about the group's organisation at the next CC session. It is decided to invite comrade Aleksandrov to make a report about the Zimmerwald Conference at the Party Conference, as well.

5.   It is decided to call a Party conference of comrades who came for the Democratic Conference plus the CC and members of the Petersburg Committee.

The Party conference agenda : 1. The current situation (speaker, comrade Trotsky). 2. The electoral campaign for the Constituent Assembly (speaker, comrade Sverdlov). 3. The Zimmerwald Conference (speaker, comrade Aleksandrov). 4. The special Party congress (report from the CC's Organisational Bureau, which is charged with working on the matter). 6. Where the special Party congress is concerned, it is decided to propose that the Party conference pass a decision to call it. The main purpose of the Party conference* must be to approve the Party pro-

---

*   Apparently a slip in the text. It should read : *congress.*

gramme[99]. The proposal to turn the conference into a special congress is rejected by all except one vote. 7. Comrade Sokolnikov makes a statement on behalf of the central organ's editorial board saying that some comrades are dissatisfied with the central organ's tone, with certain expressions in its articles, etc. Carried : while adjourning detailed discussion of the central organ's conduct, the CC affirms that its general direction wholly coincides with the CC line.

Minutes No.18
Session of the CC
September 21 [October 4] 1917

Present :
Trotsky, Kamenev, Stalin, Sverdlov, Rykov, Nogin, Miliutin, Smilga, Uritsky, Sergeev [Artem], Muranov, Krestinsky, Ioffe, Dzerzhinsky, Bukharin, Sokolnikov, Shaumian.

Agenda :
1. The Democratic Conference and the Pre-Parliament.
2. Comrade Zinoviev.

1. On the subject of the Democratic Conference, it is decided not to withdraw from it but merely to recall members of our Party from the praesidium. Where the Pre-Parliament is concerned, a decision not to go into it was passed by 9 votes to 8. But since the vote was divided almost equally, the final decision was referred to the Party meeting being organised right now from the group gathered at the Democratic Conference. Two reports – by comrade Trotsky and comrade Rykov – are planned.

At the meeting, participation in the Pre-Parliament was approved by 77 votes to 50, a decision which the CC also confirmed[100].

2. About comrade Zinoviev, it is confirmed yet again that any separation of his case from comrade Lenin's is completely unacceptable and the decision to organise a plenary session with him taking part is confirmed.

Minutes No.19
Session of the CC
September 23 [October 6] 1917

Present :

Trotsky, Kamenev, Zinoviev, Nogin, Sergeev [Artem], Bukharin, Bubnov, Krestinsky, Sokolnikov, Sverdlov, Miliutin, Dzerzhinsky, Ioffe, Shaumian, Uritsky ; representatives from the regions with a consultative vote : Sosnovsky (Urals), Piatakov (Kiev), Smirnov (Moscow).

Agenda :

1. Party Conference.
2. Democratic Conference.
3. The Pre-Parliament.
4. List of CC candidates for the Constituent Assembly.

1. As it has turned out, the agenda planned earlier[101] has had to be changed : drop 1. the current situation, 2. the Zimmerwald Conference. The first because the subject has already been discussed at a meeting of the group during the Democratic Conference[102]. The second because comrade Aleksandrov [Semashko] has left.

2. After a critical analysis of what went on at the Democratic Conference, a resolution of comrade Trotsky's was adopted.

For the Democratic Conference, which failed to reject an alliance with the imperialists and did not condemn the policy of the offensive, to endorse the principles of a democratic peace was a hypocritical gesture in the spirit of so many declarations by the French, English and American parliaments. The social-democratic group was obliged to introduce an amendment making this declaration[103] more concrete, an amendment which made certain actions binding and, in the event of the amendment being rejected, to brand the declaration as the hypocrisy of political groups who are currying favour with imperialism and hiding their servility from the masses behind a false declamation* borrowed from the socialist lexicon. For our group to join in this declaration and the

---

*   The copy of the resolution text, *ed. khr.* 27, *l.*8, has : *declaration.*

demonstration of the so-called democracy's unity in international policy that goes with it is to adopt the policy of *union sacrée** which could compromise our Party, too, in the eyes of the western revolutionary proletariat.

The resolution is adopted by 12 votes to 2, with one abstention. With regard to the commission elected at the Democratic Conference to work out the text of an appeal to all nations, it is decided : to go into the commission and there confront** the defensists' appeal with our own version. Passed by 8 votes. Trotsky and Sokolnikov are appointed to the commission.

A resolution is approved : After hearing a report that comrade Riazanov called Tsereteli 'comrade' when the declaration was being read[104], the CC suggests to comrades that people whose description as 'comrades' might offend the revolutionary feelings of the workers should not be addressed in this way in public speeches (for – 8, against – 2, abstained – 5).

3.   After a general exchange of views on work in the Pre-Parliament, a number of proposals relating to the first session are put forward.

1. If Chkheidze is elected chairman[105], to vote against after a speech giving reasons for the vote. Shaumian is charged with the speech.

2. It is decided to go into the praesidium and to demand proportional representation. For the praesidium – Rykov, Trotsky and Kamenev.

3. To respond to the report of the commission which the Democratic Conference elected to negotiate with Ministers with a critique if an agreement has already been reached and to make our own statement***[106]. Trotsky is assigned to speak.

Our attitude towards a ministry of 'similar' parties is discussed. No decision is taken.

4. It is decided to suggest to the Left SRs that they propose the immunity of members of the Pre-Parliament.

5. It is decided to prepare a resolution on the Pre-Parliament for the Party Conference. This is entrusted to Sokolnikov, Bubnov, Ioffe and Trotsky.

---

*   sacred union.
**   In the text of the minute notes : *There present our own version of the defensists' appeal.*
***   See p.70.

4.   The list of CC candidates for the Constituent Assembly[107] is approved.

5.   A decision is made to transfer Rykov to Peter to work in the Soviet.

Document
Statement made by the Bolshevik group at a session of the Pre-Parliament
September 23 [October 6] 1917

We, the RSDLP (bolsheviks) group, state that the official representatives of the Democratic Conference, in complete contradiction to their own statements at the Conference and the latter's decisions, propose to the democrats:

1.   the renunciation in practice of the revolution's rights to power; 2. the recognition in principle of Kerensky's non-accountability and 3. a coalition with property-owning and Kadet elements. We declare that to accept these conditions would be to violate openly the will of the very masses of the people whose support the Democratic Conference seeks and in whose name it wants to speak. The Petrograd Soviet of Workers' and Soldiers' Deputies, the Moscow Soviet of Workers' and Soldiers' Deputies, the Soviet of Workers', Soldiers' and Peasants' Deputies of the Caucasian area, the Finnish Regional Soviet of Workers' and Soldiers' Deputies, the Urals Regional Soviet of Workers' and Soldiers' Deputies, the Soviets of Kronstadt, Odessa, Ekaterinburg, the Donets basin, Baku, Reval, Kiev, of almost all Siberia, the Petrograd Council of Trade Unions, numerous Soviets of Peasants' Deputies and many other organs of the revolution declare by an overwhelming majority of their members that they consider that a coalition with the counter-revolutionary bourgeoisie, now ranged together under the Kadet Party banner, is unacceptable. A coalition ministry would mean that the Kadet Party had gained a decisive victory over the revolution and the people. To undertake a coalition under these circumstances would mean taking on a responsibility which would inevitably push the desperate masses of the people into elemental eruptions, that is provoke a civil war. Along with all the Soviets of Workers' and Soldiers' Deputies, along with millions of workers, soldiers and peasants, our Party will refuse to give a coalition government any support whatsoever and at the head of the masses of the people will struggle for the formation of a popular govern-

ment depending on the Soviets at the centre and in the localities. And that is why we propose to the Democratic Conference: 1. that the talks being held with the property-owning bourgeoisie under Kerensky's direction be broken off and 2. that a start be made on creating a truly revolutionary power.

Izvestiia TsIK i Petrogradskogo Soveta R i SD No. 181, September 26 1917.

Minutes No.20
Session [of the CC]
September 24 [October 7] 1917

Present :
Sverdlov, Stalin, Kamenev, Sokolnikov, Trotsky, Uritsky, Rykov, Bubnov, Shaumian.

Agenda :
1. Party conference.
3. Petrograd Soviet.
4. Railway strike.
5. Congress of Soviets.

1. Sverdlov gives information about the Party conference which was held[108] and passes on the resolution about the current situation* and the appeal, both approved in basic outline at the conference and referred to the CC for elaboration.
3. It is decided to move Rykov to Peter to work in the Soviet and to transfer several other comrades to work in the Soviets as well, including Volodarsky. Trotsky to be put forward as chairman of the Soviet and Rykov to go into the praesidium.
4. An appeal concerning our attitude to the railwaymen is approved**[109].
5. About the congress of Soviets[110], a decision is taken to campaign widely everywhere and pass resolutions in different Soviets

---

*   See p.72.
**   See p.74.

demanding that a congress be called immediately. Sverdlov is delegated to the commission for the convocation of a congress and Iurenev to help him. It would be desirable to call district and regional congresses of Soviets in advance.

6.   After hearing a communication about an offer of money[III], the following resolution is approved :

The CC heard a communication from comrade Aleksandrov [Semashko] about an offer made by the Swiss socialist K. Moor to put a certain sum of money at the CC's disposal; since it is impossible to check the real source of the money offered and to establish whether it really comes from the same fund which the offer indicated was a source of income for G. V. Plekhanov, and equally impossible to check the true purpose of Moor's offer, the CC resolved : to decline the offer and consider any further negotiations on this subject inadmissible.

Document 1
The current situation and the tasks before the proletariat
Resolution passed by the Party Conference on September 24 [October 7] 1917.

1.   Looked at from the point of view of class groupings, the characteristics of the current situation are that : a. all the bourgeois groups, the kulak upper strata of the peasantry and the cossacks included, are united under the ideological and organisational hegemony of finance capital (the Kadet Party); b. the proletariat has finally emerged from under the ideological influence of the bourgeoisie; c. the poor peasants and the soldiers have shed their last illusions, as is apparent from the formation and growth of the left wing of the SRs and the increasing influence of the party of the proletariat on these strata.

2.   In these circumstances, the ruling classes must come to rely more and more in their struggle exclusively on the naked physical force of the apparatus of oppression they have kept in their control (the army high command, a section of the cossacks, etc.) and on support from international imperialism, with its interest in stifling the Russian proletariat, ready to come to power, and in an imperialist plunder of Russia. This finds expression in the policy of repression (punitive expeditions, martial law), the organisation of military conspiracies, their active support for international capital and,

finally, in the desire to end a predatory war with a predatory peace – with the sole purpose of immediately starting a general war against the Russian proletariat.

3. The tactics of the bourgeoisie, therefore, are going through a time of sharp change. The policy of using the blind faith the masses had in the bourgeoisie, and the policy of conciliation grounded on it, which put the strength of these masses at the disposal of the bourgeoisie, has become objectively impossible. The last attempt at conciliation of that sort – the Democratic Conference – ended in failure, having shown that it was in no state to persuade the wide masses to serve the interests of the bourgeoisie. In these circumstances, its policy is directed towards a civil war against the masses of the people.

4. Foreseeing this, the proletarian party must make every effort to mobilise the broad masses of the people, organised by the Soviets of Workers', Soldiers' and Peasants' Deputies, which are now militant class organisations, and the slogan of the day becomes the transfer of power to them. The Party must direct its work along these lines and its activity in the Pre-Parliament should be merely auxiliary and completely subordinated to the tasks associated with the mass struggle.

5. With these ends in view, there must be a drive to develop the activity of the Soviets and to raise their political significance to the role of organs standing counter to the bourgeois state authorities (the government, the Pre-Parliament, etc.). The necessary conditions for this are: close links between local Soviets and contact to be established with other revolutionary organisations belonging to the proletariat, the soldiers and the peasants; a change in the Soviet's organisational apparatus (eliminating obstacles to new elections, recall of members of the *TsIK* and executive committees in the localities); the calling of regional congresses immediately and a congress of Soviets very soon.

6. Only if the broad masses, organised in the Soviets, rally all their forces can the workers, soldiers and peasants come out victorious. Only if they are victorious can a democratic peace be achieved and the cause of international revolution be moved rapidly forward.

Rabochii put' No.23, October 12 [September 29] 1917.

Document 2
Help the railwaymen
Appeal from the CC RSDLP(b)

The railway strike which has been brewing for a long time has broken out. The Provisional Government, isolated from workers' organisations and in a state of constant internal crises, has proved completely incapable of averting this railway strike. They answered the transport workers from on high with vague promises, putting off solving the problem from week to week and month to month during the very time when, at the demand of Rodzianko and Co., this same government raised bread prices by 100 per cent in a few days. This decision on its own was a direct provocation aimed at the hungry railway workers and employees whose selfless work continued throughout the revolution and who showed their heroic devotion to the revolution in the threatening days of Kornilov's plot. The railwaymen made every effort to avoid a strike, so dangerous in the country's present state of disruption. And every citizen must realise clearly that *the whole responsibility for the strike which has broken out falls on the Provisional Government* which, when decisions and actions were needed, responded with empty promises and threats.

For their part, the railwaymen, as their statements and conduct show, took every measure to prevent the strike affecting the position at the front and the provisions for the population in the towns. None the less, the bourgeois press and their claques raised a witch-hunt against the strikers, going so far as to call them traitors. The shady sections of the petty bourgeoisie, the officers and backward elements in the army were urged on against the railwaymen; the Kadet *provocateurs* strained themselves to the utmost to make the affair result in sharp conflicts among different groups of the population to give grounds for a military reprisal against the workers on the railways.

Before the whole country, we expose and denounce this bourgeois work of provocation. The railway strike undeniably affects the interests of the broadest masses of the population. But *the way out of this position is not criminally to break up the strike but to force the government to satisfy the railwaymen's legitimate demands very quickly*.

There is only one way to achieve this: the workers in every branch of industry, the politically-conscious soldiers and peasants and honest citizens in general must *surround the railwaymen with an atmosphere of total sympathy*, protect them from persecution and provo-

cative attacks by counter-revolutionary gangs and help them in
this way to end the strike thrust on them very quickly.
We appeal to all our Party organisations and members to make an
immediate effort so that the railwaymen will not find themselves
isolated and crushed. The revolutionary solidarity of the working
masses is the only salvation.

Central Committee of the RSDLP (bolsheviks)

September 24 1917
Petrograd

Archives of the IML, f. 17, op. 1, ed. khr. 395.
Printed according to the text in the newspaper, <i>Rabochii
put'</i> No.20, October 9 [September 26] 1917, collated with
the original.

Minutes No.21
Session of the Central Committee
September 29 [October 12 1917]

Present :
Zinoviev, Kamenev, Sverdlov, Uritsky, Miliutin, Sokolnikov, Bub-
nov, Dzerzhinsky, Ioffe, Muranov.
Chairman Sverdlov.

Agenda :
2. List of candidates for the Constituent Assembly.
3. Draft CC appeal on the Democratic Conference.
4. Regional congress of Finland, etc.

2. The proposal that the list of 25 be printed, indicating the
district putting them forward, is approved ; at the same time, it is
decided to increase the list of those recommended to 100 and to
print it[112]. The Electoral Commission for the Constituent Assembly,
with several comrades added, is charged with compiling the list. It
is decided to put up Kamenev for Petrograd, and to instruct the
Military Bureau under the CC to recommend candidates for the
front. Lenin[113] and Zinoviev to be put up for the Baltic fleet and
the army.

3.   The draft appeal is approved and given to the central organ's editorial board to be reviewed and confirmed[114].

4.   An announcement by Sverdlov is heard about the possibility of a congress of Northern Region Soviets on October 5[115]; it is acknowledged that a congress would be desirable.

5.   It is planned to arrange a CC session in the near future devoted to matters connected with this congress[116].

Minutes No.22
Session of the CC
October 3 [16 1917]

Present :
Kamenev, Sokolnikov, Sverdlov, Uritsky, Bubnov, Lomov [Oppokov], Ioffe, Dzerzhinsky.
Chairman Sverdlov.

Agenda :
1.   Report by Lomov on the Moscow region.
2.   Il'ich.
3.   Riazanov.
4.   Steklov.
5.   Arrangements for printing *Priboi* publications.

1.   A report by Lomov [Oppokov] is heard. It becomes clear that the mood in the region is extremely tense. We have a majority in the Soviets in many places. The masses are putting forward the demand for concrete measures of some kind. Everywhere we are marking time. It is decided not to have a debate on the report.

2.   A decision is passed to suggest to Il'ich that he move to Peter to make close and constant contact possible[117].

3.   It is decided to put Riazanov on the editorial board of *Prosveshchenie* and in this way of *Priboi*, too.

4.   An announcement is heard about Steklov joining the group in the Petersburg Soviet and the *TsIK*[118]. After this announcement, there is a move to next business.

5.   It is established that the arrangements for printing *Priboi* publications are to be sorted out by the editorial board of *Rabochii put'* and comrade Dzerzhinsky jointly.

Minutes No.23
Session of the CC
October 5 [18 1917]

Present :
Kamenev, Dzerzhinsky, Sverdlov, Sokolnikov, Lomov [Oppokov],
Ioffe, Stalin, Kollontai, Smilga, Trotsky, Bubnov.
Chairman Sverdlov.

Agenda :
1.   Organisational business.
2.   Statement from Lunacharsky.
3.   Regional Congress of the Northern Region.
4.   Pre-Parliament.
5.   Party Congress.
7.   Platform.

I.   1. Sverdlov reports on the request which has come from the
Petrograd Area Committee to be given a subsidy on the scale of
2500-3000 roubles needed to start work in the province[119].

After a discussion, Sverdlov's proposal to give 1000 roubles,
indicating that it is hoped that it will be returned, is adopted.

2.   Sverdlov reports that a Regional Bureau of our Party's Military Organisation has been formed on the south-west front and
that the Bureau requests that several thousands be given to publish
a front newspaper[120].

It is decided to give between 2 and 3 thousand roubles.

3.   A letter is read from Lunacharsky saying that a number of
contributors to *Novaia zhizn'* in the cultural section intend to leave
if Lunacharsky refuses to edit the section.

Lunacharsky raises the question of collaboration in *Novaia
zhizn'* once again.

The previous decision is confirmed[121].

4.   Comrade Kollontai gives information about the proposed
conference of women workers[122].

Comrade Sverdlov's suggestions to link the work among
women workers with the Petrograd Committee is adopted ; Kollontai's addition that CC members belonging to the Petrograd
Committee must help with this link is approved.

5.   Where *Rabotnitsa* is concerned, it is agreed that Kollontai is

the CC's representative on the editorial board and that the management side is put under a general management commission.

II.   The decision on the Northern Region Congress of Soviets is reviewed[123].

It is decided :   1.   The Petrograd Soviet is to take part in the Congress.

2.   The Congress is to be held in Petrograd.

3.   „   „   is postponed from October 8 to 10.

III.   After a discussion, the decision is passed by all except one[124] to withdraw from the Pre-Parliament on the very first day on reading the declaration*.

The theses are approved and the actual drawing up of the declaration is entrusted to the central organ's editorial board[125].

IV.   A modified proposal by Stalin to call a Party conference of the CC and our workers in Peter and Moscow is approved. The conference is timed to coincide with the Northern Region Congress of Soviets, 10. 10[126], to which the Moscow Soviet is also invited.

V.   The decision to call a Party Congress is reviewed.

Approved : the congress is postponed for a short time[127]. A commission is nominated to prepare the draft programme for the congress : Lenin, Bukharin, Trotsky, Kamenev, Sokolnikov, Kollontai.

VII.   The editorial board of the central organ is charged with considering in detail and approving Trotsky's draft platform[128].

To the CC RSDLP.

Dear comrades, I believe that your decision to withdraw from the 'Council of the Russian Republic' at the very first session commits the Party's tactics in the immediate future to a direction which I personally consider to be extremely dangerous for the Party. While submitting to the Party's decision, I ask you, comrades, to release me from duties in representative organs (*TsIK*, etc.) and to charge me with some other kind of work.

5.10.1917   Kamenev**

---

*   See p.79.

**   Kamenev's statement is written on the end of the minutes.

Document
Declaration by the Bolshevik group on withdrawing from the Pre-Parliament
October 7 [20] 1917

The officially-declared aims of the Democratic Conference called by the *TsIK* of the Soviet of Workers' and Soldiers' Deputies consisted of the abolition of an irresponsible personal regime which nourished the Kornilov plot and the formation of an accountable government capable of ending the war and getting the Constituent Assembly called at the appointed time.

Meanwhile, behind-the-scenes deals made by Mr. Kerensky, the Kadets and the SR and Menshevik leaders arrived at results behind the back of the Democratic Conference which directly contradicted the officially-declared aims.

A governing power has been created within which and around which Kornilov partisans, both open and covert, play a leading role. The non-accountability of this governing power is henceforth made secure and formally enunciated.

The 'Council of the Russian Republic' is declared a consultative institution; eight months after the revolution, an irresponsible power has made a cover for itself out of a new edition of the Bulygin Duma.

The property-owning elements had no right to be represented in such numbers in the Provisional Council, as all the elections in the country show. In spite of that, it was precisely the Kadet Party which tried to make sure and did make sure that the governing power was not accountable even to the Pre-Parliament, distorted though it is in favour of the property-owning bourgeoisie.

That same Kadet Party which was insisting only yesterday on the Provisional Government's dependence on Mr. Rodzianko's Duma secured the Provisional Government's independence of the Council of the Republic.

The property-owning elements will occupy an incomparably less favourable position in the Constituent Assembly than in the Provisional Council. The governing power cannot fail to be responsible to the Constituent Assembly. If the property-owning elements were really preparing for a Constituent Assembly in one and a half months, they would have no motive of any kind to defend the non-accountability of the governing power now. The truth of the matter is that the bourgeois classes which direct the Provisional Government's policy have set themselves the aim of *blocking* the Constituent Assembly. This is now the basic objective of the property-owning elements and their whole policy, internal and external, is subordinated to it.

In the industrial, agrarian and food-producing areas, the policy of the government and the propertied classes aggravates the disruption normally caused by war. The property-owning classes, having provoked insurrection among the peasants, are now starting to crush it, openly steering for the 'bony hand of starvation', which is to strangle the revolution and, first of all, the Constituent Assembly.

The external policy of the bourgeoisie and its government is no less criminal.

After forty months of war, deadly danger threatens the capital. The response to that is a plan to move the government to Moscow. The thought of surrendering the capital of the revolution to German troops does not disturb the bourgeois classes in the least; on the contrary, they accept it as a natural link in the general policy, designed to make their counter-revolutionary conspiracy easier.

Instead of recognising that the way to save the country is to conclude a peace; instead of openly going over the heads of the imperialist governments and the diplomatic offices and offering an immediate peace to all the exhausted peoples, thus making it impossible in practice to pursue the war any further, the Provisional Government, under orders from the Kadet counter-revolutionaries and the allied imperialists, senselessly, impotently, aimlessly drags out the murderous war, condemning yet more hundreds of thousands of soldiers and sailors to a pointless death and getting ready to surrender Petrograd and stifle the revolution. While Bolshevik soldiers and sailors perish alongside the other soldiers and sailors because of the errors and crimes of others, the so-called Supreme Commander goes on attacking the Bolshevik press (*Molot* has been closed in Minsk).

The leading parties in the Provisional Council serve as a willing cover for this whole policy.

We, the social-democratic Bolshevik group, declare: we have nothing in common with this government which betrays the people and with this Council which connives at counter-revolution. We do not want to serve as a screen for this work being done behind the official scenes, work murderous for the people – for a single day – either directly or indirectly.

The revolution is in danger! While Wilhelm's troops threaten Petrograd, the Kerensky-Konovalov government is getting ready to run from Petrograd so as to turn Moscow into a counter-revolutionary stronghold.

We appeal to the vigilance of the Moscow workers and soldiers!

As we leave the Provisional Council, we appeal to the vigilance and cour-
age of the workers, soldiers and peasants of all Russia.
Petrograd is in danger ! The revolution is in danger ! The people are in
danger !
The government makes this danger worse. The ruling parties help it.
Only the people themselves can save themselves and the country. We ap-
peal to the people.
All power to the Soviets !
All land to the people !
On with an immediate, honest, democratic peace !
On with the Constituent Assembly !

Rabochii put' No.31, October 21 [8] 1917.

Minutes No.24
Session [of the CC]
October 7 [20] 1917

Present :
Sokolnikov, Stalin, Sverdlov, Bubnov, Trotsky, Uritsky, Kamenev,
Ioffe, Dzerzhinsky.
Chairman Sverdlov.

Comrade Bubnov announces that the Petrograd Committee's Executive Commission elected two people to a bureau to as-
certain the mood of the masses and to establish close links between
them and the Party centres.

After examining and discussing the question of the need for
actions to be coordinated and information to be precise, it is decided to form : an Information Bureau under the CC for the
struggle against counter-revolution. Three are elected to the
Bureau from the CC : Trotsky, Sverdlov and Bubnov, who are
also commissioned to set up the Bureau itself.

PART TWO

The CC fighting for
the success of the October armed rising
and to consolidate Soviet power

Minutes No.25

[The minutes of the CC session of October 10 [23] 1917 (*ed.khr.*33) are the original secretarial notes written with an ordinary pencil on both sides of three sheets of paper torn from a large notebook. There are editorial corrections on the minutes in Ia. M. Sverdlov's handwriting. The minute book belonging to the secretariat of the CC RSDLP(b) contains a second set of the minutes (*ed. khr.* 59).

The text of the minutes is printed from the secretarial notes collated with the text of the minutes in the CC secretariat book.

The following documents are attached to the minutes: 1. A typewritten copy of the CC resolution about the armed rising with the CC RSDLP stamp. (The text of the original written by V. I. Lenin is kept in *f.*2, *op.*1, *ed. khr.* 4628.) The resolution is included in the text of the minutes (see p. 88). 2. The statement by Zinoviev and Kamenev 'The current situation' dated October 11 1917 (see p.89). The text is typewritten, the signatures are autographs.]

Session of the CC
October 10 [23] 1917

Present :
Lenin, Zinoviev, Kamenev, Trotsky, Stalin, Sverdlov, Uritsky, Dzerzhinsky, Kollontai, Bubnov, Sokolnikov, Lomov [Oppokov]. Chairman Sverdlov.

Agenda :
1. The Rumanian front.
2. The Lithuanians.
3. Minsk and the Northern front.
4. The current situation.
5. Regional congress.
6. Withdrawal of troops.

1. *The Rumanian front.*
Information is given by comrade Sverdlov. A conference of social democrats of all shades has taken place on the Rumanian front. A mixed list was drawn up. They went to the (unified) CC.

They got approval. They are asking what our CC's attitude is to this : out of 20 candidates, 4 Bolsheviks are nominated[129].

Resolved : Taking the Congress decision into account, no pacts of any kind are allowed[130].

2.   *The Lithuanians.*

Comrade Sverdlov reports.

The Lithuanians held a conference in Moscow where it came to light that defensists often speak in the Party's name. To counteract this, it is decided to elect a provisional centre which is to take a stand, together with the conference as a whole, under the Bolshevik banner. This centre needs to be confirmed.

Comrade Lomov [Oppokov]. He thinks it should be confirmed. But attention must be given to the fact that defensist organisations attended, too.

The provisional bureau is ratified[131].

3.   *Minsk and the Northern front.*

Report by Sv[erdlov].

Representatives who arrived from armies on the Northern front assert that there is something shady going on on that front to do with the withdrawal of troops into the interior.

There is information from Minsk that a new Kornilov-type plot is being prepared there. Because of the character of the garrison, Minsk is surrounded by cossack units. Some suspicious talks are going on between the headquarters and Supreme Command. Agitators are at work against the Bolsheviks among the Osset and certain other units of the troops. On the front, though, the mood is *for* the Bolsheviks, they follow them against Kerensky. There are no documents at all. They could be obtained if the headquarters is seized, which is technically quite possible in Minsk; at the same time, the local garrison can disarm the whole ring of forces. All the artillery has been driven into the Pinsk marshes. They can send a corps of troops from Minsk to Petrograd.

4.   *Comrade Lenin* speaks on the current situation.*

He maintains that since the beginning of September a certain indifference to the question of insurrection has been noticeable. Yet if we are seriously promoting the slogan of a seizure of power by the Soviets, this cannot be allowed. That is why attention should

---

*   In the original secretarial notes, *l.*2, Lenin's name is carefully crossed out.

have been given to the technical side of the matter long ago. Now, apparently, considerable time has been lost.

None the less, the question is urgent and the decisive moment is near. The international situation is such that we must take the initiative.

What is being done to surrender as far as the Narva and to surrender Peter[132] makes it even more imperative for us to take decisive action.

The political position is also working impressively in this direction.

On July 3-5, positive action on our part would have failed because the majority was not behind us. Since then we have gone up in leaps and bounds.

Absenteeism and indifference among the masses can be explained by the fact that the masses are fed up with words and resolutions.

The majority is now behind us. Politically, the situation is completely ripe for a transfer of power.

The agrarian movement is going in the same direction for it is clear that it would need heroic forces to quell this movement. The slogan for all land to be transferred has become the general slogan of the peasants. So the political circumstances are ripe. We have to talk about the technical side. That is the crux of the matter. Yet we, in the wake of the defensists, are inclined to regard the systematic preparation of an insurrection as something akin to a political sin.

It is senseless to wait for the Constituent Assembly, which will clearly not be on our side, for this means complicating our task.

The Regional Congress and the proposal from Minsk must be used as the starting point for decisive action.

Comrade Lomov [Oppokov] takes the floor with information about the position of the Moscow Regional Bureau and the Moscow Committee[133], and also about the situation in Moscow.

Comrade Uritsky maintains that we are not only weak technically but also in all the other aspects of our work, too. We have passed a mass of resolutions. But taken no positive action. The Petrograd Soviet is disorganised, there are few meetings etc.

What forces can we rely on?

The workers in Petrograd have 40,000 rifles but that will not settle the matter; that is nothing.

After the July days, the garrison cannot inspire great hope. But in any case, if an insurrection is the aim, then something effective must be done in this direction. We have to decide on certain actions.

Comrade Sverdlov tells what he knows about the state of affairs in Russia as a whole.

A resolution is approved in the following form :

'The CC recognises that the international position of the Russian revolution (the insurrection in the German navy[134], an extreme sign of the way the world socialist revolution has grown throughout Europe; then the imperialists' threat of a peace* aimed at stifling the revolution in Russia), as well as the military position (the decision undoubtedly made by the Russian bourgeoisie and Kerensky and Co. to surrender Peter to the Germans) and the fact that the proletarian party has acquired a majority in the Soviets – all this taken together with the peasant revolt and the swing in popular confidence towards our Party (the Moscow elections[135]) and, finally, the obvious preparations being made for a second Kornilov revolt (troops being withdrawn from Peter, cossacks moved towards Peter, Minsk encircled by cossacks, etc.) – all this puts an armed rising on the order of the day.

Recognising therefore that an armed rising is inevitable and that its time has come, the CC suggests that all Party organisations be guided by this and approach the discussion and solution of all practical issues from this point of view (the Congress of Northern Region Soviets, the withdrawal of troops from Peter, the action of our people in Moscow and Minsk, etc.)'

10 expressed themselves in favour, 2 against[136].

Comrade Dzerzhinsky suggests that a Political Bureau be created from members of the CC to provide political leadership in the days ahead.

After an exchange of views, the suggestion is approved. A Political Bureau of 7 people is created (the editorial board plus two plus Bubnov)**.

---

* I. V. Stalin, in his *Sochineniia*, vol. 6, p.345, gives the following footnote to this text: *Obviously, it should be : "of a separate peace"* I.St.

** In the original secretarial notes, *l.3*, the text – *Comrade Dzerzhinsky suggests . . . (the editorial board plus two plus Bubnov)* – is written on the back of the sheet and crossed out.

Then the question is raised of creating a Political Bureau of the CC. It is decided to form a Bureau of 7 people : Len[in], Zin[oviev], Kam[enev], Tr[otsky], Stal[in], Sok[olnikov], Bubn[ov].

Document
Statement by Kamenev and Zinoviev
October 11 [24] 1917

Dear comrades !

At the last CC session we were in a minority and the two of us voted against the theses adopted. Since the question is so important, we considered it necessary to set out a short summary of the speeches we gave at the session in a special statement attached herewith and we ask you to attach this statement of ours to the minutes of the meeting. We regard it as our duty to acquaint the Petrograd Committee, the Moscow Committee, the Moscow Regional Committee and the Regional Finnish Committee with this statement of ours. You will, of course, understand the form our statement takes without explanation.

G. Zinoviev.

Iu. Kamenev.

To the Petrograd, Moscow, Moscow Regional and Finnish Regional Committees of the RSDLP, the Bolshevik group in the TsIK, the Petrograd Executive Committee of the Soviets of Workers' and Soldiers' Deputies and the Bolshevik group in the Congress of Northern Region Soviets.

The current situation

Where the political situation as a whole is concerned, the Bolshevik departure from the Pre-Parliament raises the question for our Party : *what next?*

There is a tendency becoming established and gaining ground in workers' circles to see the immediate declaration of an armed insurrection as the only way out. All the timetables have now come together so that if one talks of such an insurrection, it has to be fixed directly and then for the very near future. The subject is already being discussed in one form or another in all the periodicals and at workers' meetings and it occupies the minds of a large circle of Party workers. We, in our turn, regard it as our duty and our right to express ourselves on this matter with complete frankness.

We are deeply convinced that to proclaim an armed insurrection now is to put at stake not only the fate of our Party but also the fate of the Russian and the international revolution.

There is no doubt that historical circumstances do exist when an oppressed class has to recognise that it is better to go on to a defeat than surrender without a fight. Is the Russian working class in just such a position today? *No, a thousand times no ! ! !*

As a result of the enormous growth in our Party's influence in the towns and particularly in the army, a position has been reached at the present moment where it is becoming more and more impossible for the bourgeoisie to block the Constituent Assembly. Through the army and the workers, we hold a revolver to the head of the bourgeoisie: the bourgeoisie has been put in such a position that if it took it into its head to try to wreck the Constituent Assembly now, the petty-bourgeois parties would again be pushed towards us and the trigger of the revolver would be squeezed.

Our Party's chances in the Constituent Assembly elections are excellent. We regard the talk put about that the influence of Bolshevism is beginning to decline and suchlike as totally without foundation. Coming from our political opponents, these assertions are simply a mode of political game calculated precisely to evoke a Bolshevik move in conditions favourable to our enemies. The influence of Bolshevism is growing. Whole sections of the working population are still only beginning to be swept up in it. With the right tactics, we can get a third of the seats in the Constituent Assembly, or even more. The position of the petty-bourgeois parties in the Constituent Assembly will not be exactly the same as it is now. First of all, their slogan 'For land, for freedom, wait for the Constituent Assembly' lapses. But the intensification of need and hunger and the peasant movement will bring more and more pressure to bear on them and they will be forced to seek an alliance with the proletarian party against the landowners and capitalists represented by the Kadet Party.

The Constituent Assembly cannot by itself, of course, change the real relationship between social forces. But it will prevent this relationship being disguised as at present. There is no getting rid of the Soviets, which have taken root in the life we live. Already the Soviets in practice exercise power in a number of places.

The Constituent Assembly too, can only rely on the Soviets in its revolutionary work. The Constituent Assembly plus the Soviets – here is that mixed type of state institution we are going towards. Based on this, our Party's policy gets a tremendous chance of a real victory.

We have never said that the Russian working class *on its own*, relying only on its own resources, can successfully accomplish the present revolution. We did not forget, and still must not forget, that between us and the bourgeoisie stands a huge third camp: the petty bourgeoisie. This camp aligned itself with us in the days of the Kornilov revolt and brought us victory. It will join us again, more than once. One must not allow oneself to be mesmerised by what exists at a given moment. There is no doubt that now this camp is far nearer to the bourgeoisie than it is to us. But the present position is not eternal and immutable. And it only takes one careless step, some ill-considered move which makes the whole fate of the revolution depend on an immediate insurrection, for the proletarian party to push the petty bourgeoisie into Miliukov's arms *for a long time.*

They say: 1. The majority of the people in Russia are already on our side and 2. the majority of the international proletariat is on our side. Alas! Neither one nor the other is true, and that is the whole point.

In Russia we have the majority of the workers and a considerable section of the soldiers on our side. But all the rest are doubtful. We are all convinced, for example, that if things now get as far as the Constituent Assembly elections, the peasants will vote in the main for the SRs. What is this then – chance? The masses of the soldiers support us not for the cry of war but for the cry of peace. This factor is extremely important and if we do not take account of it we risk building all our calculations on sand. If, after taking power now and alone, we are faced (because of the world situation as a whole) with the need to wage a revolutionary war, the soldier masses will leave us in a rush. The best young soldiers will stay with us, of course, but the masses of the soldiers will go. The criminal nature of the imperialist government is summed up in this very fact, that by serving the interests of the Russian and the allied bourgeoisie, it radically undermined the economic strength of the country and disorganised it in such a way that the revolutionary people are being more and more deprived of the possibility of defending themselves from the appetites of world imperialism by a revolutionary war. After forty months of an imperialist war in a country ravaged by the rule of marauders, in the midst of the devastation created by Tsarism and perpetuated by bourgeois supremacy, the soldiers are drained and less and less capable of waging a successful revolutionary war against all international capitalism in alliance.

The same delegates from the front who are now agitating so much against the war, ask our public speakers straight out not to mention a revolutionary war because it will drive away the soldiers. That is a very important symptom.

Undoubtedly, a proletarian government would immediately go on to make sure that it laid the economic burden of the war on the bourgeoisie – that it left the bourgeoisie 'only crusts of bread' and 'took its boots away'. This should arouse enthusiasm among the masses. But it still does not guarantee victory over German imperialism in a revolutionary war. Present-day Russia, having allowed itself in spite of the working class to be drained dry by the imperialist war, would still remain a country with comparatively backward technology, with a disrupted railway system, shortages of goods, a lack of the necessary military and technical equipment, etc. The fact that the workers' party had taken power would, undoubtedly, be a blow to Wilhelm. It would be more difficult for him to make war against a revolutionary Russia which was offering an immediate and democratic peace. That is so. But would the blow be hard enough in the situation after Riga, etc, for Russia to shake off the grasp of German imperialism? If the German and British imperialists have begun separate talks – and this is almost beyond doubt – will they not go on with them even after our victory, and will Wilhelm not succeed in reaching Peter then, too? Where are the facts which say that the proletarian party alone – opposed by the petty-bourgeois democrats – must now take the responsibility, the *sole* responsibility for such a state of affairs and its inevitable consequences?

And now we come to the second assertion – that the majority of the international proletariat now supports us. Unfortunately, it is not so. The revolt in the German navy has enormous significance as a symptom. The first signs of a serious movement exist in Italy. But from this to any active support of proletarian revolution in Russia, declaring war on the whole bourgeois world, is still a very long way. It can do great harm to overestimate one's strength. There is no doubt that much is given to us and much is required of us. But if we stake everything now and suffer defeat, we will also be striking a cruel blow at the international proletarian revolution, which is growing extremely slowly but undoubtedly growing all the same. And yet it is only the growth of revolution in Europe which would make it obligatory for us, with no hesitation at all, to take power into our hands immediately. This is also the only guarantee of victory for a proletarian rising in Russia. It will come but it is not here yet.

What do we see ahead then for the immediate future? This is our answer.

Of course, our course does not depend on us alone. The opposition *may compel* us to engage in a decisive fight before the Constituent Assembly elections. Attempts at a new Kornilov revolt would, of course, leave us no choice. We would naturally join unanimously in the only decision possible then. But then, too, a considerable section of the petty-bourgeois camp would certainly support us again. The government's flight to Moscow will push the petty-bourgeois masses in our direction. And then the conditions will be right for our victory, then it will not be we who are defeated but our opponents.

But, so long as the choice depends on us, we can and must confine ourselves now to a *defensive position.* The Provisional Government is often powerless to put its counter-revolutionary intentions into practice. It is shaky. The soldiers and workers are strong enough to prevent such moves by Kerensky and Co. from being carried out. The peasant movement is still only beginning. In the present mood of the army, the Kadets cannot succeed in a mass suppression of the peasant movement. The Provisional Government has not the power to rig the Constituent Assembly elections. There will be growing sympathy for our Party. The bloc between the Kadets and the Mensheviks and SRs will disintegrate. In the Constituent Assembly, we will be so strong as an opposition party that, with universal suffrage in the country, our opponents will be forced to yield to us at every step, or we will form a ruling bloc with the Left SRs, the non-party peasants and others which will basically have to promote our programme. That is our opinion.

We do not have the right before history, before the international proletariat, before the Russian revolution and the Russian working class to stake the whole future on the card of an armed insurrection now. It would be wrong to think that such an action now would, in the event of failure, only lead to the consequences that followed July 3-5. Now it is a question of something bigger. It is a question of a final battle, and defeat *in this* battle would be the defeat of the revolution.

That is the general situation. But anyone who wants to do more than just talk about a rising is also obliged to weigh its chances soberly. And here we feel it our duty to say that at this moment the most harmful thing of all would be to underestimate the enemy's strength and overestimate our own. The strength of the opposition is greater than it seems. Petrograd is the key and in Petrograd the enemies of the proletarian party have amassed considerable forces: 5,000 junkers *magnificently* armed, *organised,* eager (because of their class position) and knowing how to fight, then the headquarters staff, the shock troops, the cossacks, an important section of the garrison, and a large amount of artillery deployed in a fan round Peter. Then our opponents, with the help of the *TsIK,* will almost certainly try to bring forces from the front. The balance of forces under which the proletarian party would have to fight at the present moment is completely different from that of the Kornilov days. Then we were fighting alongside the SRs, the Mensheviks and even in part with the supporters of Kerensky. But the proletarian party would have to fight the Black Hundreds, plus the Kadets, plus Kerensky and the Provisional Government, plus the *TsIK* (SRs and Mensheviks).

Of course, the proletarian party has very considerable forces but the decisive question is whether the workers and soldiers in the capital are really yet in a mood where they themselves see the only salvation in a street battle, in a mood to erupt on to the streets. No. This mood does not exist. Even those who advocate action declare that the mood among the masses of workers and soldiers is far from reminiscent of, say, the feelings before July 3. If a militant mood for street demonstrations existed deep among the masses of the city's poor, it would serve as a guarantee that once they had started to act, they would also carry along behind them those very large and important organisations (the railway and post and telegraph unions, etc.) where our Party's influence is weak. But since this mood does not even exist in the factories and barracks, to calculate on it would be to deceive ourselves.

They say: but the railwaymen and the post and telegraph employees are hungry, oppressed by poverty, angry with the Provisional Government. Of course, all that is true. But that is still no guarantee that they will support an insurrection against the government in defiance of the SRs and Mensheviks. The railway employees and workers were oppressed by poverty in 1906, too, and they are suffering in Germany and France as well. This is no guarantee, however, that they will support an insurrection. If everyone oppressed by poverty were always ready to support an armed rising of socialists, we would have won socialism long ago.

This underlines our next task. The Congress of Soviets is fixed for October 20. It must be held whatever happens. It must consolidate the growing influence of the proletarian party in an organised way. It must become a centre for rallying all the proletarian and semi-proletarian organisations, such as those very unions of railwaymen, postmen, bank employees, etc., round the Soviets. There is still no fixed organisational link between these organisations and the Soviets. This can only be judged as a symptom of the proletarian party's organisational weakness. And this kind of a link is, in any event, a prerequisite for the effective realisation, the effective implementation of the slogan 'All power to the Soviets'. At any particular moment, this slogan signifies, of course, the most determined resistance to the slightest encroachment made by the authorities on the rights of the Soviets and the organisations they have created.

Under these conditions, it would be a grave historical error to put the
question of transferring power into the hands of the proletarian
party in the terms: now or never!

No! The party of the proletariat will grow and its programme will be
made clear ever more widely to the masses. It will have the opportunity to go on exposing, mercilessly and in a still wider form, the
policy of the Mensheviks and SRs, who obstructed the way to an
effective transfer of power into the hands of the majority of the
people. And there is only one way to block its success and that is
precisely by it assuming the initiative for a rising in the present circumstances, thus putting the proletariat under attack from the
whole unified counter-revolution, supported by the petty-bourgeois
democrats.

It is against this fatal policy we raise our voice in warning.

G. Zinoviev
Iu. Kamenev

11.10.1917.

Archives of the IML, *f*.17, *op*.1, *ed. khr*. 33, *ll*.15, 23-29.

Minutes No.26

[The minutes of the CC session of October 16 [29] 1917 (*ed.khr*.
34) are the original secretarial notes written with an indelible and an
ordinary pencil in two columns on both sides of four large sheets of writing paper. A second set of short minute notes is in the minute book
belonging to the secretariat of the CC RSDLP(b) (*ed. khr*. 59).

The text of the minutes is printed according to the secretarial
notes, collated with the text of the minutes in the CC secretariat book.

The following documents are attached to the minutes:

1. The CC decision to organise a Military Revolutionary Centre.
Written in pencil on a small sheet of paper in F. E. Dzerzhinsky's handwriting. The decision is included in the minutes (see p. 109).

2. The typewritten text of V. I. Lenin's resolution, written in the old
orthography. (The text of the original resolution is kept in *f*.2, *op*.1, *ed.
khr*. 4630). The resolution is included in the text (see p. 108).

3. Zinoviev's resolution written in ink on a scrap of paper, also included in the text (see pp. 108-109).

4.   Original statements: by Kamenev about withdrawing from the CC; by Kamenev and Zinoviev demanding that a CC plenum be called and a statement by Nogin, Miliutin and Rykov (see pp. 108-110).]

Session
October 16 [29 1917]

Present:
Members of the CC, the Executive Commission of the Petrograd Committee, the Military Organisation, the Petrograd Soviet, trade unions, factory committees, the Petrograd Area Committee and the railwaymen.

Comrade Sv[erdlov] in the chair.
Comrade S[verdlov] proposes an agenda:

1.   Report on the last CC meeting.
2.   Short reports from representatives.
3.   The current situation.

1.   Report on the last CC meeting.

Comrade Lenin reads out the resolution the CC adopted at its last session*. He announces that the resolution was passed with two votes against. If the dissenting comrades want to say something, a debate can be held but in the meantime he gives the reasons for this resolution.

If the Menshevik and SR Parties had broken with conciliation, it might have been possible to offer them a compromise. The proposal had been made but it was clear that the Parties in question rejected this compromise. By that time, on the other hand, it had already become clear that the masses were supporting us. That was before the Kornilov revolt. He cites the election figures in Peter and in Moscow as evidence. The Kornilov revolt itself pushed the masses even more decisively towards us. The balance of forces at the Democratic Conference. The position is clear: either a Kornilov dictatorship or a dictatorship of the proletariat

---

*   See p.88.

and the poorest strata of the peasants. One cannot be guided by the mood of the masses for it is changeable and not to be calculated; we must go by an objective analysis and assessment of the revolution. The masses have put their faith in the Bolsheviks and demand deeds not words from them, a determined policy in both the struggle against the war and the struggle with disruption. On the basis of a political analysis of the revolution, it becomes quite clear that even anarchic outbursts confirm this now.

He goes on to analyse the situation in Europe and shows that revolution is even more difficult there than here; if things have gone as far as a revolt in the navy in a country like Germany, then this shows that things have already gone a long way there, too. Certain objective facts about the international situation indicate that in acting now we will have the whole European proletariat on our side; he shows that the bourgeoisie wants to surrender Peter. We can only escape that when we have taken control of Petrograd. From all this, the conclusion is clear, the armed insurrection talked of in the CC resolution is on the agenda.

As far as practical conclusions to be drawn from the resolution are concerned, it would be better to deal with them after hearing the reports from representatives from the centres.

A political analysis of the class struggle both in Russia and in Europe points to the need for a very determined and active policy, which can only be an armed insurrection.

[2.   Reports from representatives.]

Comrade Sverdlov of the CC reports on behalf of the CC secretariat on the state of affairs in the localities.

The Party has grown on a gigantic scale; it can be estimated that it now encompasses no fewer than 400,000 (he furnishes evidence).

Our influence has grown in the same way, especially in the Soviets (evidence) and similarly in the army and navy. He goes on to give the facts about the mobilisation of counter-revolutionary forces (Donetsk district, Minsk, Northern front).

Comrade Boky of the Petrograd Committee. He gives information district by district:

Vasil'evskii Island – mood not militant, military preparations being made.

Vyborg District the same but they are preparing for an insurrection; a Military Council has been formed; if there were action, the masses would be in support. They consider that the initiative ought to come from above.

1st City District	The mood is difficult to assess. There is a Red Guard.
2nd [City District]	A better mood.
Moscow District	A reckless mood, will come out if the Soviet calls but not the Party.
Narva District	Not eager for action but no falling off in the Party's authority. The anarchists are getting stronger at the Putilov [factory].
Neva District	The mood has swung sharply in our favour. Everyone will follow the Soviet.
Okhten District	Things are bad.
Petersburg District	An expectant mood.
Rozhdestvensk District	Doubt here, too, on whether they will rise, anarchists have strengthened their influence.
Porokhov District	The mood has improved in our favour.
Schluesselburg	Mood in our favour.

Comrade Krylenko of the Military Bureau announces that they differ sharply in their assessment of the mood.

Personal observations of the mood in the regiments indicate that they are ours to a man, but information from comrades working in the districts differs; they say that they would have to be positively stung by something for a rising, that is : the withdrawal of troops. The Bureau believes that morale is falling. Most of the Bureau thinks there is no need to do anything in practice to intensify things, but the minority thinks that it is possible to take the initiative oneself.

Comrade Step[anov] of the Area Organisation. In Sestroretsk, Kolpino* the workers are arming, the mood is militant and they are preparing for a rising. In Kolpino, an anarchist mood is developing.

---

*   Crossed out in the original secretarial notes, *l.* 1 *ob.*: *and Narva.*

The atmosphere in Narva is grave because of the dismissals. 3000 have already been dismissed.

Where the garrisons are concerned, the mood is depressed but Bolshevik influence is very strong (2 machine-gun regiments). Work in the regiment in N[ovyi] Petergof has fallen off a lot and the regiment is disorganised. Krasnoe Selo – 176th [regiment] is completely Bolshevik, the 172nd [regiment] nearly, but apart from that the cavalry is there. Luga – a garrison of 30,000; the Soviet is defensist. A Bolshevik mood and there are elections ahead.

In Gdov – the regiment is Bolshevik.

Comrade Boky adds that according to the information he has, matters are not so good in Krasnoe Selo.

In Kronstadt, morale has fallen and the local garrison there is no use for anything in a militant sense.

Comrade Volodarsky from the Petrograd Soviet. The general impression is that no one is ready to rush out on the streets but everyone will come if the Soviet calls.

Comrade Ravich confirms this and adds that some have indicated that also at the Party's call.

Comrade Shmidt of the trade unions. The total number organised is more than 500,000. Our Party's influence predominates but it is weak in unions more of the handicraft type (especially among the office workers and the printers) but even there it is beginning to grow, particularly since there is dissatisfaction with pay regulations. The mood is one where active demonstrations cannot be expected, especially because of the fear of dismissals. To a certain extent, this is a restraining factor. Because of certain economic conditions, colossal unemployment can be anticipated in the near future; this, too, makes the mood expectant. Everyone recognises that there is no way out of the situation apart from a struggle for power. They demand all power to the Soviets.

Comrade Shliapnikov adds that Bolshevik influence predominates in the metalworkers' union but a Bolshevik rising is not popular; rumours of this even produce panic. The mood among metalworkers in Russia as a whole is also predominantly Bolshevik; they pass Bolshevik resolutions but they are not conscious that they are capable of organising production for themselves. The union faces the struggle to raise wages. The issue of control will be linked with this fight.

Comrade Skrypnik from the factory committees. He states

that a craving for practical results has been noted everywhere; resolutions are no longer enough. It is felt that the leaders do not fully reflect the mood of the masses; the former are more conservative; a growth of anarcho-syndicalist influence is noted, particularly in the Narva and Moscow Districts.

Comrade Sverdlov gives additional information that as a result of the CC resolution, steps have been taken in Moscow to clarify the position about a possible insurrection.

Comrade Moskvin* *from the railwaymen.* The railwaymen are starving and embittered, organisation is weak, especially among the telegraph employees.

Comrade Shmidt adds that the strike has led to a crisis among the railwaymen. Dissatisfaction with the committee[137] is especially marked at the Moscow junction. In general, the Peter and Moscow junctions are closer to the Bolsheviks.

Comrade Boky. *The post and telegraph employees.* There is no separate organisation. The telegraph apparatus is mostly under the control of the Kadets. The postmen report that they will be able to take control of the post offices at the decisive moment.

Comrade Shmidt. The postal workers' union is more radical than the railwaymen. The lower employees are essentially Bolshevik but not the higher ones; while they keep control of the union, there has to be a struggle with them.

3.   The current situation.

Comrade Miliutin considers that the resolution should be made more concrete on the basis of all the reports. He believes that the slogan 'All power to the Soviets' has come to fruition, particularly in the provinces, where the Soviets are effectively in power in places. Agitation is not really the issue – actions not words are needed now. The matter is not resolved by moods and bulletins but by organised forces. Either we take the first step or it will be taken by our enemies. The resolution does not take enough account of the possibility of this second prospect, i.e. the possibility not of an insurrection, which presupposes our initiative, but of a conflict resulting from objective conditions. Personally, he believes that we

---

*   The name *Moskvin* is included from the minutes book of the CC secretariat, *l.*97.

are not ready to strike the first blow. We are unable to depose and arrest the authorities in the immediate future.

Another prospect arises : an armed conflict; he shows that this is developing and the possibility approaching. And we must be ready for this conflict. But this is a different prospect from an insurrection. He thinks the resolution should be developed in this direction.

Comrade Shotman says the mood was far more pessimistic at the City Conference and in the Petrograd Committee and the *Voenka*. He shows that we are unable to take action but must prepare ourselves.

Comrade Lenin argues against Miliutin and Shotman and demonstrates that it is not a matter of armed forces, not a matter of fighting against the troops but of a struggle between one part of the army and another. He sees no pessimism in what has been said here. He shows that the bourgeoisie do not have large forces on their side. The facts show that we have the edge over the enemy. Why is it not possible for the CC to begin? No reason emerges from all the facts. To throw out the CC resolution, it must be shown that there is no economic disruption and that the international position is not leading to complications. If the trade union leaders are demanding full power, they know very well what they want. Objective conditions show that the peasants have to be led; they will follow the proletariat.

There is a fear that we will not hold on to power, but just now our chances of retaining power are particularly good.

He expresses the wish that the debate be confined to a discussion of the substance of the resolution.

Comrade Krylenko declares that the whole Bureau is unanimous on one point, that things are near enough to the boil; it would be the greatest mistake to pass a resolution rescinding this resolution. Our task is to bring armed force to the support of an insurrection if one flares up anywhere. But the mood described here is the result of our mistakes.

He differs from V. I. [Lenin] on the subject of who will start it and how. He considers it unnecessary to enter into the technical details of the insurrection too much and, on the other hand, also regards it as inadvisable to make a definite date for it. But the issue of withdrawing the troops is crucial, the very moment to give rise to a fight. It will be argued at the Cherem[isov] conference[138] that it is necessary for the troops to retreat; we will not be able to make an answer to this but must reply that even if it is necessary, it will not be done because there is no faith in the generals : thus, the offensive against us is already a fact and it can be used. Agitation cannot be diminished and there is no point in worrying about who is to begin since a beginning already exists.

Comrade Rakh'ia shows that the masses are consciously preparing for an uprising. If the Petersburg proletariat had been armed, it would have been on the streets already regardless of any CC resolutions. There is no sign of pessimism. There is no need to wait for a counter-revolutionary attack for it already exists. The masses are waiting for slogans and weapons. They will erupt into the streets because famine awaits them. Apparently, our rallying cry is already overdue for there is doubt whether we are going to live up to our exhortations. It is not our task to reconsider but, on the contrary, to reinforce.

Comrade Grigory [Zinoviev]. Evidently the resolution is not being interpreted as an order otherwise it would not be possible to discuss it.

On its substance, he expresses doubt about whether a rising would be successful. First of all, we do not control the railway and post and telegraph. The influence of the *TsIK* is still quite strong.

The issue has to be decided on the very first day, and in Peter, for otherwise demoralisation will set in. One cannot count on reinforcements from Finland and Kronstadt. And we do not have the strength in Peter yet. In addition, our enemies have a huge organised headquarters staff. The noise we have made in recent times is wrong, even from the point of view of the CC resolution. For why do we have to give them a chance to prepare? The mood in the factories is no longer what it was in June. It is clear that there is not the mood now there was in June.

It is said there is no way out of the position in which we find ourselves; I do not think the position is like that yet. I think our attitude to the Constituent Assembly is wrong. Of course, it cannot be regarded as a panacea but the Constituent Assembly will take place in a highly revolutionary atmosphere. Until then, we will be gaining strength. It is not out of the question that with the Left SRs we will be in a majority there. It cannot be that the peasants will hesitate on the land question. I stood for withdrawal from the Pre-Parliament but I do not think that this mass is lost to us forever. He talks of international relations and shows that it is our duty to the international proletariat, too, to exercise the greatest caution : our influence is still growing. The surrender of Peter is not to be expected before the Constituent Assembly. We have no right to take risks, to stake everything on one card.

I propose : that if the Congress meets on the 20th, we should suggest that it does not disperse until the moment the Constituent Assembly meets. In the context of the Provisional Government's complete inertia, our tactics must be defensive, biding our time. One must not totally isolate oneself. The Constituent Assembly does not mean freedom from civil war either but it is a very important stage. The CC resolution must be reconsidered, if possible. We must tell ourselves squarely that we are not going to organise an insurrection in the next five days.

Comrade Kamenev. A week has passed since the resolution was adopted and this is also the reason this resolution shows how not to organise an insurrection : during that week, nothing was done; it only spoiled what should have been done. The week's results demonstrate that there are no factors to favour a rising now. It cannot be said that the resolution was only to inspire the idea, it called for a move from words to action. But nothing was done. We have no apparatus for an insurrection; our enemies' apparatus is far stronger and has probably grown even more in this week. He shows that we did nothing in the past week, either in a military and technical sense or in provisioning. This resolution only gave the government the opportunity to get itself organised. All the masses who do not support us are now on their side. We strengthened them at our own expense. The matter is more serious than in the July days. Socially, the crisis is ripe but there is no evidence of any kind that we must begin the fight before the 20th. It is not a question of now or never. I have more faith in the Russian revolution. Social battles lie before us and in preparing for the Constituent Assembly, we will certainly not be taking the path of parliamentarianism. We are not strong enough to go into an insurrection with the certainty of victory but we are strong enough to prevent any extremism by the reaction. Two tactics are in conflict here : conspiracy and faith in the motive forces of the Russian revolution.

Comrade Fenigstein considers that the armed rising is not a question of weeks but of days. That is a political position, and he agrees with it, but he is not in favour of immediately going over to bayonets.

He goes on to show that we have not made technical preparations for an armed insurrection. We do not even have a centre yet. We are going half-consciously to defeat. There are moments when one has to go on all the same. But if this is not one of them, it is necessary to look at things from the practical side.

Comrade Stalin. The right day must be chosen for the rising. This is the only way to understand the resolution.

It may be said that we have to wait to be attacked but it must be understood what such an attack is; the rise in bread prices, cossacks sent to the Donetsk district, etc. – all this already constitutes an attack. How long is one to wait if there is no military attack? The objective result of what Kamenev and Zinoviev propose is that the counter-revolution will be given the opportunity to organise itself; we will retreat endlessly and lose the whole revolution. Why not give ourselves the chance to choose the day and the conditions so the counter-revolution has no opportunity to organise itself. He moves on to an analysis of international relations and he shows that now there ought to be more faith. There are two lines here : one steers for the victory of the revolution and relies on Europe, the second has no faith in the revolution and reckons on being only an opposition. The Petrograd Soviet has already taken its stand on the road to insurrection by refusing to sanction the withdrawal of troops. The navy has already rebelled since it has gone against Kerensky.

Comrade Kalinin does not interpret the resolution as meaning a rising tomorrow but as taking the matter out of the realm of policy into that of strategy and appealing for specific action. Conspiracy is not to be feared, it must always be in view; there is no need to slip on to the path of the parliamentary struggle, that would be wrong. Neither should we wait till they attack, because the very fact of attack improves the chance of victory.

Comrade Sverdlov analyses the resolution. From one point of view, it was an order but it is true that the matter has moved out of the political sphere into the technical sphere. He speaks about the preparations made by the counter-revolution. He takes issue with Kamenev's assertion that the weakness of the resolution is that so far nothing has been done in practice to implement it. The conclusion to be drawn from that is that it is necessary to work more energetically. One does not have to conclude that the majority is against us, it is only not yet for us. In Peter itself, we have the strength; the junkers are not so terrible, especially if we act first. He does not share the pessimistic feelings about the garrison which have been expressed here. The balance of forces is in our favour. The resolution should not be rescinded but amended to make the technical preparations more energetic.

Comrade Skrypnik. If we do not have the strength now, we are not going to have any more later; if we will not retain power now, it will be even worse then. It is said that it is an advantage to be in a defensive position – perhaps! But later we will not even have the strength for defence.

All the arguments used here are only postponements. There is no guarantee of victory. They are repeating here what the Mensheviks and SRs said when the proposal was made to them to take power. Now we are talking too much when we should act. The masses are appealing to us and if we do not give them anything, they will regard it as a crime. What is needed is preparation for insurrection and an appeal to the masses.

Comrade Volodarsky. If the resolution is an order then it has already been disobeyed. If the question of an insurrection is put in terms of tomorrow, we must say straight out that we have nothing to do it with. I made speeches daily but I must say that the masses met our appeal with bewilderment; this week, a change has occurred.

If there had not been a current of thought in the CC wanting to reduce the class struggle to a parliamentary one, we would have been ready for a rising now, but not as it is. The positive side of the resolution is that it forces us to go to the masses with a new slogan. The resolution must be understood as putting us on a course for insurrection and we must not stop our technical preparations.

A concrete motion: to continue to make technical preparations and to bring the question before the Congress, but not to regard the moment as having arrived already.

Comrade Dzerzhinsky thinks that Volod[arsky] is wrong to think that our Party made a mistake when it pursued, as he puts it, parliamentary tactics. On the contrary, it was the change in the situation which led to the change in our decision. Two months ago, illusions still existed and had not been overcome and that was why it was impossible to present the idea of an insurrection then. Conspiracy is just the demand that everything should be technically prepared for a rising. When the rising comes, the technical resources will be there, too. The same goes for food.

Comrade Ravich. To rescind the resolution would be to rescind all our slogans and our whole policy. The masses have already taken the view for themselves that an insurrection is inevitable. If the masses are too revolutionary, it will start from below, but if there is also a call from above, no one can doubt that the masses will support it. There is no going back.

Comrade Sokolnikov. Kamenev's objections carry no conviction. He blames us for broadcasting our insurrection, i.e. a conspiracy is what is needed. Our most unusual feature, and our strength, lies precisely in the openness of our preparations for a rising. He recalls the events of February, when nothing was prepared either, yet the revolution succeeded. No better balance of forces can be expected.

On the subject of the resolution, there is absolutely no point in interpreting it as an order to act.

If it turns out that events give us a respite then we will, of course, make use of it. It is possible that the Congress will be earlier. If the Congress adopts all power to the Soviets, it will be necessary then to deal with the question of what to do, appeal to the masses or not.

Comrade Skalov argues that the right relationship of forces is needed for power to pass to the Soviets. Once the Soviets are in power, the food problem will be solved. Now we are turning into defensists; if we do not take power, maybe the navy will abandon its position and the army, too. He talks of breaking treaties, etc. He thinks an insurrection cannot be organised before the meeting [of the Congress] of Soviets but it is necessary to take power at the Congress.

Comrade Miliutin. The resolution was not written in the sense it has been given here; it is being interpreted to mean that we should orient ourselves towards an insurrection. That was already planned in September. The discussion is still about the political and not about the technical side of the problem. No one is arguing about our general direction. Those who talk about an insurrection picture it in a very primitive way. The first need is to take power and to replace the old regime, but to act like a stereotype – that is absurd. We gained from the fact that there was no insurrection on [July] 3-5 and if there is not one now, it will not be the end of us. This resolution must be for internal consumption.

Comrade Ioffe argues that the resolution cannot be understood as an order to rise; it is a rejection of the tactics of refraining from action and a recognition that insurrection is a possibility and a duty on the first suitable occasion. In this sense, it is to be welcomed. But it is not true, on the other hand, that it is now a purely technical matter; even now, the moment for insurrection must be considered from a political point of view. The spirit of the resolution is the need to use the first suitable occasion to seize power and that is why it should be welcomed.

Comrade Shmidt. The matter is becoming clearer now, and there is no reason to object to preparations for a revolution.

Comrade Diadia [Latsis]. It is grievous that the resolution has not gone into action so far. I am convinced the resolution will be approved. I took the floor to amend the assessment given of the mood of the masses. The eagerness with which the masses seize on arms is an indication of how they feel. Our strategy is also strange. When they talk of junkers, I have already said they can be crossed off.

Comrade Le[nin]. If all resolutions were defeated in this manner, one could not wish for anything better. Now Zinoviev is saying down with the 'power to the Soviets' slogan and bring pressure on the government. To say that an insurrection is ripe means there is no need to talk of conspiracy. If an insurrection is inevitable politically, it must be treated as an art. And politically, its time has come.

There is only bread for one day, and that is why we cannot wait for the Constituent Assembly. He moves that the resolution be confirmed, that preparations get positively under way and that it should be for the CC and the Soviet to decide when.

Comrade Zinoviev. This revolution has been compared with the February revolution. There is no comparison because then* the old regime had nothing on its side and now it is a war against the whole bourgeois world. We did not launch the slogan 'power to the Soviets' in the abstract. If the Congress puts pressure on the Constituent Assembly, this cannot be compared with Menshevik policy. If the insurrection is tabled as a long-term prospect, there can be no objection, but if it is an order for tomorrow or the day after, then this is adventurism. We must not start an insurrection before our comrades have held the Congress and there has been consultation.

---

*   Crossed out in the original secretarial notes, *l.*4 : *all.*

Comrade Stepanov. The resolution has historic significance; I saw it as a barometer pointing to a storm. He goes on to object to Kamenev about his arguments about the lack of food.

The Cheremisov conference apart, the reduction in the soldiers' rations could be the moment for an insurrection.

The objective situation is growing from minute to minute and this resolution has played an important role. It has clarified a lot of things for us. He contends that the masses make a distinction between the *TsIK* and the Peter Soviet; he suggests that this resolution be kept intact as a barometer.

Comrade Kamenev shows that the present interpretation of the resolution is a retreat because earlier it was said that the rising must be before the 20th and now it is a question of steering towards a revolution. The question is posed politically. To fix a date for the rising is adventurism. We ought to explain to the masses that we will not summon them to a rising in the next three days but that we consider an insurrection inevitable.

He moves a vote on the resolution, and makes a proposal that the central organ should publish a statement that there will be no appeal for a rising before the congresses.

Comrade Skrypnik proposes an appeal to the masses to get ready for an insurrection.

Comrade Lenin objects to Zinoviev that this revolution should not be seen in contrast to the February revolution.

On the substance, he proposes the resolution :

'The meeting unreservedly welcomes and entirely supports the CC resolution, calls on all organisations and all workers and soldiers to make comprehensive and intensive preparations for an armed insurrection and to support the Centre created for this by the Central Committee and expresses its full confidence that the CC and the Soviet will be timely in indicating the favourable* moment and the appropriate methods of attack'.

Zinoviev. He replies to Lenin on the subject of the February revolution. These two months will not be the worst in the pages of our Party's history. On the substance, he moves his own resolution :

While going ahead with the work of reconnaissance and pre-

---

*   *will be timely in indicating the favourable* – is written over the crossed out : *will not let slip the occasion to indicate the correct* (see *f.2, op.1, ed.khr.4630.* Original.)

paration, to consider that any demonstrations in advance of a conference with the Bolshevik section of the Congress of Soviets are inadmissible.

Comrade Lenin's resolution voted on in principle. In favour 20, against 2, abstained 3.

An amendment by comrade Miliutin to substitute the words 'armed conflict' is rejected.

An amendment by comrade Skrypnik to take out the words 'expressing confidence' etc. is rejected.

An amendment by comrade Fenigstein : to replace the word 'attack' with the word 'action'. Rejected.

An amendment [introduced by] comrade Volodarsky :

To move comrade Zinoviev's resolution in the form of an amendment to the approved resolution.

Rejected.

An amendment by comrade Fenigstein :

'The centre consisting of the Executive Commission and the *Voenka*'. Withdrawn.

The resolution as a whole :

In favour – 19; 2 – against; abstained – 4.

Comrade Zinoviev's resolution : in favour – 6; against –15; abstained – 3.

The CC sits alone and adopts the following decision :

The CC organises a Military Revolutionary Centre† consisting of the following : Sverdlov, Stalin, Bubnov, Uritsky and Dzerzhinsky. This Centre is included in the Soviet Revolutionary Committee.**

Documents

We insist on a CC plenum being called by telegraph immediately.

Oct. 16 1917.   G. Zinoviev.
                                                     Kamenev.

Archives of the IML, *f*.17, *op*.1, *ed.khr*.34, *l*.17.

---

†   See note on p.287.
**   *The CC sits . . . Soviet revolutionary committee* is included in the text in the minute book of the CC secretariat, *l*.99. In the original secretarial notes, *l*.14, the decision is attached to the minutes.

To the CC RSDLP.

Being unable to defend the point of view which is expressed in the latest decisions of the CC and which determines the whole character of its work, and considering as I do that this position will lead the Party and the proletariat to defeat — I ask the CC to cease to regard me as one of its members.

16.10.1917.   Iu.Kamenev.

Archives of the I M L, *f*.17, *op*.1, *ed.khr*.34, *l*.16.

To the CC RSDLP

Dear comrades !

We ask that the statement we have submitted[139] be given to the central organ for publication.

> V. Nogin.
> V. Miliutin.
> A. Rykov.

Archives of the I M L, *f*.17, *op*.1, *ed. khr*. 34, *l*.18.

Minutes No.27

[The minutes of the CC session of October 20 [November 2] 1917 (*ed. khr.* 35) are the original secretarial notes written in ink on one side of two large sheets of paper torn out of a pad. There are editorial corrections on the minutes in ink in Ia.M.Sverdlov's handwriting. The second set of minutes is in the minute book of the secretariat of the CC RSDLP(b) (*ed.khr*.59).

The text of the minutes is printed from the secretarial notes collated with the text of the minutes in the CC secretariat book.]

Session of the CC

October 20 [November 2 1917]

Present :

Trotsky, Stalin, Sokolnikov, Dzerzhinsky, Uritsky, Ioffe, Sverdlov, Miliutin and, later, comrade Kollontai.

Agenda :
1. Statement by comrade Lenin.
2. Statement from the *Voenka*.
3. Statement by Trotsky.
4. Security Commission.
5. Statement apropos of an article by comrade Lenin.

1. Statement by comrade Lenin.

Comrade Sverdlov reads out a letter to the CC from comrade Lenin*[140].

Comrade Dzerzhinsky proposes that Kamenev be required to abstain from political activity completely, bearing it in mind that Zinoviev is keeping to himself and not doing any Party work even without this.

Comrade Stalin considers that comrade Lenin's proposal should be dealt with at a plenum and suggests that no decision be made at the moment.

Comrade Miliutin associates himself with comrade Stalin's opinion but contends that in general nothing special has happened.

Comrade Uritsky gives information about the mood in the provinces ; he states that the majority of the delegates in Moscow have said they are against an armed insurrection ; on the subject of K[amenev] and Z[inoviev], he also asks for the question to be referred to a plenum for consideration.

Comrade Sverdlov argues that there is an enormous difference between the behaviour of Kamenev and Il'ich ; he considers that nothing can justify the behaviour of the first ; but the CC does not have the right of expulsion from the Party ; he considers that the question must be dealt with now, that the meeting has enough authority and must give an answer both to Lenin's statement and to Kamenev's statement about leaving the CC. Kamenev's resignation ought to be accepted.

Comrade Trotsky accounts for his statement in the Soviet[141], explains that it was forced on him by comrade Kamenev and considers that the situation which has been created is completely intolerable and the letters to the central organ (from Zinoviev and

---

* See p.116.

Lunacharsky, together with an editorial comment)*, published
...** inadmissible ; he considers that Kamenev's resignation ought
to be accepted.

Comrade Ioffe suggests that it be announced that Zinoviev
and Kamenev are not members of the CC and that a resolution be
passed that not a single Party member may come out against Party
decisions, otherwise things will run wild in the Party.

Comrade Stalin considers that K[amenev] and Z[inoviev]
will submit to CC decisions and shows that our whole position is
contradictory ; he considers that expulsion from the Party is no
remedy, what is needed is to preserve Party unity ; he proposes
that these two comrades should be required to submit but be kept
in the CC.

Comrade Sokolnikov reports that he had no part in the editorial statement on the subject of Kamenev's letter, etc., and considers this statement a mistake.

Comrade Trotsky requests that his statement about the circumstances in which he made his statement in the Soviet be entered in the minutes, that is, he was forced into it by Kamenev's
statement that he intended to make his resolution public.

Decisions taken : the question of K[amenev] and Z[inoviev]
to be decided now. Kamenev's resignation to be accepted. For – 5,
against – 3.

To put off a decision until the plenum – rejected.

The duty is imposed on K[amenev] and Z[inoviev] to refrain
from any statements against the decisions of the CC and its pro-
jected line of work. For – 6.

Comrade Miliutin's proposal that not a single member of the
CC should have the right to come out against decisions passed by
the CC – unanimous.

Comrade Stalin announces that he is leaving the editorial
board.

It is resolved : in view of the fact that comrade Stalin's
statement in today's issue was made in the name of the editorial
board and has to be discussed by the editorial board, it is decided

---

*   See pp. 120 - 121.
**   Two words difficult to make out, possibly : *published today.*

to pass on to next business without discussing comrade Stalin's statement or accepting his resignation.

2.   The statement from the *Voenka*[142].

Read out by comrade Sverdlov.

Comrade Ioffe proposes that a resolution be passed; to reject the *Voenka*'s proposal since everyone wanting to work can go into the revolutionary centre attached to the Soviet.

Comrade Trotsky moves an amendment that all our organisations can go into the revolutionary centre and discuss any question of interest to them in our group there.

(Approved with the amendment.)

4.   The Congress of Soviets.

Adjourned to the next session (tomorrow).

5.   The Security Commission (under the City Duma).

Comrade Uritsky reports on how things stand in this Commission (the plan to organise a voluntary guard). He raises the question of whether we can stay in this Commission.

Comrade Trotsky suggests telling the Commission that it is necessary to keep in contact with the Military Revolutionary Committee attached to the Soviet.

If they refuse – to resign.

Comrade Sverdlov suggests that we should not leave the Commission but advocate the project for universal militia service. This is approved.

6.   Comrade Kollontai gives information about the state of affairs in Finland; it is possible that the social-democrats will walk out of the seim*; this will make the situation much more acute; the Finnish social-democrats think that this is not the time to separate from Russia since we have a struggle for power on our hands.

It is decided to adjourn this question, too, until tomorrow.

---

*   In the original secretarial notes, *l.2*: *the possibility of the social-democrats walking out of the seim.*

Document 1
Letter to Bolshevik Party members

Comrades! I have not yet been able to get the Peter newspapers for Wednesday, October 18. When the full text of Kamenev's and Zinoviev's statement in the non-Party newspaper *Novaia zhizn'** was transmitted to me by telephone, I refused to believe it. But it turns out that there can be no doubt and I am forced to take the opportunity to get this letter to Party members by Thursday evening or Friday morning, for it would be a crime to stay silent in the face of such unheard-of *strike-breaking*.

The more important the practical issue, the more responsible – and 'prominent' – the people who acted as blacklegs, the more dangerous it is and the more determined must we be in throwing out the strike-breakers, for any hesitation, even on account of the strike-breakers' past 'services', is made all the more unforgivable.

Just think! It has been known in Party circles that the Party has been considering the question of an insurrection since September. No one has heard of a single letter or leaflet by either of the people in question! Now, on the eve, it can be said, of a Congress of Soviets, two prominent Bolsheviks came out *against* the majority and, the matter is clear, *against the CC*. This is not said outright but this does even more harm to the cause for it is even more dangerous to speak in hints.

The text of Kamenev's and Zinoviev's statement makes it quite clear that they went against the CC for otherwise their statement makes no sense, but they do not say exactly *which* CC decision they disputed.

Why?

The reason is clear: because the CC did not publish it.

What then does all this come to?

On a vitally important issue, on the eve of the critical day of October 20, two 'prominent Bolsheviks' attack an *un*published decision by the Party centre in the *non*-Party press, and moreover in the very newspaper which, on the issue in question, *is hand in glove with the bourgeoisie against the workers' party*.

Why, this is a thousand times more despicable and *a million times more damaging* than all those statements which Plekhanov, for example, made in the non-Party press in 1906-1907 and which the Party so sharply condemned! Then it was only a matter of elections, now it involves an insurrection to win power!

---

*   See p.121.

On a question like this, *after* the centre has made a decision, to dispute this *unpublished* decision in front of the Rodziankos and Kerenskys, in a non-Party newspaper – can one imagine a more treacherous and strike-breaking action?

I would consider it a disgrace to even hesitate to condemn these former comrades because I was once close to them. I say outright that I do not regard either of them as comrades any more and that I will fight with everything I have, both in the CC and at the Congress, to have them both expelled from the Party.

For a workers' party which events increasingly face with the prospect of an insurrection is in no position to accomplish this difficult task if the centre's unpublished decisions are disputed in the non-Party press after they have been adopted, and if hesitation and discord are introduced into the ranks of our supporters.

Let Mr. Zinoviev and Mr. Kamenev found their own Party with a few dozens of confused people or candidates for the Constituent Assembly. Workers will not join that Party for its first slogan will be: 'Central Committee members who are defeated at a CC meeting on the question of a decisive fight are allowed to resort to the non-Party press to attack the Party's unpublished decisions.'

Let them build *that* kind of Party for themselves; our workers' Bolshevik Party can only gain from it.

When all the documents are published, Zinoviev's and Kamenev's strike-breaking will stand out more clearly than ever. And meanwhile, let the question be put to the workers:

'Suppose that the executive of an all-Russian trade union decided, after a month's discussion and by a majority of more than 80 per cent, that preparations had to be made for a strike but nothing was to be published about the time or anything else for the time being. Suppose that *after* the decision, two members, under the false pretext of a 'dissenting opinion', not only began to write to local groups about a reconsideration of the decision but also allowed their letters to be communicated to *non*-Party newspapers. Suppose, finally, they even attacked the decision themselves in non-Party newspapers, though it had still not been made public, and began to run down the strike in front of the capitalists.

The question is, would the workers hesitate to expel strike-breakers like that from their midst?'

*   *   *

As to the position with regard to an insurrection now, so close to October 20, I am too far away to be able to judge just how much the cause has been compromised by the blacklegging statement in the non-

Party press. There is no doubt that the *practical* damage is very great. The first thing to do to set the matter right is to restore the unity of the Bolshevik front by expelling the strike-breakers.

The weakness of the ideological arguments against an insurrection will become clearer the more we drag them out into the daylight. I have just sent an article about this to *Rabochii put'*[143], and if the editorial board does not think it can publish it, Party members will acquaint themselves with it in manuscript.

These 'ideological' arguments, if one may call them that, come down to two: first, to 'waiting' for the Constituent Assembly. Let us wait, perhaps we can hold out till then – that is all the argument consists of. Perhaps, with famine and disruption, with the patience of the soldiers exhausted, with Rodzianko taking steps to surrender Peter to the Germans, with lock-outs, perhaps we can still hold out.

Perhaps and maybe – that is the whole force of the argument.

The second, loud pessimism. Everything is fine with the bourgeoisie and Kerensky, everything is wrong with us. The capitalists have everything marvellously prepared, among the workers things are all bad. The 'pessimists' are shouting their heads off about the military side of the work while the 'optimists' are silent, for no one finds it pleasant to make disclosures in front of Rodzianko and Kerensky, except for strike-breakers.

Difficult times. A weighty task. A grave betrayal.

Nevertheless, the task will be accomplished, the workers will unite, the peasant revolt and the extreme impatience of the soldiers at the front will do their work! Let us close ranks more tightly – the proletariat must win!

N. Lenin.

Written October 18 [31] 1917.
V. I. Lenin, *Sochineniia*, 4th. ed., vol. 26, pp.185-188.

Document 2
Letter to the Central Committee of the RSDLP

Dear comrades!

No self-respecting party can tolerate strike-breaking and strike-breakers in its midst. That is obvious. The more one thinks about Zinoviev's and Kamenev's statements in the non-Party press, the clearer it becomes that their action constitutes strike-breaking in the full sense of the term. Kamenev's evasion at the session of the Petrograd Soviet is something really low; he is, don't you see, in full agreement with Trotsky. But is it really so difficult to understand that in front of enemies Trotsky *could not,* had no right to, was not permitted to say more than he did? Is it really so difficult to understand that it is the *duty* of a party which has concealed *its own* decision from the enemy (that an armed insurrection is necessary, that its time has come, that full-scale preparations are to be made, etc), that this decision makes it an *obligation* when making public pronouncements to shift the initiative as well as the blame on to the enemy. Only a child could fail to understand this. Kamenev's gambit was pure fraud. The same must be said for Zinoviev's evasion. At least, his letter 'justifying himself' (addressed to the central organ, it seems)[144], a letter which is all I have seen (for as to the dissenting opinion, the alleged dissenting opinion the *bourgeois* press is trumpeting about, I, a member of the CC, have not seen it *to this day*). One of Zinoviev's 'arguments': Lenin sent out his letters 'before decisions of any kind were taken' and you did not protest. This is literally what Zinoviev writes, himself underlining the word *before* four times. Is it really so difficult to understand that *before* the centre has come to a decision on the question of a strike, there can be agitation both for and against, but *after* a decision in favour of a strike (and after an additional decision to conceal this from the enemy), to campaign against the strike after that is strike-breaking? Any worker will understand it. The question of an armed insurrection has been discussed in the centre since September. That is when Zinoviev and Kamenev could and *should* have put their views in writing so that *everyone,* seeing their arguments, so that *everyone* could judge for themselves the full extent of their confusion. To conceal your views from the Party for a whole month *before* a decision is taken and to circulate a dissenting opinion *after* the decision – that makes you a strike-breaker.

Zinoviev pretends not to understand this difference, not to understand that after a decision to strike, a decision made by the centre, it is only a strike-breaker who could campaign in the lower bodies against the decision. Any worker will understand it.

But Zinoviev did campaign against the centre's decision, attacking it both at Sunday's meeting, where he and Kamenev did not get a single vote, and in their present letter. For Zinoviev is brazen enough to assert that 'the Party has not been consulted' and that such questions 'are not to be settled by ten people'. Just think about it. Everyone in the Central Committee knows that there were more than ten CC members at the meeting which took the decision, that the *majority of the plenum* was there, that Kamenev himself declared at the meeting: 'This meeting decides', and that it was known with certainty that the majority of those CC members who were absent *did not agree with* Zinoviev and Kamenev. And now, *after* the CC's decision which even Kamenev recognised as a deciding one, a CC member has the nerve to write: 'The Party has not been consulted'. 'Such questions are not to be settled by ten people'; this is real strike-breaking. Until the Party congress, the CC takes the decisions. The CC decided. Kamenev and Zinoviev, not having come out in writing *before* the decision, began to *contest* the CC decision *after* it had gone through.

This is real strike-breaking. When the matter concerns immediate and *secret* preparations for a strike, any kind of dispute after the decision has been taken is *inadmissible*. Now Zinoviev has the insolence to blame *us* for 'warning the enemy'. Where does his shamelessness end? Who was it really who damaged the cause and wrecked the strike by 'warning the enemy' if not the people who appeared in the *non-Party* press?

To come out *against* a 'decisive' resolution of the Party in a newspaper which, on this *particular* issue, is of one mind with the whole bourgeoisie.

If this is tolerated, there can be no Party, the Party will be destroyed.

It makes a mockery of the Party to call something which Bazarov finds out about and prints in a non-Party newspaper a 'dissenting opinion'.

Kamenev's and Zinoviev's statement in the non-Party press was particularly despicable, too, because the Party cannot publicly refute their *slanderous lie*: I know of no decisions about a date, writes Kamenev, publishing it in his own name and that of Zinoviev. (After this statement, Zinoviev takes full responsibility for what Kamenev has said and done.)

How can the CC refute this?

We cannot tell the truth in front of the capitalists, that is, that we *have decided* on a strike and have decided to *keep its timing secret.*

We cannot refute Zinoviev's and Kamenev's slanderous lie *without further damage to the cause*. The infinite baseness and the real treachery of these two individuals lies in the fact that they gave away the strikers' plan to the capitalists, for since we keep silent in the press, everyone will guess *how* things stand.

Kamenev and Zinoviev *betrayed* to Rodzianko and Kerensky the decision made by their Party CC about an armed insurrection and its decision to conceal the preparations and the choice of date for it from the enemy. This is a fact. A fact which no amount of evasion can refute. By a slanderous lie in front of the capitalists, two CC members gave away the workers' decision. There can and must be only one response to this; an immediate CC decision:

'The CC, considering that Zinoviev's and Kamenev's statement in the non-Party press fully constitutes strike-breaking, expels them both from the Party.'

It is not easy for me to write this about people who were once close comrades but it would seem to me a crime to hesitate here, for a party of revolutionaries which did not punish prominent strike-breakers would *perish*.

Even if the question of an armed insurrection has been postponed for a long time by the strike-breakers who betrayed it to Rodzianko and Kerensky, it has not been *taken off the agenda,* not by the Party. But how is it possible to get ready for an armed rising and organise it while 'prominent' strike-breakers are *tolerated* in our midst. The more prominent they are, the more *dangerous* and the more unworthy of 'pardon'. *On n'est trahi que par les siens,* the French say. Only your *own* can betray you.

The more *'prominent'* the strike-breakers, the greater the obligation to punish them instantly by expulsion.

This is the only way to make the workers' party healthy again, to purge ourselves of a dozen or so spineless intellectuals and, having united the ranks of the revolutionaries, go on to meet great and momentous difficulties, go forward *with the revolutionary workers*.

We cannot print the truth: that *after* the deciding meeting of the CC, Zinoviev and Kamenev had the insolence to demand a *reconsideration* at Sunday's meeting, that Kamenev shamelessly cried: 'The CC has collapsed because nothing was done all week' (I could *not* refute it for I could not say *exactly what was done*) and Zinoviev with an innocent air moved the resolution which the meeting turned down: 'To take no action until a meeting with the Bolsheviks due to arrive on the 20th for the Congress of Soviets.'

Just think: after the *centre* has taken a decision to call a strike, to propose to a meeting of the rank and file that it be postponed and referred (until the Congress on the 20th, a Congress later put off . . . the Zinovievs have faith in the Liberdans), referred to a body of *this kind,* not recognised by the Party rules, which has *no* authority over the CC and does *not* know Peter.

And after this, Zinoviev still has the nerve to write: 'They are hardly strengthening the unity of the Party this way.'

Can this be called anything other than the threat of a split?

To such a threat, I answer that I will do my utmost, I will get myself the freedom to speak in front of the workers and, *come what may*, I will brand Zinoviev as a strike-breaker. To the threat of a split, I answer by declaring war to the end, a war to expel both strike-breakers from the Party.

After debating for a month, a trade union executive has come to a decision: a strike is inevitable and due, and we will conceal the timing from the bosses. After this, two of the executive go *to the rank and file* to contest the decision and they are defeated. Then these two go to press in full view of the capitalists and betray the executive's decision through a slanderous lie and in doing so more than half-wreck the strike or postpone it to a worse time, giving the enemy warning.

This is real strike-breaking. And this is why I demand the expulsion of both strike-breakers, keeping the right (in view of their threat of a split) to publish *everything* when it can be made public.

Written October 19 [November 1] 1917.
V. I. Lenin, *Sochineniia,* 4th ed., vol. 26, pp.192-196.

Document 3
Letter to the editorial board of Rabochii put'

In his 'Letter to comrades' published in yesterday's issue of *Rabochii put'*, comrade Lenin argued against the views of 'two comrades'; I am one of them.

For a number of reasons, I am obliged to refrain from making a detailed answer to this polemic now. I will only say that my real views on the subject in dispute are very far from those with which comrade Lenin takes issue. Endorsing yesterday's statement by comrade Trotsky in the Petrograd Soviet of Workers' and Soldiers' Deputies, I think that we are quite able to close ranks and defer our dispute until circumstances are more favourable.

G. Zinoviev.

FROM THE EDITORIAL BOARD. We in our turn express the hope that with comrade Zinoviev's statement (and also comrade Kamenev's statement in the Soviet) the matter may be considered closed. The sharp tone of comrade Lenin's article does not change the fact that, fundamentally, we remain of one mind.

To the editorial board of Rabochii put'

In the last two numbers of *Birzhevye vedomosti,* the rumour is assiduously put out that I have received inquiries from official representatives of the city militia about an insurrection allegedly being prepared. My answer to them is also given, accompanied by all sorts of malicious comments by the editorial board.

I declare that this whole story is fictitious from first to last. If anyone were to make such inquiries, I would answer, word for word, what comrade Trotsky stated at the October 18 session of the Petrograd Soviet of Workers' and Soldiers' Deputies.

A. Lunacharsky.

Rabochii put' No. 41, November 2 [October 20] 1917.

Document 4
Iu. Kamenev's statement to the newspaper Novaia zhizn'
Iu. Kamenev on a 'rising'.

Yesterday's article by V. Bazarov mentioned a tract against a rising issued in the name of two prominent Bolsheviks.

On this subject, Iu. Kamenev states: in view of the intensive discussion about the question of a rising, comrade Zinoviev and I sent a letter to the largest organisations of our Party in Petrograd, Moscow and Finland expressing ourselves emphatically against our Party initiating armed demonstrations of any kind in the immediate future.

I must say that I am not aware of any decisions by our Party which fix a rising of any sort for this or any other date.

The Party has made no such decisions. Everyone realises that as the revolution stands at present, there can be no question of any 'armed demonstration'. There can only be question of an armed seizure of power and the people responsible to the proletariat cannot fail to understand that they can only go for a mass 'rising' of some sort when they have given clear and definite attention to the objective of an armed insurrection. Not only comrade Zinoviev and I but also a number of comrades with experience in the field consider it would be inadmissible, and fatal for the proletariat and the revolution, for us to initiate an armed insurrection at the present moment, with the prevailing relationship of social forces, independently of and only a few days before a Congress of Soviets.

No party, and least of all ours, in which the hopes and faith of the masses are increasingly concentrated, can fail to strive for power, to carry out their own programme with the resources of the state. No revolutionary party, and least of all ours, a party of the proletariat, of the urban and rural poor, can or has the right to renounce insurrection. It is the inalienable right of the working masses to rebel against a governing power destroying the country, and also at certain moments the sacred duty of those parties in whom the masses trust. But insurrection, in Marx's expression, is an art. And that is just why we believe that it is our duty now, in the present circumstances, to speak out against any attempt to initiate an armed insurrection which would be doomed to defeat and would bring in its train the most disastrous consequences for the Party, for the proletariat, for the destiny of the revolution. To stake all this on a rising in the coming days would be an act of despair. And our Party is too strong, it has too great a future, to take such desperate steps.

Novaia zhizn' No. 156, October 18 [31] 1917.

Minutes No.28

[The minutes of the CC session of October 21 [November 3] 1917 (*ed. khr.* 36) are the original secretarial notes written in ink on both sides of a large sheet of paper torn out of a pad. The second set of minutes is in the minute book of the secretariat of the CC RSDLP(b) (*ed. khr.* 59).

The text of the minutes is printed from the secretarial notes collated with the text of the minutes in the CC secretariat book.]

Session of the CC
October 21 [November 3] 1917

Present :
Trotsky, Sverdlov, Dzerzhinsky, Stalin, Ioffe, Sokolnikov, Muranov, Miliutin.

1. Report on the Northern front.
2. Petrograd Executive Committee of the Soviet.
3. Deployment of manpower.
4. Publication of Lenin's letter as a brochure.
5. Congress of Soviets.

1. Report on the Northern front.
Comrade Sverdlov reports on the state of affairs on the Northern front.

2.   The Petrograd Executive Committee of the Soviet of Workers' and Soldiers' Deputies.

Comrade Dzerzhinsky announces that the Executive Committee is completely disorganised and proposes that all Bolshevik members of the Executive Committee be required to work reliably in it or else leave it.

It is resolved : that comrades Volodarsky, Iurenev, Miliutin, Skalov, Pakhomov, Zorin, Dzerzhinsky, Stalin, Lashevich and Ioffe should go into the Executive Committee to work there.

4.   The publication of Lenin's letter as a brochure[145].

Comrade Dzerzhinsky announces that Lenin's letter has been given to the printers to be published as a brochure. He suggests that it should not be published as a brochure.

It is decided not to publish it as a separate brochure.

5.   The Congress of Soviets[146].

Comrade Stalin proposes that reports be prepared on the subjects : 1. The war ; 2. State power ; 3. Control ; 4. The nationality question ; 5. Land.

Comrade Sokolnikov proposes getting the Congress opened on the 25th without fail.

Comrade Trotsky talks about the problem of the praesidium ; he considers that the method of forming the praesidium which the last Congress adopted is not to our advantage and proposes that the praesidium be formed using a scale of representation of 1 : 100.

Comrade Sverdlov considers that a preliminary meeting of the group is necessary and that there is a need for special work : he proposes Sverdlov, Stalin and Miliutin for this work in the group. Il'ich must be brought into the work of preparing theses for the reports.

Comrade Stalin suggests sending a comrade to Moscow demanding that the Moscow delegation come immediately; the range of questions to be covered by theses must be defined :

Land, the war and power – to be given to comrade Lenin.

Workers' control – comrade Miliutin.

The nationality question – comrade Stalin.

Report on the current situation – comrade Trotsky.

Comrade Miliutin suggests an additional report on rules of procedure, to be entrusted to comrade Sverdlov.

All this is approved.

Minutes No.29

[The minutes of the CC session of October 24 [November 6] 1917 (*ed. khr.* 37) are the original secretarial notes. They are written in ink on two large sheets of paper torn out of a pad. The first sheet has writing on both sides, the second on one side. The second set of minutes is in the minute book of the secretariat of the CC RSDLP(b) (*ed. khr.* 59).

The text of the minutes is printed from the secretarial notes collated with the text of the minutes in the CC secretariat book.]

Session of the CC
October 24 [November 6] 1917

Present[147] :
Dzerzhinsky, Kamenev, Nogin, Lomov [Oppokov], Miliutin, Ioffe, Uritsky, Bubnov, Sverdlov, Trotsky, Vinter [Berzin].

Comrade Kamenev proposes that no CC member should be able to leave Smolny today without special permission from the CC. Approved.

An arrangement to be made with the Executive Commission [of the Petersburg Committee] about permanent manning at both Smolny and the Petersburg Committee. Approved.

Agenda :
1. Report from the Military Revolutionary Committee.
2. Congress of Soviets.
3. The CC plenum.

1. Comrade Kamenev's report.
He reports on talks with representatives from headquarters[148].
2. The printers and the newspaper.

It is resolved : to send an immediate guard to the printers and see to it* that the next issue of the newspaper comes out on time[149].

---

* The original secretarial notes, *l*.1, has: *send the printers and see to it.*

3. Our attitude to the Bureau of the $TsIK$[150].

Comrade Nogin insists on the need to clarify our attitude to the $TsIK$ Bureau because the railwaymen are subject to what the $TsIK$ decides and if we have a disagreement with the latter, we will be cut off from the rest of Russia.

Other comrades object to this apprehension about the railwaymen.

Comrade Trotsky proposes that we put two CC members at the disposal of the Military Revolutionary Committee to improve our ties with the post and telegraph employees and the railwaymen; a third CC member for observation of the Provisional Government. With regard to the $TsIK$, we should declare at today's session, no matter which delegates are present, that the $TsIK$, whose authority has long since expired, is undermining the cause of the revolutionary democracy.

Comrade Vinter [Berzin] protests that there is a risk of the CC being dispersed so it would be better to use others as well as CC members.

Comrade Kamenev considers that we must exploit yesterday's talks with the $TsIK$, now broken off because of the banning of *Rabochii put'*, and that is why a breach with the $TsIK$ must be founded on just these grounds. He also considers it necessary to begin talks with the Left SRs and establish political contact with them.

Comrade Sverdlov sees a need to make comrade Bubnov responsible for contacts with the railwaymen and the post and telegraph employees. He suggests telling our comrades in the $TsIK$ Bureau immediately that we have no solidarity with the latter.

A vote is taken on the first proposal by comrade Trotsky to delegate CC members to the functions described: (1. railways, 2. post and telegraph, 3, food). Approved.

Comrade Bubnov – to the railways.

Comrade Dzerzhinsky – post and telegraph.

Comrade Dzerzhinsky protests and suggests comrade Liubovich who has connections with the post [and] telegraph.

Comrade Dzerzhinsky is given the responsibility; he is to organise it.

Comrade Miliutin is charged with organising food matters.

Comrade Podvoisky to be commissioned to organise observation of the Provisional Government and the orders it issues.

(Objections to comrade Podvoisky; *assigned* to comrade Sverdlov.)

It is proposed that three be put in charge of negotiations with the Left SRs ; one is suggested.

Assigned to comrade Kamenev and comrade Vinter [Berzin].

Comrades Lomov and Nogin are instructed to inform Moscow immediately of everything that is happening here.

The Moscow comrades contend that at least one ought to go to Moscow.

Comrade Miliutin suggests setting up continuous contact with Moscow; for that reason, Lomov and Nogin should not both be released but only one of them; one will go tomorrow and the other after a few days. An amendment is moved, that one will go off today, and the other tomorrow.

Comrade Trotsky suggests organising a reserve headquarters in the Peter-Paul fortress and assigning one CC member there for that purpose.

Comrade Kamenev considers that if Smolny is destroyed, we must have a base on the 'Aurora'.

But Uritsky moves an amendment about the mine-layer.

Comrade Trotsky insists that the political base should be in the Peter-Paul fortress.

Comrade Sverdlov proposes that comrade Lashevich and not a CC member be entrusted with observation at the summit.

It is decided to supply all members of the CC with passes to the fortress[151].

General observation is entrusted to Lashevich and Blagonravov.

Sverdlov is charged with maintaining constant communication with the fortress.

Minutes No.30

[The minutes of the CC session of October 29 [November 11] 1917 (*ed.khr*.403) are the original secretarial notes written with an ordinary pencil on both sides of two half-sheets of writing paper. The second set of minutes is in the minute book of the secretariat of the CC RSDLP (b) (*ed.khr*.59).

The text of the minutes is printed from the secretarial notes collated with the text of the minutes in the CC secretariat book.]

Session of the CC
October 29 [November 11 1917]

Present :
Vinter [Berzin], Kamenev, Miliutin, Rykov, Sokolnikov, Ioffe, Dzerzhinsky, Kollontai, Sverdlov, Bubnov, Uritsky.

1.   A vote is taken : the CC considers that the base of the government has to be widened and that some changes in its composition are possible (approved unanimously)[152].
2.   Comrade Vinter's proposal (appended) is voted on. Approved (with amendments)[153].
3.   The proposal is put to the vote : The government is formed by the *TsIK* and is responsible to it. (Approved.)*
4.   The government confirms the decrees on peace and land. (Approved.)
5.   The proposal is put to the vote : we do not make it a matter for an ultimatum if all the Soviet parties join the government, the Popular Socialists included**. For – 7 ; against – 3.
6.   The proposal is put to the vote : the right to make reciprocal objections to party candidatures is allowed. Approved : 5 for, 1 against, 3 abstained.

There is a proposal to vote by name on the fifth point and to take a poll of CC members not present. (Approved.)

Voting by name on the fifth point.

For	*Against*
Kamenev	Ioffe
Miliutin	Dzerzhinsky
Rykov	Vinter
Sokolnikov	A. Kollontai
	Ia. **Sverdlov**
	A. Bubnov
	M. Uritsky

---

*   In the original secretarial notes, *l.*1, there follows this text, crossed out : *The proposal is put to the vote : we will not go into a government which includes the Right Internationalists.*

**   In the original secretarial notes, *l.*1, there follows this text, crossed out : *and we agree to renounce the candidature of Trotsky and Lenin if they demand this.* After the crossed-out words is written : (*Approved*).

Comrade Bubnov asks to record his personal opinion : I am
voting against the point about the ultimatum because the formulation does not point out that power at the centre and in the localities
belongs to the Soviets.

Sokolnikov and Kamenev are delegated to the Conference[154]
from the CC.

Ioffe's proposal to make an ultimatum of the demand : all
power at the centre and in the localities belongs to the Soviets was
not put to the vote because it was acknowledged that it lapses after
the vote on the third point.

7. The *TsI K* must be supplemented by representatives of the
parties which left the Congress, proportionately.

8. Representatives of the railwaymen, the post and telegraph
union and similar organisations should be brought into the *TsI K*.

Minutes No.31

[The minutes of the CC session of November 1 [14] 1917 (*ed.khr.*
39) are the original secretarial notes written in ink on both sides of five
sheets of writing paper. The second set of minutes is in the minute book
of the secretariat of the CC RSDLP(b) (*ed.khr.*59).

The text of the minutes is printed from the secretarial notes collated with the text of the minutes in the CC secretariat book.

Attached to the minutes are: 1. The text of the CC resolution
written in ink on half a sheet of paper in Ia.M.Sverdlov's writing (see p.
136); 2. The original (*l.* 17) and draft (*l.* 18) note of the CC resolution to
continue talks, written in indelible pencil on two small sheets of writing
paper. The resolution included in the text of the minutes is taken from
the original note (*l.* 17) (see p. 136).]

Session of the CC
November 1 [14] 1917[155]

Present :

12 members of the Central Committee, 5 members of the Executive Commission of the Petersburg Committee, 1 member of the

Military Organisation, 3 members of the government who are not in the CC, comrade Lozovsky – the representative of the trade unions and comrade Riazanov as delegate to the conference*.

Agenda :
Comrade Kamenev makes a report on the talks between representatives of the parties, *Vikzhel'*, etc.[15f]

What came out of the proposals was that an organ should be created to which the government would be responsible : consisting of 100 members of the *TsI K*, 75 representing the peasants, 80 from the navy, 100 from Peter and Moscow [City] Dumas; 15 from *Vikzhel'*, 20 from the All-Russian Trade Union.

Comrade Riazanov states that the first part of the talks was official.

Comrade Kamenev adds that the delegation was sent only to learn the opinion of the parties.

Comrade Trotsky considers that one thing is clear from the report and that is that the parties which took no part in the insurrection want to grab power from the people who overthrew them. There was no point in organising the insurrection if we do not get the majority; if the others do not want that, it is obvious they do not want our programme. We must have 75 per cent. It is clear that we cannot give a right of objection, just as we cannot yield on Lenin's chairmanship; such a concession is completely unacceptable. We can approve representation from the Dumas so long as there are new elections in a week's time. The programme is the issue on which we must break with them and explain to the masses what it is we want to put into practice and that we need a ministerial apparatus to do it.

Comrade Dzerzhinsky considers that the delegates did not observe the CC's instructions. The CC definitely decided that the government must be responsible to the *TsI K*[157]. It was clearly said yesterday that we put the most importance on our programme. We also stated definitely that we would not allow objections to Lenin and Trotsky[158]. None of this was implemented and I propose an expression of no confidence in the delegation and that they be recalled and others sent.

Comrade Kamenev reads out the decision of the last meeting

---

*   In the original secretarial notes, *l*.21, the word *conference* is written above the crossed-out : *talks*.

and contends that the delegation did not discuss candidatures and did not bargain but only listened to the opinions of others; a show-down was not the point; that is why I could only listen and report to the CC; if the latter decides on a break, this can be done today.

Comrade Dzerzhinsky considers that it was what was decided yesterday that the delegation failed to implement. There was no decision that the government must be designated and for that reason the delegation must be recalled.

Comrade Rykov, referring to the agenda, proposes passing on to the next question.

Comrade Kamenev suggests that the proposals be discussed first and the conduct of the delegation afterwards.

Comrade Uritsky considers that the CC has taken a firm stand on the position of all power to the Soviets and that means there can be no question of supplementation. He objects to repre-sentation from the Dumas and considers that a majority of Bolshe-viks in the *TsIK* is obligatory[159]. This must be established conclu-sively. The same for ministerial posts; we must have a solid major-ity. The next question about objections; there is no doubt that we must not yield on either Lenin or Trotsky, for in a certain sense this would be renunciation of our programme; there is no need to insist on the others, but L[enin] must remain Chairman, and Tr[otsky] Minister of Foreign Affairs. We can make no concessions on the decrees. These are our demands and we cannot yield on them.

Comrade Lunacharsky considers that the CC cannot go back on its decisions; we made a definite decision : a majority in the *TsIK*; a majority in the government, and our programme. There was no point in referring back to us and the delegation could have decided what to reply itself. But on the other hand, he protests against the statements that we have to have 75 per cent because there was no such decision. I think that there is no need to alter any decisions.

Comrade Lenin considers that Kamenev's policy must be halted instantly. This is not the moment to have talks with *Vik-zhel'*. Troops must be sent to Moscow[160]. He moves a resolution on *Vikzhel'*[161]. *Vikzhel'* is not represented in the Soviet and cannot be admitted there; the Soviets are voluntary organs and *Vikzhel'* has no support among the masses.

Comrade Riazanov makes an additional report as the *TsIK* representative that when the question of an institution endowed with full powers was raised, he protested against it having representatives from the cities and said that there could only be a *delegation* from the Peter and Moscow Dumas, of not more than 50. This was turned down. With a reminder that the *TsIK* has to have an answer[162], he asks to be told what he should report.

Comrade Dzerzhinsky recalls that there was no delegation from the *TsIK* but delegation by groups.

Comrade Slutsky considers that it is clear from the article in *Izvestiia*[163] and from Kamenev's report that some CC members act in contradiction to all the decisions of the workers. The question is settled on this plane as far as the masses are concerned and there is no occasion to talk of enlarged Soviets of any kind. He reports on the meetings of railwaymen who resolved to elect a new *Vikzhel'*, and announces that Military Revolutionary Committees have been formed on the railways. He recommends paying attention to the will of the masses.

Comrade Sokolnikov reports on the statements he made there. He declared that the plan proposed by Mart[ov] and Co. was a political fiction, pointed out that the *TsIK* (the old one) could not be recognised and stated on behalf of the CC RSDLP that the plan was unacceptable to the Party.

Comrade Kamenev declared that he stated in front of Sokolnikov that he judged this meeting to be one capable of electing Kerensky in place of Lenin.

Comrade Trotsky endorses Lenin's statement on *Vikzhel'* and considers that our complicity and undercover attitude to *Vikzhel'* is giving heart to them and weakening us; he has told their representatives that we will implement our decisions against them.

He reads out a resolution on the structure of power[164].

Comrade Riazanov (on a point of order) asks for information on whether the meeting knows that Kerensky sent a telegram offering peace negotiations and what our headquarters answered[165]?

Comrade Vinter [Berzin] calls for calm in spite of the disagreements. There are points on which we are all agreed; we are all agreed that there are points on which we can concede nothing; this applies to 1. the point : all power to the Soviets. This does not exclude the possibility of supplementation but on this we have already said and resolved that the only enlargement permissible is from Soviets who were not present*.

---

*   In the minute book of the CC secretariat, *l.*125 : *unrepresented*.

Then we cannot yield on our programme. It is clear that we cannot be satisfied by the recognition of our decrees alone, but that we must have an organ capable of carrying them out; I do not insist on a majority in the government but I cannot allow a change in the character of the *TsIK*. This must be our ultimatum.

Comrade Bubnov (on a point of order) suggests closing the general debate; no retreat from yesterday's decision and the discussion to move on to the question put forward by Lenin.

A reduction of the time taken by speakers is approved.

Comrade Lenin considers that the negotiations were to serve as a diplomatic cover for military operations. The only correct decision would be to end the hesitation of the waverers and become extremely positive. We have to come to the aid of the Muscovites and our victory is assured.

Comrade Rykov declares that there is a gap between us; he took the negotiations seriously. If we break them off, we will lose the groups who are supporting us as well and we will be in no position to keep power. Kamenev conducted the talks absolutely correctly. Essentially, we have to fight for predominance in the *TsIK*, for a defensist *TsIK* is quite inadmissible. All discussions on the subject of *Vikzhel'*, the peasants' union, etc. are entirely acceptable to us.* Elections cannot take place straight away and we are not assured of a Bolshevik *Vikzhel'*. He proposes the confirmation of the decisions of the last CC meeting, including approval of representation from the Peter Duma. He suggests that at this critical moment all those standing for conciliation* should be suspended.

Comrade Zinoviev considers that it would be very important if our Party were to get an agreement now. But the proposals made to us are not acceptable to anyone. For us, two points have the status of an ultimatum; our programme and the responsibility of the governing power to the Soviet as the source of power.

Comrade Sokolnikov considers that up to now there has been manoeuvring to gain time. Now that the defensists are going for an agreement, our situation has become considerably worse. If there is an agreement on supplementation now, we will find ourselves in a minority in the *TsIK,* especially if you take into account the

---

*   Like this in the text of the minute notes.

inclusion of peasant representatives. The conclusion is that these negotiations have to be broken off and efforts made in the future to prevent an enlargement destroying our majority.

Comrade Miliutin raises the question of whether we are going to insist on keeping power exclusively in our own hands. If the answer is yes, there is no point in all these negotiations. But if we do not get too carried away, and not only in a military sense, it will become clear to us that we cannot sustain a long civil war. Objectively, we have already put our programme into effect. Soviet power is a necessity and under Soviet power, an agreement is a necessity.

Comrade Riazanov states that he went in to these talks as a way out of the position we involuntarily find ourselves in. Even in Peter, power is not in our hands but in the hands of the Soviet, and this has to be faced. If we abandon this course, we will be utterly and hopelessly alone. We already made a mistake when we headed the government and insisted on names; if we had not done this, the middle levels of the bureaucracy would have supported us. He goes on to recall that in 2 or 3 days time we face the obligation to issue quarter-pound rations of bread. If we reject agreement today, we will be without the Left S Rs, without anything*, we will be left with the fact that we deceived the masses when we promised them a Soviet government. While the masses felt they were defending themselves, they were full of enthusiasm. But the consequences of an offensive will be even more terrible than the offensive on the 18th [June]. A split will begin within. No one denies that the proposed agreement is unacceptable. We have to clarify what can be demanded now from the *TsIK*. Are we going to insist that the *TsIK* be enlarged. The question is how can we get a majority on *TsIK*. He proposes the creation of a Provisional Government on the basis of the decrees passed by the All-Russian Congress, a rejection of 'antechamber' politics and the reservation of the key posts in the government for ourselves. In the agreement [it is necessary] to make sure of as much as possible [for ourselves]. But an agreement is unavoidable.

Comrade Zinoviev reports on yesterday's talks with the men

---

* The words: *we will be without the Left S Rs, without anything* – do not appear in the minute book of the C C secretariat, *l.* 128.

from the front. Everything will be in our favour if it is shown that the opposite side made the agreement founder because of the programme. The issue must be presented in just this way and stress laid, too, on a Soviet government.

Comrade Kamenev considers that even in time of victory an agreement is needed. A suggestion has been made to break off negotiations but if the agreement breaks down, it will put us in real jeopardy. He points out that *Vikzhel'* has great power in its hands; if this apparatus, which has so far been neutral, turns against us, it may be that our military force alone will not be enough. While we are coping with a strike, several weeks will pass and then we will lose. He cites the facts: the Obukhovo delegation[166], Kaledin, etc. We can fight with *Vikzhel'*, not against it. I stand for an agreement but that does not mean that every proposal has to be adopted.

Comrade Lenin. This question is fundamental and it is time to make an end of vacillation. It is clear that *Vikzhel'* is on the side of the Kaledins and the Kornilovs. There can be no wavering. The majority of the workers, peasants and army are for us. No one here has proved that the rank and file are against us; choose between Kaledin's agents and the rank and file. We must rely on the masses, and send agitators into the villages. A call was made to *Vikzhel'* to get troops to Moscow and it refused; we must appeal to the masses and they will throw it out[167].

Comrade Sverdlov considers that the talks should not be broken off but their direction sharply changed. He recalls that everyone is asking who, apart from the Bolsheviks, are to have ministerial posts; the second question has always been about a Soviet government and we cannot yield on that whatever happens. We cannot break off the talks; it would not do any harm to arrest someone from *Vikzhel'* – it has no support among the masses but there may be a response nevertheless to its appeal for a strike in some places. We have to keep to the fundamental point of supplementing the Soviet as it was decided at the Congress.

Comrade Sokolnikov quotes figures on the composition of the Congress, based on data from the mandate commission[168].

Trotsky's resolution is read out.

Lenin's *Vikzhel'* ,, ,, ,, ,,
Kamenev's ,, ,, ,, ,,
Zinoviev's[169] ,, ,, ,, ,,

The question of whether or not to break off the talks is put to the vote. For – 4, against – 10.

Tr[otsky] moves a resolution to make the decision adopted more concrete.

It is voted on in parts[170] :

First part :

For – 8, against – 4, abstained – 1.

Second part :

For – 9, against – 4*, abstained – 1.

The resolution on the ultimatum to be presented is put to the vote[171].

The CC resolves : to continue the talks.

To state that the *programme* has the force of an ultimatum for us.

I.   1. Peace ⎫
       2. Land   ⎬ Decree
       3. Workers' control.
       4. The food question.
       5. A ruthless struggle against counter-revolution (Kaledin, Kerensky).

II.   Soviet power.

The source of power is the *TsI K*, which may be enlarged**

Voting on points   1. unanimous.

                2. unanimous.

                3. for – 8, against – 3.

                4. unanimous, 3 abstaining.

                5.

The ultimatum must be accepted or rejected within two hours – for 5***, against – 4.

Put to the vote again.

The proposal not to wait at all; rejected.

---

*   In the original secretarial notes, *l*.25 *ob*. the figure *3* put initially is corrected to *4*.

**   On this, the note of the resolution stops short.

*** In the original secretarial notes. *l*.25 *ob*. the figure *4* put initially is corrected to *5*.

Document
Resolution of the CC[172]
[Passed at the session of November 1 [14] 1917.]

Considering, on the basis of its experience of previous talks, that the conciliation parties are pursuing these negotiations not to create a united Soviet power but to cause a split among the workers and soldiers, to undermine Soviet power and finally to attach the Left SRs to a policy of conciliation with the bourgeoisie,

The CC resolves: to allow the members of our Party, in view of the decision already taken by the *TsIK*, to take part today in a last attempt by the Left SRs to form a so-called homogenous power in order to expose the unviability of this attempt for the last time and to put a conclusive end to further negotiations on a coalition power*.

In place of Minutes No.32

[No minute notes of CC sessions have been found for the period between November 1 and 8 [14-21] 1917; nevertheless, judging by the documents which have been preserved and which are published below, CC sessions did take place.

The 'Resolution by the CC RSDLP(b) on the opposition within the CC' printed here was approved at the CC session of November 2 [15] 1917. The resolution was written by V.I.Lenin.

Documents relating to the struggle against the opposition inside the CC which have been preserved in the archives of the Institute of Marxism-Leninism or published in the press are printed as an appendix.]

Resolution by the CC RSDLP(b) on the opposition within the CC
November 2 [15] 1917[173].

The Central Committee recognises that the present meeting is of historic importance and therefore finds it necessary to set out clearly the two positions which have been revealed here.

1.   The Central Committee takes the view that the opposition

---

*   On the original of the resolution, *l*.20, there are the notes: *Resolution of the CC, endorsed by the representative of the M. Reg. Bureau, November 1 or 2.*

which has arisen within the CC totally disregards all the fundamental tenets of Bolshevism and the proletarian class struggle in
general, repeating deeply unMarxist phrases about a socialist revolution being impossible in Russia and the need to yield to ultimatums and threats of resignation made by an obvious minority in
the Soviet organisation, and in so doing frustrates the will and the
decision of the Second All-Russian Congress of Soviets and sabo-
tages the dictatorship of the proletariat and the poor peasants
which has been inaugurated.

2.   The Central Committee considers that this opposition must
take full responsibility for the way revolutionary work has been
hampered and for vacillations criminal at a moment like this and
invites it to remove itself from practical work it does not believe in
and to transfer its discussion and its scepticism to the press. For
apart from a fear of the bourgeoisie and a state of mind which re-
flects that of the exhausted (and not the revolutionary) section of
the population, there is nothing in this opposition.

3.   The Central Committee confirms that there can be no re-
pudiation of the purely Bolshevik government without betraying
the slogan of Soviet power, since a majority of the Second All-
Russian Congress of Soviets, barring no one from the Congress, entrusted power to this government.

4.   The Central Committee affirms that if the slogan of rule by
the Soviets of Workers', Soldiers' and Peasants' Deputies is not to
be betrayed, there can be no resort to petty bargaining over the
affiliation to the Soviets of organisations which are not of the
Soviet type, that is of organisations which are not voluntary associations of the revolutionary vanguard of the masses fighting to overthrow the landowners and the capitalists.

5.   The Central Committee affirms that to concede to ultimatums and threats from the minority in the Soviets amounts to a
complete renunciation not only of Soviet power but of democracy,
too, for such concessions add up to a fear of the majority to use its
majority, inviting anarchy and new ultimatums from any minority.

6.   The Central Committee affirms that, not having excluded
anyone from the Second All-Russian Congress of Soviets, it is fully
prepared even now to reinstate those who walked out and to agree
to a coalition within the Soviets with those who left; therefore the
claim that the Bolsheviks do not want to share power with anyone
is absolutely false.

7.   The Central Committee affirms that on the day the present

government was formed, some hours before that formation, the CC invited three representatives of the Left Socialist-Revolutionaries to its meeting[174] and formally proposed that they join the government. The Left SRs' refusal, though temporary and conditional, means that all responsibility for the failure to reach an agreement with them must be put fairly and squarely on these Left SRs.

8.   The Central Committee recalls that the Second All-Russian Congress of Soviets adopted a resolution moved by the Bolshevik group which said that it was prepared to supplement the Soviet with soldiers from the trenches and peasants from the localities, from the villages – and therefore the assertion that the Bolshevik government is against a coalition with the peasants is completely false. On the contrary, the CC declares that our government's land law, embodying the SR mandate, has proved in practice that the Bolsheviks are completely and very sincerely ready to establish a coalition with the vast majority of Russia's population.

9.   The Central Committee affirms, finally, that no matter what the difficulties, the policy of the present government must be continued unswervingly if the victory of socialism both in Russia and in Europe is to be ensured. The Central Committee expresses its complete faith in the victory of this socialist revolution and invites all sceptics and waverers to abandon their hesitations and give wholehearted and energetic support to the activity of this government.

V. I. Lenin, Sochineniia, 4th ed., vol. 26, pp. 244 - 246.

Document 1
Ultimatum from the majority of the CC RSDLP(b) to the minority[175]

The majority of the CC RSDLP(b), fully approving the policy pursued by the Council of People's Commissars up to the present, considers it necessary to address the following categorical statement to the minority in the CC.

Our Party's policy at this moment is defined in the resolution moved by comrade Lenin and passed yesterday, November 2, by the CC*.

---

*   See preceding document.

This resolution brands any attempt to force our Party to renounce power as a betrayal of the proletariat's cause since the All-Russian Congress of Soviets on behalf of millions of workers, soldiers and peasants entrusted this power to our Party's representatives on the basis of our programme. This is our basic tactical line, which flows from our whole struggle against the conciliators and which guided us in the insurrecton against Kerensky's government, and it now constitutes the revolutionary essence of Bolshevism and is endorsed once again by the CC – it is unconditionally binding on all Party members and, first and foremost, on the CC minority.

Yet representatives of the minority, before yesterday's CC meeting and after the meeting, too, pursued and are still pursuing a policy which is clearly directed against our Party's basic line and which is demoralising for our own ranks, sowing doubt at the very moment when the greatest firmness and steadfastness is needed.

Thus, at the *TsIK* meeting yesterday, the Bolshevik group, with CC members belonging to the minority taking a direct part, openly voted against a CC decision (on the question of how many and who should represent our Party in the government)[176]. Such an unheard-of breach of discipline committed by CC members behind the CC's back, after so many hours of debate in the CC provoked by these very same representatives of the opposition, makes it obvious to us that the opposition intends to take our Party institutions by attrition, sabotaging the Party's work at the very moment when the fate of the Party, the fate of the revolution depends on that work having immediate results.

We cannot and do not want to bear the responsibility for such a state of affairs.

In addressing this statement to the CC minority, we demand a categorical reply in writing to the question: does the minority undertake to submit to Party discipline and carry out the policy formulated in comrade Lenin's resolution adopted by the CC?

If the reply to this question is in the negative or is indeterminate, we will make an immediate appeal to the PC, the Moscow Committee, the Bolshevik group in the *TsIK,* the Petrograd City Conference and to a special party congress, proposing these alternatives:

Either the Party must commission the present opposition to form a new governing power together with their allies on whose behalf the opposition is sabotaging our work now – and then we will count ourselves completely free in relation to that new governing power, which can produce nothing but vacillation, impotence and chaos.

Or – and we have no doubt of this – the Party will endorse the only possible revolutionary line, the one expressed in yesterday's CC decision, and then the Party must emphatically suggest to the representatives of the opposition that they take their disorganising activities outside our Party organisation. There is no other way out, and there cannot be. A split would be a very regrettable fact, of course. But an honest and open split now is incomparably better than internal sabotage, the blocking of our own decisions, disorganisation and prostration. In any event, we do not doubt for a moment that if our disagreements (repeating essentially our differences with the *Novaia zhizn'* and Martov groups) were submitted to the judgement of the masses, our policy would secure the unconditional and devoted support of the revolutionary workers, soldiers and peasants and the vacillating opposition would very soon be condemned to impotent isolation.

N. Lenin, L. Trotsky, I. Stalin, Ia. Sverdlov, M. Uritsky, F. Dzerzhinsky, A. Ioffe, A. Bubnov, V. Sokolnikov, M. Muranov*.

Written November 3 [16] 1917.
V.I.Lenin, *Sochineniia*, 4th ed., vol.26, pp.247-249.

Document 2
Statement to the CC of the RSD Labour Party (bolsheviks)
[November 4 (17) 1917]

The CC RSDLP (bolsheviks) passed a resolution on November 1** rejecting in effect an agreement with parties belonging to the Soviet of Workers' and Soldiers' Deputies on forming a socialist Soviet government.

We consider that only an immediate agreement on the conditions we have indicated would give the proletariat and the revolutionary army the chance to make the gains of the October revolution secure, to fortify themselves in new positions and to gather strength to struggle further for socialism.

We consider that a government of this sort has to be created to avoid further bloodshed and impending starvation, to prevent Kaledin's men destroying the revolution, to secure the convocation of the Constituent Assembly at the appointed time and to effectively carry out the programme of peace adopted by the Second All-Russian Congress of Soviets of Workers' and Soldiers' Deputies.

---

*   Signatures given from a typewritten copy of the document kept in the archives of the IML, *f.17, op.1, ed.khr.*40.

**   See p.136.

By an incredible effort, we managed to get a revision of the CC decision
and a new resolution[177] which could have become the basis for
creating a Soviet government.

However, this new decision produced a number of actions on the part of
the leading group in the CC which clearly showed that it had
firmly made up its mind not to allow a government to be formed
from the Soviet parties and to defend a purely Bolshevik government whatever happened and at whatever the cost to the workers
and soldiers.

We cannot take responsibility for this fatal policy of the CC, pursued
contrary to the will of a vast proportion of the proletariat and
soldiers, who crave a speedy end to the bloodshed between different sections of the democracy.

For that reason, we relinquish the title of members of the CC so that we
can have the right to state our view frankly to the masses of the
workers and soldiers and appeal to them to support our call: on
with a government of Soviet parties ! An immediate agreement on
this condition.

We leave the CC at a moment of victory, at a moment when our Party
is in control, we leave because we cannot watch unmoved as the
policy of CC's leading group causes the workers' party to lose the
fruits of that victory, causes the proletariat to be crushed.

Remaining in the ranks of the proletariat party, we hope that the proletariat will overcome all obstacles and will recognise that our step
was dictated by a consciousness of our duty and responsibility to
the socialist proletariat.

Iu. Kamenev, A. I. Rykov, V. Miliutin, G. Zinoviev,
V. Nogin.

Izvestiia TsIK i Petrogradskogo Soveta R i SD No. 217,
November 5 1917.

Document 3
Statement by a group of People's Commissars at a session of the VTsIK
November 4 [17] 1917

It is our view that a socialist government must be formed from all the
parties in the Soviet. We consider that only if such a government
is formed will there be an opportunity for the fruits of the heroic
struggle waged by the working class and the revolutionary army in
the October and November days to be made secure.

We believe that, apart from this, there is only one other path: the retention of a purely Bolshevik government by means of political terror. The Council of People's Commissars has embarked on that path. We cannot and will not take it. We see that it leads to the mass proletarian organisations being cut off from the leadership of political life, to the establishment of an unaccountable regime and to the destruction of the revolution and the country. We cannot be responsible for this policy and so, before the *TsIK*, we relinquish our titles of People's Commissars.

> People's Commissar of Trade and Industry *V. Nogin.*
> People's Commissar for Internal Affairs *A. Rykov.*
> People's Commissar of Agriculture *V. Miliutin.*
> People's Commissar for the Food Supply *Teodorovich.*
> Associating themselves with this statement: *D. Riazanov.*
> Commissar for Press Affairs *N. Derbyshev.*
> Commissar of the State Printers *S. Arbuzov.*
> Commissar of the Red Guard *Iurenev.*
> Director of the department of disputes in the Ministry of Labour *G. Fedorov* (chairman of the workers' section).
> Director of the department of legisl. Chm. Commissar. L.*Iu. Larin.*

While I endorse the general assessment of the political situation with regard to the need for an agreement, I consider it inadmissible to relinquish my responsibility and obligations.

> People's Commissar for Labour *A. Shliapnikov.*

Izvestiia TsIK i Petrogradskogo Soveta R i SD No. 217,
November 5 1917.

Document 4
From the Central Committee of the Russian Social-Democratic Labour Party (bolsheviks)[178]
To comrades Kamenev, Zinoviev, Riazanov and Larin

The CC has already presented one ultimatum to the most prominent spokesmen for your policy (Kamenev and Zinoviev) demanding that they submit fully to decisions of the CC and to its policy line, give up sabotaging its work and stop their disruptive activity*.

---

* See p.138.

In leaving the CC but remaining in the Party*, the exponents of your
    policy put themselves under an obligation to observe CC resolu-
    tions. Yet you have not confined yourselves to criticism within the
    Party but are bringing uncertainty into the ranks of the people
    fighting in an insurrection which is still unfinished and you con-
    tinue, in defiance of Party discipline, to thwart CC decisions *out-
side* the bounds of our Party, in the Soviets, in municipal institu-
    tions, in trade unions, etc., and to obstruct the CC's work.
In view of this, the CC is forced to repeat its ultimatum and to suggest
    that you either give an immediate undertaking in writing to sub-
    mit to CC decisions and to promote its policy in all your speeches,
    or withdraw from all public Party activity and resign all respons-
    ible posts in the workers' movement until the Party congress.
If you refuse to make one of these two pledges, the CC will be obliged
    to raise the question of your immediate expulsion from the Party.

Written on November 5 or 6 [18 or 19] 1917.
V.I.Lenin, *Sochineniia*, 4th ed., vol.26, p.268.

Document 5
To the CC RSDLP(b)

In your letter** it claims that I 'continue, in defiance of Party discipline,
    to thwart CC decisions *outside* the bounds of our Party, in the
    Soviets, in municipal institutions, etc.' I bring it to your notice
    that *nowhere outside the Party* have I spoken against CC decisions
    and at sessions of the *TsIK*, I voted according to what the maj-
    ority of the group decided. For that reason, I ask you to indicate
    exactly how you consider CC decisions were thwarted *outside* the
    bounds of our Party.

Kamenev.

CC decisions were in fact thwarted, not by me but by Sokolnikov,
    for example, when he moved a resolution in the Petrograd Soviet
    to break off negotiations at a time when the CC was continuing to
    take a stand for going on with negotiations, promoted this point
    of view in the *TsIK* and sent comrade Sverdlov to pursue the

---

*   See pp.140-141.
**   See p.137.

talks. CC decisions were also defied by those who called an adopted resolution 'Kaledinist', etc., at the meeting of Petrograd workers[179]. I hope the CC has demanded explanations from these comrades, too.

Kamenev.

Archives of the IML, *f.17, op.1, ed.khr.40, l.6.*

Document 6
From the Central Committee of the Russian Social-Democratic Labour Party (bolsheviks)
To all Party members and all the working classes of Russia.

Comrades !

Everyone knows that the majority of the delegates at the Second All-Russian Congress of Workers' and Soldiers' Deputies were from the Bolshevik Party.

This fact is fundamental to an understanding of the revolution which has just taken place and triumphed in Petrograd and Moscow and in Russia as a whole. Yet this fact is constantly forgotten and ignored by all the supporters of the capitalists and their unwitting helpers, who are undermining the basic principle of the new revolution, that is: *all power to the Soviets.* There must be no other government in Russia but a *Soviet government.* Soviet power has been won in Russia and the government can be transferred out of the hands of one Soviet party into the hands of another party without any revolution, simply by a decision of the Soviets, simply by new elections of deputies to the Soviets. The Bolshevik Party was in the majority at the Second All-Russian Congress of Soviets. Only a government formed by that Party is, therefore, a Soviet government. And everyone knows that a few hours before the new government was formed and before the list of its members was proposed to the Second All-Russian Congress of Soviets, the Central Committee of the Bolshevik Party called three of the most prominent members of the Left SR group, comrades Kamkov, Spiro and Karelin to its meeting *and invited them* to join the new government. We are extremely sorry that the Left SR comrades refused, for we consider such a refusal unthinkable for revolutionaries and partisans of the workers and we are always ready to include Left SRs in the government, but we declare that, as the majority party in the Second All-Russian Congress of Soviets, we have the right *and the obligation* to the people to form a government.

Everyone knows that the Central Committee of our Party submitted a purely Bolshevik list of People's Commissars to the Second All-Russian Congress of Soviets and that the *Congress approved this list of a purely Bolshevik government.*

The fraudulent statements to the effect that a Bolshevik government is *not* a Soviet government are therefore complete lies and come and can only come from enemies of the people, from enemies of Soviet power. On the contrary, *only* a Bolshevik government now, after the Second All-Russian Congress of Soviets and until the convocation of the Third or new elections to the Soviets or until the Central Executive Committee forms a new government – *only* a Bolshevik government can now be regarded as a *Soviet* government.

*   *   *

Comrades! Several members of our Party's CC and of the Council of People's Commissars, Kamenev, Zinoviev, Nogin, Rykov, Miliutin and some others, resigned yesterday, November 4, from the CC of our Party and – the last three – from the Council of People's Commissars*.

In such a large party as ours, there were bound to be, in spite of the proletarian and revolutionary bent of our policy, certain comrades who turned out not to be stalwart and firm enough when it came to struggling with the enemies of the people. The tasks now facing our Party are truly immense and the difficulties enormous – and some members of our Party who held responsible posts in the past trembled at the onslaught of the bourgeoisie and fled from our midst. The whole bourgeoisie and all its helpmates are exultant about it, gloating, shouting about disintegration and predicting the fall of the Bolshevik government.

Comrades! Do not believe these lies. The comrades who resigned behaved like deserters for they not only abandoned the posts they were entrusted with but also defied our Party CC's express decision that they should at least wait for the decisions of the Petrograd and Moscow Party organisations before they resigned. We strongly condemn this desertion. We are deeply convinced that all politically-conscious workers, soldiers and peasants, belonging to

---

*   See pp. 140-142.

our Party or sympathising with it, will be just as emphatic in condemning what the deserters have done.

But we declare that the desertion of a few people from the top of our Party will not ruffle the unity of the *masses* supporting our Party for a single moment or by a single hair and, consequently, will not shake our Party.

Remember, comrades, that two of the deserters, Kamenev and Zinoviev, acted as deserters and strike-breakers even before the insurrection in Petrograd. They not only voted against the insurrection at the decisive CC meeting of October 10 1917, but also campaigned among Party workers against an insurrection *after* the CC had passed the decision. Everyone knows that newspapers which are afraid to range themselves with the workers and are inclined to side with the bourgeoisie (*Novaia zhizn'*, for example) raised a hue and cry then, along with the entire bourgeois press, about the 'break-up' of our Party, the 'collapse of the insurrection' and so on. But events quickly refuted the lies and slanders of some, the doubts, hesitations and cowardice of others. The 'storm' they wanted to stir up round Kamenev's and Zinoviev's moves to wreck the Petrograd insurrection turned out to be a *storm in a teacup* and the way the masses rose in a great surge, the great heroism of millions of workers, soldiers and peasants in Peter and Moscow, on the front, in the trenches and in the villages pushed the deserters aside with as much ease as a railway train casts off splinters of wood.

Shame on all the sceptics then, all the waverers and the doubters, all those who let themselves be frightened by the bourgeoisie or believed the cries of their direct and indirect supporters. There is *no shadow* of hesitation in the Petrograd and Moscow *masses* and the other workers and soldiers. Our Party stands together and strong as one man in defence of Soviet power, in defence of the interests of all the working people and first and foremost the interests of the workers and poor peasants!

Bourgeois hacks and people who let themselves be frightened by the bourgeoisie accuse us in chorus of being unyielding and uncompromising, of being unwilling to share power with any other party. That is not true, comrades! *We offered* to share power with the Left SRs and the offer is still open. It is not our fault that *they refused*. We began negotiations and, after the Second Congress had dispersed, we made all sorts of concessions in those negotiations, even to the point of provisionally agreeing to allow representatives from part of the Petrograd City Duma, from that nest of Kornilov supporters which will be the first to be swept away by the people if the unsavoury Kornilovites, the darling sons of the capitalists and landlords, the junkers again try to resist the will of the people as they tried last Sunday in Petrograd[180] and as they would like to do again (as is proved by the exposure of Purishkevich's plot and the papers seized on him yesterday, November 3). But the gentlemen standing behind the Left S Rs and acting through them in the interests of the bourgeoisie interpreted our willingness to make concessions as our weakness and took advantage of it to present new ultimatums to us. Mr. Abramovich and Mr. Martov were at the November 3 conference[181] and they presented an ultimatum: no negotiations until our government stops making arrests and closing bourgeois newspapers.

Our Party and the *TsIK* of the Congress of Soviets both *refused* to obey this ultimatum which had clearly come from supporters of Kaledin, the bourgeoisie, Kerensky and Kornilov. Purishkevich's plot and the appearance in Petrograd on November 5 of a delegation from a unit of the 17th Corps, threatening us with a march on Peter (a ridiculous threat since advance detachments of these Kornilov men have already been beaten and routed at Gatchina and most of them have refused to march against the Soviets) – all these events have shown whom Mr. Abramovich's and Mr. Martov's ultimatum *really* came from and whom these people were *really* serving.

Let the working people stay calm and firm ! Our Party will never yield to ultimatums from the minority in the Soviets, a minority which has let itself be intimidated by the bourgeoisie and which is, in reality, for all its 'good intentions', acting as the puppets of the Kornilovites.

We take a firm stand on the principle of Soviet power, that is, the rule of the *majority* at the last Congress of the Soviets; we agreed and *we still agree* to share power with the Soviet minority, on condition that that minority loyally and honestly undertakes to submit to the majority and carry out the programme *approved by the whole* All-Russian Second Congress of Soviets, consisting of gradual but firm and undeviating steps towards socialism.

But we are not going to submit to any ultimatums from groups of intellectuals who are not backed by the masses, who are only backed *in reality* by the Kornilov people, the Savinkov people, the junkers and others.

Let the workers stay calm and firm ! Our Party, the party of the Soviet majority, stands steadfast and united in defence of their interests and behind our Party, as before, are ranged millions of workers in the towns, soldiers in the trenches, peasants in the villages, ready to bring about, come what may, the triumph of peace and the triumph of socialism !

Written on November 5-6 [18-19] 1917.

V.I.Lenin, *Sochineniia*, 4th ed., vol.26, pp.269-273.

Document 7
To the CC RSDLP(b)

In answer to your letter*, we inform you that we do not consider our disagreements with the CC to be a breach of the Party rules, which we consider it our duty to observe as a submission to Party directives. But at the same time, we consider that it is totally inadmissible to create a special regime for particular Party members, both by treating them in the pogrom style of the CC proclamation against us and also by demanding special assurances of any kind from us. Your demand 'in all speeches to promote the policy of the CC' with which we radically disagree represents an unprecedented demand to speak against our own convictions. Our suspension from all work can only be accomplished by a special resolution of the CC.

Riazanov, Iu. Kamenev, Iu. Larin.
7.11.1917

Although the ultimatum in question was not given to us, we nevertheless fully share the position expressed in this answer and add our signatures:

V. Miliutin, N. Derbyshev.

Archives of the IML, f.17, op.1, ed. khr.40, l.5.

Document 8
To the CC RSDLP(b)

In answer to your communication*, may I state the following:
Since I continue to consider the policy of the CC majority deeply mistaken, and in so far as it contradicts the principles of revolutionary social democracy, I cannot renounce the right to criticise it.
I regard myself even less bound by CC decisions such as, for instance, the one to make an ultimatum out of Lenin's and Trotsky's candidature, demands which only compromise the party of the prole-

---

* See p.142.

tariat. In all such cases, where CC decisions are only dictated by political combinations and do not rest on decisions of the supreme Party body – the congress – I consider it my duty to fight against them.

7.11.1917.   Riazanov.

Archives of the IML, *f.*17, *op.*1, *ed. khr.*40, *l.*4.

* * *

Document 9
Statement by a spokesman for the Moscow Regional Committee

With reference to the resignation of Kamenev, Zinoviev and others from their posts of responsibility at a critical moment for the revolution, I declare on behalf of the Moscow Regional Committee that, in responding to this action, the Moscow Regional Committee will even go as far as to demand the expulsion of the people mentioned above from the Party.

In. Stukov.

Archives of the IML, *f.*17, *op.*1, *ed.khr.*40, *l.*7.

Document 10
A letter to comrades[182]

Comrades ! I made a statement on my resignation from the CC of our Party*. You will understand that it was not easy for me to come out publicly against comrades with whom I have been working side by side for 15 years now. I considered it my duty, however, to take even that step so as to induce the most intransigent of my comrades to reach an agreement with all the socialist parties and groups which recognise Soviet power.

---

*   See p.140.

I had to listen to many bitter reproaches from comrades on my statement. In *Pravda,* they rained accusations on me and my colleagues
which were, of course, exaggerated and only determined by the
fevered atmosphere in which we live and work. I remain convinced
that *it was necessary to do everything possible* to try to clarify
which groups were ready to support Soviet power.

The *TsIK* of the All-Russian Congress of Soviets put forward a concrete
plan for an agreement (November 3 resolution) which I completely
agree with, for it demands immediate recognition of the decrees
on land, peace and workers' control and the recognition of Soviet
power.

In response to this resolution by the Central Executive Committee, the
Mensheviks made a number of preliminary conditions. Not wanting to make negotiations more difficult, the *TsIK* approved, at our
suggestion (and in spite of the intransigents), a decision which
cleared the way for these negotiations.

In spite of that, the other side did not want to come to meet the *TsIK.*
The conditions it put forward were rejected by the Mensheviks
and SRs. Although the attempt at agreement was pursued to the
end in spite of all the obstacles, it was not crowned with success,
through no fault of ours. Now it has been proved that *Mensheviks
and SRs did not want an agreement* and were only looking for an
excuse to wreck it. Now all the workers and soldiers will know
where to put the responsibility for the breakdown of the agreement. Now – I am convinced of this – the Left SRs will also put
the responsibility for the breakdown of the agreement on the Mensheviks and enter our government.

Numerous comrades and several workers' delegations have been insisting
that I and my colleagues withdraw our resignation from responsible Party posts and submit to Party discipline. As things stand
now, after the Mensheviks have rejected talks on the conditions the
TsIK proposed, I am assenting to the comrades' proposal and
withdraw my statement.

I appeal to those who share my views most closely. Comrades! We have
made a great sacrifice in protesting openly against the majority of
our CC and demanding an agreement. However, this agreement
has been turned down by the other side. As things are now, we are
obliged to reunite with our old comrades-in-arms. It is a difficult
time, a very crucial time. It is our right and our duty to warn the
Party against mistakes. But we remain attached to the Party, we
prefer to make mistakes together with millions of workers and
soldiers and to die together with them than to step to one side
at this decisive, historic moment. We may still have our differences
and we have done everything we could to get the issue decided our

way. But as things are at present, we are bound, in my opinion, to submit to Party discipline and to act as the Left Bolsheviks did when they were in the minority about taking part in the Pre-Parliament and nevertheless committed themselves to pursue the policy of the majority.

There will not be, and must not be, a split in our Party.

November 7 1917.   G.Zinoviev.

Pravda No.183, November 21 [8] 1917.

Minutes No.33

[The minutes of the CC session of November 8 [21] 1917 (*ed. khr.* 41) are the original secretarial notes written in ink on one side of a large sheet of writing paper. Part of the second point and much of point three is written in pencil in Ia. M. Sverdlov's handwriting. The second set of minutes is in the minute book of the secretariat of the CC RSDLP(b) (*ed. khr.* 59).

The text of the minutes is printed from the secretarial notes collated with the text of the minutes in the CC secretariat book.]

Session of the CC
November 8 [21 1917]

[No list of those present in the original.]

2.   About Kamenev, Riazanov and the others.

On grounds of principle (the basic reason being the disparity between the policy line taken by the CC and the Bolshevik group and Kamenev's line)*, comrade Kamenev is relieved of the chairmanship of the $TsIK^{183}$.

---

*   In the original secretarial notes, *l.*1, the text in brackets from the words: *the basic reason* to the words: *and Kamenev's line* is inserted in pencil.

The question of Riazanov and the others is adjourned.

Comrades Trotsky, Stalin and Ioffe are to see to the implementation of the resolution in the group.

3.   The *TsIK**.

Raise the food problem in the *TsIK,* pointing out that it needs enormous resources to put the food supply right. A direction that money must be provided by the Treasury is the conclusion to be reached. The resolution on financial means is adopted.

(The newspapers say that the *TsIK* adopted it unanimously.)**[184]

Document
On sabotage
Resolution adopted at the TsIK *session of November 8 [21] 1917.*

The *TsIK* states that senior officials in the Ministry of Finance and the
State Bank do not recognise Soviet power and dispose of the income of the Treasury and the State Bank at will, issuing credits in some cases, withholding them in others and refusing credits to the Council of People's Commissars for the most urgent and vital needs, above all for special measures to supply food to the front and organise elections for the Constituent Assembly. Since the *TsIK* regards this conduct by senior officials of the Ministry of Finance, particularly in the State Bank and the Treasury, as criminal sabotage, which can have results affecting the lives of millions of soldiers, peasants and workers in the most disastrous way and which can interfere with getting the Constituent Assembly convened at the appointed time, the *TsIK* proposes to the Council of People's Commissars that it take very energetic measures to get rid of counter-revolutionary sabotage in the State Bank immediately and it calls on all remaining employees who are faithful to the people's cause to co-operate with Soviet rule in every way in the business of supplying state work with the necessary financial resources.

---

*   In the original secretarial notes, *l.*1, crossed out: *cancel Teodorovich's report.*
**   See below.

Meanwhile, until the Constituent Assembly, the *TsIK* is assuming control over allocating money sums to particular requirements of the Council of People's Commissars and the *TsIK* is setting up a financial commission of 9 members for this purpose.
The resolution is adopted unanimously.

Pravda No.185, November 23 [10] 1917.

Minutes No.34

[The minutes of the CC session of November 29 [December 12] 1917 (*ed. khr.* 42) are the original secretarial notes written with an ordinary pencil on both sides of six small sheets of paper torn out of a pad. The second set of minute notes is in the minute book of the secretariat of the CC RSDLP(b) (*ed. khr.* 59).

Since they diverge in a great many places, the texts of both sets of minutes are printed. The minute notes from the CC secretariat book are given in the lefthand column – the text of the secretarial minute notes in the right.

A CC resolution written in ink in E.D. Stasova's handwriting on both sides of two and a quarter sheets of small-size writing paper is appended to the secretarial notes (see pp. 162 - 164).]

Session of the CC
November 29 [December 12] 1917

Present: Bukharin, Oppokov [Lomov], Lenin, Trotsky, Uritsky, Muranov, Stalin, Sverdlov, Stasova, towards the end after the fourth point, Dzerzhinsky.

Present: Bukh[arin], Opp[okov – Lomov], Len[in], Trots[ky], Ur[itsky], Mur[anov], St[alin], Sv[erdlov], Stasova. After the fourth point, Dzerzhinsky.

Agenda:
1. Constituent Assembly.
2. Redistribution of manpower. (*Pravda* and Party work.)

Agenda:
II. 1. *Pravda*
2. Party work. } redistribution of manpower

3. Congresses in the army and on the front.
4. Statement of the Four.
6. The Ukrainian question.

IV. 4. Letter of the 4.
  I. 5. Constituent Assembly.
III. 6. Congresses in the army and on the front.
 VI. 7. The Ukrainian question.

Comrade Sverdlov raises the question of the need for CC sanction even retrospectively regarding the decision to declare the Kadets enemies of the people*[185].

Sverdlov. The question of the Kadets – enemies of the people. Sanction.

Comrade Uritsky feels that the CC must plan out what it is going to do about the Constituent Assembly because it turns out there are two commissions which do not recognise each other, so two convocations[186]. The question of candidatures also has to be decided.

Uritsky. How to act. Two convocations. Candidatures.

Comrade Bukharin puts the question of whether there is a need to call the Constituent Assembly or whether not to call it? What is better for us, to beat the Kadets bit by bit or to convene the Constituent Assembly and then drive the Kadets out of it all at once. He prefers the second course because constitutional illusions are still alive in the masses at large, and so he proposes organising the Left part, chucking out the Kadets and declaring the Left part of the Constituent Assembly a

Bukharin. To call or not to call the Constituent Assembly. Beat bit by bit. Convene and kick out the Kadets. 2nd path better because constitutional attitude on the part of the Bolsheviks. We organise the Left part, driving out the Kadets. Declare the Left part a revolutionary convention. The Left SRs and the Bolsheviks with a colossal preponderance of Bolsheviks. If others appear, too, we will arrest them.

---

*   See p.164.

revolutionary convention. This will be all the easier because the Bolsheviks and the Left SRs together will have a colossal preponderance[187].

Comrade Oppokov [Lomov] points out that the Kadets will turn heel and go off to the Ukraine or to Kaledin and that then Russia will not only be divided politically but also geographically. He suggests that the delegates should not be kept waiting in Peter for the Constituent Assembly to open but be allowed to go to the localities because work is so very important.

Comrade Stalin considers that comrade Bukharin's proposal has come a day late because at this moment two commissions exist and two constituent assemblies are being convened, and it is impossible to unite them because they do not recognise each other. We must definitely finish off the Kadets at this time or they will finish us off, because they have opened fire on us*.

Comrade Bukharin points out that he analysed alternatives theoretically, since this is the only way to establish our political line. Of course, we must create a revolutionary

Oppokov [Lomov]. The Kadets will turn round and go to the Ukraine or to Kaledin. There will also be a geographical division. Not to keep the delegates but adjourn.

Stalin. The future, yes, but there are urgent needs. Too late. Two commissions, two constituent assemblies. Impossible to unite them. Registration and that is all. The two commissions and the two sections do not recognise each other. They have opened fire and we must finish off the Kadets or they will finish us off.

Bukharin. Theoretically analysed alternatives. We must pursue a political line. We must create a revolutionary convention. An explanation is needed for the masses. We have been

---

*   See p.165.

convention but an explanation is needed for the masses because we have been working and trumpeting about getting the Constituent Assembly convened for $1\frac{1}{2}$ months.

At the end of the debate, comrade Sverdlov suggests putting the following two motions to the vote :

1. In view of the fact that elections to the Constituent Assembly have not finished everywhere yet, the opening of the Constituent Assembly is put off until December 10. (Rejected).

2. A commission of three people to be formed to determine who withdraws their candidature where. Approved.

The question is discussed in passing of whether to call all the candidates to Peter to tell them what the situation is or whether to consult with regional representatives so that they on their part would inform the regions.

It is decided to approve the latter and summon the candidates by telegraph when it becomes necessary, so as not to tear them away from work at this important time.

Sverdlov and Stasova are commissioned to scrutinise the candidatures and compile a list.

working and trumpeting about securing the convocation of the Constituent Assembly for $1\frac{1}{2}$ months. It is necessary to call the convention.

1. In view of the fact that elections to the Constituent Assembly have not finished everywhere yet, the opening of the assembly to be postponed until December 10 – rejected.

2. A commission of 3 to be formed to determine who cancels their candidature where. Approved. Speed up arrival or delay it.

Trotsky. Gather all the candidates in Peter to tell them about the situation.

Lomov. Consult with the regional representatives. Commission Sverdlov and Stasova.

Bukharin. How to promote our line in the press.

Trotsky. 400 people, that is no answer. We will pursue the line for a convention[188]. Summon by telegraph immediately.

II. Because the best people have moved into work for the state as a whole, Party work has suffered greatly, something which is particularly noticeable in the Party newspaper which is failing to satisfy its readers, not publishing articles explaining decrees, etc.

The explanation is that the whole editorial collegium stopped doing editorial work and in practice comrade Sokolnikov did the editing on his own, in addition to his Bank work.

Comrade Trotsky points out that close ties must be established between the Council of People's Commissars and the editorial boards of our newspapers and to this end, he suggests that all the editors gather for information every day towards evening at Smolny. In this way, there will be close links between the Council's policy and the policy of our Party. He suggests that it would both liven up our publications and thus also strengthen the Party's influence if *Priboi* has its own stenographers to take down all the speeches needed in shorthand. These speeches are the most vital material on the current situation.

Comrade Bukharin points out that this still will not put the matter right because there

II. *Redistribution of manpower.*

Only Bukharin at the Economic Conference; he goes to *Pravda* and *Priboi*.

Change. *Stalin.*

Joint editorial with *Krasnaia gazeta* assigned to Sokolnikov. Volodarsky and Slutsky.

An institute of control not to be created.

Close ties between the Council of People's Commissars and the editorial boards of our newspapers. The Council's policy closely linked with the policy of our Party.

Shorthand records of speeches, vital literature.

The most important is that we must write ourselves.

If there are no empty

is not enough material for the newspaper and if there are no empty patches, it is only because the newspaper is filled up with governmental decrees. The editors will have to write themselves, and as much as possible, so he suggests that he be relieved of work in the Economic Conference and comrades Obolensky and Smirnov sent there instead and that he could then devote himself to work in *Pravda*.

Comrade Lenin asserts that so far the Economic Conference has not been given the attention it deserves, yet it is one of largest elements in the current state structure and so has a need of experienced people like comrade Bukharin; that is why he insists that comrade Bukharin should not be included in *Pravda's* editorial collegium.

Comrade Stasova points out that of course comrade Bukharin is badly needed in the Economic Conference but he is needed in *Pravda* far, far more.

That aside, it is quite possible to combine ideological direction of the Economic Conference with work in *Pravda*, and organisational work does not suit comrade Bukharin in any case and can be confided to someone else. She proposes an editorial col-

patches it is because there are governmental decrees.

To the Economic Council : Obolensky and Smirnov.

Collegium of 3 : Sokolnikov, Stalin and Bukharin.

Obolensky and Smirnov.

legium of three : Stalin, Sokolnikov, Bukharin.

Comrade Uritsky supports
the proposal and, apart from
that, supports comrade Trotsky
about keeping the editorial
boards informed and in touch
and so he suggests that Trotsky
be included in the editorial collegium as a fourth.

Adopt Trotsky's proposal.

Comrade Lenin suggests a
different three : Sokolnikov,
Stalin, Trotsky.

Sverdlov supports a three-
some.

The evening three plus our
two. Sokolnikov and Stalin.

Lenin's three : Sokoln[ikov],
Stalin, Trotsky.

There is a vote on the proposal for an editorial board
consisting of three : Bukharin,
Stalin, Sokolnikov and it is approved by all except one ;
approval is also given to the
proposal that Trotsky be included for the special purpose
of information.

Then comrades Stalin and
Sokolnikov are charged with
getting together with the editorial board chosen by the
Petrograd Committee to work
out an agreement on replacing
the evening *Pravda* by *Krasnaia gazeta**[189].

Stalin. A directing collegium
of three for all the newspapers :
Sok[olnikov], St[alin], Tr[otsky].

Gather all the editors in the
evening for guidance.

Uritsky supports Bukharin,
Trotsky as a fourth.

A directing collegium of all
the editorials.

The editorial collegium of
Pravda : Stalin, Sokolnikov,
Bukharin, Trotsky included as
a fourth. Stalin and Sokol-
nikov** to work out an agreement on replacing the evening
Pravda by *Krasnaia gazeta*.

---

*   Written by mistake in the CC secretariat minute book : *Krasnaia
        zvezda.*
**   In the original secretarial notes, *l.*3 *ob.*, the words are crossed out :
        to come to an agreement with the Petrograd Committee.

III. Comrade Sverdlov reports that in the coming days, namely the 1st, 3rd, 5th, 6th, 7th and 10th, a whole series of regional army and front congresses are envisaged and CC representatives must be delegated to them because the situation is critical and we must bring them under our banner. But he has absolutely no one at his disposal and for that reason he asks them to spare one of the comrades for these congresses.

It is resolved to put comrades Lashevich, Muranov and Ordzhonikidze at comrade Sverdlov's disposal.

III. *Congresses in the army and on the front.*

Need for Central Committee members.

1 - 11 army.

3. Regional Congress.

5. Rumanian.

6.

7.

10.

*Lashevich, Muranov, Ordzhonikidze.

Sergo for S.W. front.

IV. The statement by Rykov, Kamenev, Miliutin and Nogin (see attached) is read through[190].

IV. *Statement of the 4.*

Comrade Uritsky feels that we cannot take them back into the CC because there is absolutely no guarantee that if they are left in the minority again on any question they will not once again come out with the same kind of letters and statements as just recently.

Uritsky's opinion. We cannot accept them since there is no guarantee that if they are left in the minority again, they will not behave in the same way.

Comrade Lenin reads an outline of his reply to this communication[191] in which he points out that a complete divergence between them and us

Lenin. Outline.

Concrete proposal. Let them indicate in writing where they want their letter to appear, i.e. do they want it in the press.

---

* Crossed out in the original secretarial notes, *l.*4 : *Bubnov, Ar*[tem].

comes out clearly from the statements of the Four since they consider that the CC went so far as to make concessions. Concretely, he proposes that the Four be required to make a written statement* on where they want their letter to appear, that is, do they want to put it in the press. We will not put it in the press on our own initiative but reply in writing that we are not accepting them back.

We are not putting it in the press.

We reply in writing.

We are not accepting them back.

Comrade Sverdlov poses the question of whether formally we can refuse them entry to the CC again.

Sverdlov. Formally, can we refuse them entry.

Comrade Uritsky states that there can be no question of their coming in unless they give us formal guarantees that they will not act subversively.

Uritsky. Come in only if they give formal guarantees.

It is decided to approve comrade Lenin's reply and to hand it over to any three CC members for editing. If they issue a statement about having their letter published, we will publish it but simultaneously with our reply.

Approve Il'ich's reply as a basis and hand it over to a commission of any three**.

If they issue a statement about publication ?

We publish with our reply.

Adopted.

VI. The Ukrainian social-democrats are asking permission to call themselves the

VI. The Ukrainian question. SDLP of the Ukraine.

---

* Crossed out in the CC secretariat minute book, *l.*144: *that they want to publish their statement and then we will publish it.*

** In the original secretarial notes, *l.*5, crossed out: *Bukharin, Lenin, Stalin.*

Social-Democratic Labour Party of the Ukraine since *Russia's* SDLP means *Russian* in Ukrainian. Because all the factors for and against have to be discussed and time is short, this question is referred to the CC Bureau (Stalin, Lenin, Trotsky and Sverdlov).

As it is so difficult to assemble a session of the CC, it is decided that these four shall be given the right to decide all urgent matters, but that they are obliged to include all the CC members in Smolny at the time in the decision-making.

Four decide urgent matters. Stalin, Sverdlov, Lenin, Trotsky. With the obligation to include all CC members.

CC Resolution of November 29.

The question of the Constituent Assembly.
1. A commission to be created to determine where to withdraw candidatures of comrades who are CC members or recommended by the CC.

Entrusted to comrades Sverdlov and Stasova.
2. No urgent summons to the candidates for the time being but they are to be called quickly by telegraph if it becomes necessary.

The editorial board of *Pravda.**

---

* In the original resolution, *l.*7, this item was initially formulated: *The editorial board of Pravda. Entrusted to comrade Sokolnikov to compose a common editorial board of Krasnaia gazeta with Volodarsky, Slutsky and,*

1. For close ties between the Council of People's Commissars and the editorial boards of our newspapers it is resolved that all the newspaper editors should gather at about 3-4 o'clock at Smolny where comrade Trotsky will bring them up to date.

2. The editorial board of *Pravda* is to be composed of four comrades : Sokolnikov, Stalin, Bukharin and Trotsky.

3.* Comrades Stalin and Sokolnikov are charged with working out an agreement on replacing the evening *Pravda* by *Krasnaia gazeta* (Molotov, Volodarsky and Slutsky – Petrograd Committee newspaper).

The congresses in the army and on the front.

Comrades Lashevich, Muranov and Ordzhonikidze are put at comrade Sverdlov's disposal to be sent to these congresses.

The statement of the Four.

It is decided to demand a written reply from them on whether they want their state-

---

* In the original resolution, *l.*7, point 3 was initially formulated in the following manner : *It is proposed to replace the evening* Pravda *with the Petrograd Committee newspaper* Krasnaia gazeta *and negotiations on the replacement and on setting up a joint editorial board with the editorial board chosen by the Petrograd Committee (Molotov, Volodarsky, Slutsky) is entrusted to comrades Sokolnikov and Stalin.*

ment published. If they do produce this statement in writing, the CC's reply is to be printed alongside it. Lenin's reply serves* as a basis for this reply and any three from the CC can be charged with drawing it up.

The Ukrainian question.

Four are commissioned to resolve it : Stalin, Lenin, Trotsky, Sverdlov. These four decide all urgent matters, but they are obliged to include all the CC members in Smolny at the time in the decision-making.

Document 1
Decree on the arrest of the leaders of the civil war against the revolution

Members of the governing bodies of the Kadet Party, as a Party of enemies of the people, are liable to arrest and trial by revolutionary tribunal.

Local Soviets are required to keep the Kadet Party under special surveillance because of its connection with the Kornilov and Kaledin civil war against the revolution.

This decree comes into force the moment it is signed.

Chairman of the Council of People's Commissars
Vl. Ul'ianov (Lenin)
Petr., November 28 1917, 10.30 p.m.

V.I.Lenin, *Sochineniia*, 4th ed., vol.26, p.315.

---

*   Crossed out in the original resolution, *l.*8 *ob,* : *to be adopted.*

Document 2
To all the workers and the exploited
Governmental announcement.

The bourgeoisie, under the direction of the Kadet Party, made all its
forces ready for a counter-revolutionary coup the moment the
Constituent Assembly was convened. In the Urals and on the Don,
Kornilov, Kaledin and Dutov raised the standard of civil war
against the Soviets of Peasants, Workers' and Soldiers' Deputies.
Bogaevsky, Kaledin's aide, declares openly that the insurrection
was begun at the express demand of the Kadet Party, which long
ago established official ties with the counter-revolutionary section
of the cossacks. In the Urals, the Kadet bourgeoisie gives money
and goods to support the counter-revolutionary rebellion. The first
bloody clashes between the revolutionary forces and detachments
from the bourgeois conspirators have occurred at Belgorod. Thus,
outright civil war has begun on the initiative of the Kadet Party
and under its direction. That Party's Central Committee is now
the political headquarters for all the counter-revolutionary forces
of the country.

This work, directly threatening the cause of peace and everything the
revolution has won, is being pursued under the pretext of defending the Constituent Assembly. The Kadet Central Electoral Commission carried on its work in secret from the Soviets, hiding all
the data about the elections to avoid any chance that the Kadets'
failure would be revealed before the conspiracy of Miliukov,
Kaledin, Kornilov and Dutov could be crowned with success. The
Council of People's Commissars resolved to open the Constituent
Assembly as soon as half its members had assembled, that is 400
out of 800. This resolution contained the best refutation of the
malicious slanders that the Council of People's Commissars,
resting on the support of all the working classes of the country, do
not want to convene the Constituent Assembly. But this was just
the reason why the bourgeoisie could not wait patiently for the
representatives of the people to be lawfully convened. Several
dozen people calling themselves Deputies but not showing their
documents broke into the Tavricheskii Palace on the evening of
November 28 accompanied by armed white guards, junkers and
several thousand bourgeoisie and saboteurs from the bureaucracy.

The Kadet Party's objective was to create a cover of 'apparent' legality
for the Kadet and Kaledin counter-revolutionary insurrection.
They wanted to present the voice of a few dozen bourgeois Deputies as the voice of the Constituent Assembly.

The Council of People's Commissars brings this conspiracy to the attention of the whole people. Everything the people have won, and this includes an imminent peace, is put at risk. In the South, Kaledin; in the East, Dutov; and finally, in the political centre of the country, in Petrograd, a conspiracy by the Kadet Party's Central Committee, which regularly sends Kornilovite officers to the South to help Kaledin. The slightest irresoluteness or weakness on the part of the people can result in the destruction of the Soviets, the destruction of the cause of peace, the extinction of the land reform and a new reign of landowners and capitalists.

Fully conscious of the enormous responsibility for the destiny of the people and the revolution now being placed on the shoulders of Soviet power, the Council of People's Commissars declares that the Kadet Party, being an organisation for counter-revolutionary rebellion, is a party of *enemies of the people*.

The Council of People's Commissars pledges itself not to lay down arms in the struggle against the Kadet Party and Kaledin's troops supporting it.

The political leaders of the counter-revolutionary civil war will be arrested. The bourgeois revolt will be suppressed whatever the price.

In this struggle, the Council of People's Commissars firmly counts on the support and indestructible loyalty to the revolution of all the revolutionary workers, peasants, sailors, soldiers, cossacks, of all honest citizens.

Down with the bourgeoisie! There must be no place in the Constituent Assembly for enemies of the people, for landowners and capitalists! The country can only be saved by a Constituent Assembly of representatives of the working and exploited classes of the people! On with the revolution! On with the Soviets! On with peace!

Council of People's Commissars.

Izvestiia TsIK i Petrogradskogo Soveta R i S D No.239,
November 29 1917.

Minutes No.35

[The minutes of the CC session of December 11 [24] 1917 (*ed. khr.* 43) are the original secretarial notes written with an ordinary pencil on both sides of one small sheet of paper torn out of a pad. The second set of minute notes are in the minute book of the secretariat of the CC RSDLP(b) (*ed. khr.* 59).

Because the secretarial notes are so short, the text of the minutes is printed from the minute notes from the CC secretariat book.]

Session of the CC
December 11 [24 1917]

Present :
Zinoviev, Sverdlov, Lenin, Sokolnikov, Stalin, Bukharin, Uritsky, Trotsky, Dzerzhinsky, Stasova.

Only one item on the agenda, about the group in the Constituent Assembly, because right-wing attitudes have taken hold in the group and its views differ from those of the CC[192].

A proposal is made to establish a constitution for the group, to arrange lectures for it and to join it up with the work of the Peter organisation.

Second proposal : a. To delegate one or several CC members to work with the group; b. To give them an opportunity to say what they think about the Constituent Assembly ; c. To take up the fight only when more people have assembled.

Comrade Lenin proposes : 1. to remove the bureau of the Constituent Assembly group[193] ; 2. to set out our attitude to the Constituent Assembly for the group in the form of theses[194] ; 3. to draw up an address to the group reminding them of Party rules that all representative bodies come under CC authority ; 4. to appoint a CC member to guide the group ; 5. to draw up rules for the group.

Comrade Zinoviev* proposes :

1. to write CC theses on the Constituent Assembly ; 2. to make no protest against the group's wishes to send out telegrams to candidates asking them to come to Peter ; 3. to appoint a CC member to the group ; 4. rules for the group ; 5. the CC considers the convocation of a Party congress or conference not desirable at the present time.

Comrade Sverdlov proposes : 1. to arrange new elections for the bureau immediately ; 2. to appoint a CC member to work in the group ; 3. to obtain signed assurances from all candidates that they will withdraw from the list at the request of the CC ; 4. telegrams summoning candidates not be sent by the bureau of the group but by the CC. The CC's answer to the group's demand

---

*   In the minute book of the CC secretariat, *l.*148 : *Zinoviev* is written over the crossed-out *Sverdlov*.

about telegrams is that, in accordance with the CC resolution of November 29[195], it is sending telegrams summoning the candidates to Peter.

It is decided to arrange a meeting of the group at Smolny on Tuesday, December 12 at 4 o'clock and comrade Sverdlov is to inform its bureau about it. The agenda of the group's meeting is planned as follows : 1. CC report ; 2. theses ; 3. new elections for the bureau.

The reply to the demand about telegrams is to be that the CC has already taken a decision to summon the members of the Constituent Assembly and is already sending for them, the telegrams having already gone out.

Comrades Sokolnikov and Bukharin are commissioned to work in the group.

PART THREE

The CC during the struggle to withdraw from the imperialist war and the conclusion of the Brest peace

Minutes No.36

[The minutes of the CC session of January 9 [22] 1918 (*ed. khr.* 404) are the original secretarial notes written in ink on one side of two half-sheets of writing paper.

The text of the minutes is printed from the original for the first time.]

[Session of the CC]
January 9 [22 1918]

Present :
Lenin, Zinoviev, Smilga, Sokolnikov, Krestinsky, Sergeev, Sverdlov, Lashevich, Ioffe, Shmidt, Stalin, Stasova, Vladimirsky.

Agenda :
Distribution of manpower
Central organ
Commissariats : Trotsky and Chicherin
Banks

(Leave the praesidium of the Petrograd Soviet as it is. The *TsIK* praesidium (Lander). Governmental military centre.

List of people in the praesidium : Krestinsky, Menzhinsky, Lunacharsky, Lashevich, Zinoviev, (Stalin), Smilga, Stuchka) – Uritsky gets an assignment from the CC.

We are strengthening the Petrograd Soviet with the remaining commissars, who will have a consultative vote.

The distribution of manpower as it affects departures from Peter without CC permission.

2 against, the remainder – in favour.

[Commissariat of] Foreign Affairs : Chicherin temporarily Deputy.

Dissolution of the Petrograd Committee (Zinoviev, Smilga and Lashevich).

Radek and Uritsky to the War Commissariat – approved.

Pravda is evacuated to Moscow. Editorial board : Sokolnikov, Stalin.

Bystriansky will remain in Peter for *Petrogradskaia pravda**[196]*. CC organ.

The editorial board of *Petrogradskaia pravda* – Bystriansky, Zinoviev and Smilga.

1. Central organ in Moscow, title *Pravda*.
2. Temporarily *Pravda petrogradskaia*.
3. Until it ceases to come out without a sub-title. 200,000 to *Pravda* from**.

For the central organ : Sokolnikov and Stalin.

For *Petrogradskaia pravda* : Zinoviev, Smilga and Bystriansky.

*Banks**** : Gukovsky to the banks for the time being. A conference in Moscow on bank policy.

C C Bureau.

1. CC to Moscow.
2. Bureau to Moscow as in the April days.

Lenin, Stalin, Sverdlov, Sokolnikov, Trotsky.

Banks : Menzhinsky, Spunde, Krestinsky.

Council of National Economy. Miliutin.

Menzhinsky's deputy – Aksel'rod.

Minutes No.37

[The minutes of the CC session of January 11 [24] 1918 (*ed. khr.* 405, *ll.*1 - 13) are the original secretarial notes written with an ordinary pencil on one side of thirteen small sheets of paper torn out of a pad. A second set of minute notes is written out again in ink in the same handwriting (*ll.*14 - 18) on both sides of five half-sheets of writing paper. A third set of minute notes is in the minute book of the secretariat of the CC RSDLP(b) (*ed. khr.* 59).

The text of the minutes is printed from the secretarial notes (*ll.*14 - 18) collated with the text of the two other sets of minutes.]

---

*   In the original notes written by mistake : *Peterburgskaia pravda.*
**   Then a gap in the minute notes.
***   The words are crossed out in the minute notes : *Menzhinsky proposes Gukovsky.*

Session of the CC
January 11 [24] 1918

Present :
Lomov [Oppokov], Krestinsky, Muranov, Uritsky, Dzerzhinsky,
Sergeev [Artem], Sverdlov, Trotsky, Lenin, Stalin, Bukharin,
Sokolnikov, Bubnov, Kollontai, Zinoviev and Stasova*.

Agenda :
1. The admission of a representative from the Petersburg Committee to the session with a consultative vote.
2. The election of praesidium members of the trade union
centre.
3. The peace.

1. The first question is decided in the affirmative and comrade
Kosior attends the session.
2. From the candidates proposed by the Bolshevik group in
the Trade Union Congress[197] for the posts of chairman, secretary
and editor of the trade union organ, it is decided to nominate
comrade Shliapnikov for chairman, two comrades for secretary :
Shmidt and Tomsky (in general, it is decided to have two secre-
taries) and comrade Glebov as editor.
3. The peace[198].
The first to speak is comrade Lenin, who points out that at
the January 8 meeting three points of view crystallised on this issue
and he asks whether the discussion should follow the points in the
theses he presented[199] or whether to open a general debate.
The latter is favoured and the floor given to comrade Lenin.
He begins by setting out the three points of view which
emerged at the previous meeting : 1. a separate peace with annexations ; 2. a revolutionary war and 3. declare a halt to the war,
demobilise the army but not sign a peace. At the earlier meeting,
the first point of view gained 15 votes, the second 32 and the
third – 16.
Comrade Lenin asserts that the Bolsheviks have never rejec-

---

* In the original secretarial notes, *l.*1, it goes on to say: *With a
consultative vote Kosior, Glebov, Sokolnikov.*

ted defence but that there had to be definite and concrete circumstances for that defence and protection of the homeland, and these exist at the present time, namely : the protection of a socialist republic from an extraordinarily strong international imperialism. It is now only a question of how we must defend the homeland – the socialist republic. The army is utterly exhausted by war ; our supply of horses is such that in an attack we will not be able to withdraw the artillery ; the German position on the Baltic islands is so good that if they attacked they could take Reval and Petrograd with their bare hands. If we continue the war in conditions like this, we will strengthen German imperialism enormously and will have to make peace all the same, but the peace will be worse then because we will not be the ones to conclude it. There is no doubt that it is a shameful peace which we are forced to conclude now, but if we embark on a war, our government will be swept away and another government will make peace. Now we not only have the support of the proletariat but of the poor peasants, too, and that will leave us if we continue the war. It is in the interests of French, English and American imperialism to drag out the war and the offer made by the Americans in Krylenko's headquarters, for example, of 100 roubles for each Russian soldier, proves it. Those who advocate a revolutionary war point out that this will involve us in a civil war with German imperialism and in this way we will awaken revolution in Germany. But Germany is only just **pregnant with revolution and** we have already given birth to a completely healthy child, a socialist republic which we may kill if we start a war. We have a circular letter belonging to the German social-democrats in our hands and there is information about how two centrist currents regard us ; one thinks we have been bribed and that a comedy is now being played out in Brest, with the roles defined in advance. This section attacks us for the armistice. The other section of Kautskyites declares that the personal integrity of the Bolshevik leaders is beyond doubt but that the conduct of the Bolsheviks is a psychological mystery[200]. We do not know the opinions of the Left social-democrats. The English workers support our desire for peace. Of course, this peace we are going to conclude will be a shameful peace but we need a respite to put social reforms into practice (take only transport) ; we need to gain strength and for that we need time. The bourgeoisie has to be throttled and for that, we need both hands free. When that is done, we will have nothing on our hands and then we can wage a revolutionary war against international imperialism. The troops of the revolutionary and volunteer army created today will be the officers of our future army.

What comrade Trotsky suggests – halting the war, refusing to sign a peace and demobilising the army – this is international political showmanship. The only thing we will achieve by withdrawing our troops is that we will give the Estonian socialist republic to the Germans. It is said that if we conclude peace, we will untie the hands of the Japanese and the Americans, who will immediately take possession of Vladivostok. But before they have reached Irkutsk, we will have been able to make our socialist republic strong. By signing peace, we will, of course, be handing over independent Poland but we will keep the socialist Estonian republic and get a chance to consolidate what we have won[201]. Of course, we are making a turn to the right and it means we have to rub our noses in the dirt but it has to be done. If the Germans start to attack, we will be forced to sign any peace at all and then, of course, it will be a worse one. To save the socialist republic, reparation of three milliards is not too high a price. If we sign a peace now, the broad masses will see with their own eyes that the imperialists (of Germany, England and France), having taken Riga and Baghdad, are going on fighting while we are developing, the socialist republic is developing.

Comrade Bukharin feels that comrade Trotsky's position is the most correct and he discerns two contradictions in comrade Lenin's position. He says that our stance must be one of defence, but defence presupposes war and in waging that war, we are crawling behind imperialism. We have to look at the socialist republic from the point of view of internationalism, since here we have a common front in the class struggle. From this point of view, we can say that we have already conquered, elsewhere detachments are not advancing and in another place again, they are only just beginning to move. Comrade Lenin is wrong to condemn political showmanship, because renouncing war and fraternising are ways to demoralise an army. We beat Kornilov by demoralising his army, that is, precisely by political showmanship. We want to apply this very method to the German army, too. Let the Germans strike, let them advance another 100 versts, what interests us is how this affects the international movement. The German social-democrats are concerned that we should not sign a treaty because in Germany and Vienna the movement is growing out of this struggle for peace. A general strike is developing in Vienna in connection with the Brest negotiation and if we sign peace, we will wreck that struggle. In preserving our socialist republic, we will lose the chance of an international movement. What has caused the movement in the West to intensify? The peace issue. Of course, this is evidence of weakness in the movement but if it is to be encouraged, we must kindle it on the peace issue, not give the governments in Berlin and Vienna the opportunity to say that peace has been concluded. Every opportunity must be taken to spin things out and not sign a shameful peace, because this way we will keep the Western European masses on the alert.

Comrade Uritsky considers that comrade Lenin's mistake at this moment is the same as it was in 1915 – that is, he looks at the matter from Russia's angle and not from an international point of view[202]. Of course, we cannot wage a revolutionary war – cannot because the moment we begin it, we will lose our army, the soldiers; and the bourgeoisie will immediately conclude a peace. But if we sign a peace, we will lose the proletariat because the Peter proletariat will certainly not accept the signature of a peace and will consider that we have abandoned our line. By refusing to sign a peace, demobilising the army and thus making a political gesture, we will of course be opening the way for the Germans but then the instinct of self-preservation will undoubtedly awaken in the people and the revolutionary war will begin. On the subject of political showmanship, the whole policy of the People's Commissariat of Foreign Affairs was none other than a political gesture. This is just how our policy, too, will be understood by the German soldiers when we have refused to sign peace, halted the war and demobilised the army.

Comrade Trotsky raises the question of how a revolutionary war fits into the context of world international relations. At this moment, the essence of the whole question is in the balance of forces. Whether we take an active part in the imperialist war or stay passive, we will still be taking part in the war. We have to assess what would be more profitable for us. To convert all our resources into military power – that is utopia. That is why the question of a revolutionary war is an unreal one. The army has to be disbanded, but disbanding the army does not mean signing a peace. During the negotiations, we could not manage to discover the relations between Austro-Hungary and Germany. By refusing to sign a peace and demobilising the army, we force the facts into the open, because when we demobilise, the Germans will attack. This will be a clear demonstration to the German social-democrats that this is no game with previously-determined roles. We could not discover, either, how strong the forces of opposition were in Germany because the Germans do not know the printed peace conditions and the German censor falsifies the negotiations. Comrade Stuchka suggested that we should propose a court of arbitration to the Germans and this seems to me acceptable as a way of delaying the negotiations further and if it is rejected, we break off the negotiations but state that we are not going to fight.

Comrade Oppokov [Lomov] feels that even if we get a respite, nothing will be achieved because there is no doubt that all our measures to introduce socialism will meet such opposition from German imperialism that we will be completely powerless. He considers that one cannot say that a revolutionary war is impossible because we have done nothing up to now to prepare one. He considers comrade Lenin's position of renouncing war because we want to save the child, the socialist republic, to be wrong. It is precisely the demoralisation of the German army, precisely a civil war with German imperialism, precisely our suffocation which can arouse revolution in the West. There is no stopping halfway but we must go on to the end, holding on to our position, but by concluding peace, we capitulate to German imperialism. He believes that we have to adopt Trotsky's position but combine it with maximum activity in preparing for a revolutionary war.

Comrade Stalin considers that adopting the slogan of a revolutionary war is playing into the hands of imperialism. Comrade Trotsky's position is no position at all. There is no revolutionary movement in the West, nothing existing, only a potential and we cannot count on a potential. If the Germans start to attack, it will strengthen the counter-revolution here. Germany will be able to attack because she has her own Kornilovite troops – the guards. In October, we talked of a holy war because they told us that just the word 'peace' would raise a revolution in the West. But this turned out not to be true. The socialist reforms we bring in will stir things up in the West but we need time to implement them. If we adopt comrade Trotsky's policy, we will make conditions much worse for the movement in the West, so he proposes that comrade Lenin's proposal be approved.

Comrade Zinoviev says that, of course, we face a grave surgical operation because a peace will strengthen chauvinism in Germany and for a time weaken the movement everywhere in the West. But beyond, another perspective opens up – that is the extinction of the socialist republic. Trotsky's proposal is unacceptable because of course Kuehlmann will answer in parliamentary fashion that since no peace has been signed, we remain in a state of war with them. Comrade Zinoviev puts the question : should we not delay the resumption of negotiations for some time longer and hold a national referendum on the question of a peace in the interval.

Comrade Bubnov observes that three points of view figured at the January 8 meeting and now there are only two, since no one is advocating the point of view of the revolutionary war.

Comrade Lenin indicates that he disagrees on some points with his fellow-thinkers, Stalin and Zinoviev. On the one side, of course, a mass movement does exist in the West but the revolution has not yet started there. If we were to change our tactics on the strength of that, however, then we would be betraying international socialism. With Zinoviev, he disagrees that concluding a peace will weaken the movement in the West for a time. If we believe that the German movement can immediately develop if the peace negotiations are broken off, then we must sacrifice ourselves, for the power of the German revolution will be much greater than ours. But the point is that the movement has not yet started there and here it already has a newborn, lusty child and if we do not make it clear now that we agree to a peace, then we will perish. It is important for us to hold out until the general socialist revolution and this can only be achieved when we have concluded peace.

Comrade Dzerzhinsky states that to sign a peace is to capitulate on our whole programme. He considers that comrade Lenin is doing in a disguised form what Zinoviev and Kamenev did in October. We must behave in a way which strengthens the West. Comrade Lenin pointed out that the socialist republic relies on the poor peasants and the proletariat. We are a party of the proletariat and must see clearly that the proletariat will not support us if we sign a peace.

Comrade Kosior says that the Petersburg organisation is protesting and will protest as long as it can against comrade Lenin's point of view and considers that the position of a revolutionary war is the only possible one[203].

Comrade Bukharin advances the slogan of a peace in the trenches as a possibility.

Comrade Sergeev [Artem] points out that all the speakers agree that our socialist republic is threatened with destruction in the absence of a socialist revolution in the West and he considers that time is needed for it to develop from a potential into an active, effective force, so that we must get this time and the only way to get it is by concluding a peace; a peace is our salvation.

Comrade Krestinsky says that the chief argument cited against a revolutionary war is our lack of an army as a fighting unit. But we must continue to demobilise because the old army cannot be considered suitable to fight a revolutionary war. We must build up our Red Guard since that will both make us strong and we will be able to rely on it and not on the garrison. Only when we have created our own Red Army will we be able to wage a revolutionary war.

Comrade Sokolnikov points out that there is no harm in dragging out the peace negotiations but that we have nothing to fear from signing a peace because in reality the peace will be only a truce and the conclusion of the peace will mark the start of our preparations for a revolutionary war. He thinks it would even pay us to sign a capitulation since this would show the whole world still more clearly that we are fighting in a political way for the right of nations to self-determination and not by reconquering occupied territories. History shows clearly that the key point on the earth is gradually moving towards the East. In the 18th century, it was France, in the 19th, Germany, now it is Russia.

Comrade Bukharin suggests defining what we consider to be a revolutionary war : an attack or staying where we are?

Comrade Trotsky suggests asking the question : do we intend to appeal for a revolutionary war?

It is put to the vote.

For 2, against 11, abstained 1.

Comrade Lenin suggests it is put to the vote that we do everything to drag out signing the peace.

It is put to the vote.

For – 12, against 1*.

---

* In the original secretarial notes, *l.*13, the text continues: [Lenin]. *In doing this, we are spinning out a preliminary peace into a permanent peace, even if we have to pay 1 000 000 000.* *Bukharin. Do we decide demonstr.*

Comrade Trotsky suggests putting the following formula to the vote : we halt the war, do not conclude peace and demobilise the army.

It is put to the vote.

For – 9*, against – 7**.

(Comrade Smilga's written statement was taken into account when the votes were counted.)[204]

Minutes No.38

[The minutes of the CC session of January 19 [February 1] 1918 (*ed.khr.* 406, *ll.*1 - 12) are the original secretarial notes written in ordinary pencil on one side of twelve small sheets of paper torn out of a pad. The second set of minute notes (*ll.*13 - 15) is written in ink in the same handwriting on both sides of three large sheets of paper torn out of a pad. The third set of minute notes is in the minute books of the secretariat of the CC RSDLP(b) (*ed. khr.* 59).

The text of the minutes is printed from the secretarial notes (*ll.*13 - 15) collated with the text of the two other sets of minutes.

The following documents preserved in the archives are given after the minutes : 1. The original statement to the CC RSDLP from a group of CC members and People's Commissars about calling an immediate conference (p.188). 2. The typewritten text of a statement from the Executive Commission of the Petersburg Committee to the CC RSDLP. The statement is written on headed paper with the Petersburg Committee imprint. The signatures are autographs (see pp.190 - 191). 3. A typewritten copy of the theses by the Petrograd Committee on the current situation and the war (see pp.191 - 192). 4. The statement to the CC about calling a Party conference (see p.196) is from the original document written in indelible pencil. The signatures are autographs. 5. The statement to the CC from a group of Urals Party workers (see p.197) is from the original document written in ink. The signatures are autographs. 6. The Moscow Committee's resolution of February 20 (see p.195) is from a handwritten copy written in ink on one side of a sheet of writing paper.]

---

*   In the original secretarial notes. *l.*13 : 7 corrected to 9.
**   In the original secretarial notes, *l.*13 : 6 corrected to 7.

Session of the CC
January 19 [February 1] 1918[205]

Present :
Sokolnikov, Sverdlov, Oppokov [Lomov], Uritsky, Stalin, Krestin-
sky, Sergeev [Artem], Bubnov, Zinoviev, Bukharin, Muranov,
Lenin, Stasova.

Agenda :
1. Conference.
2. Congress.
3. The *TsI K* delegation abroad.
4. The praesidium of the *TsI K*.
5. Food supply.
6. Allocation of portfolios.

I. Conference.
Comrade Oppokov [Lomov] says that as a result of comrade
Trotsky's and especially Zinoviev's speeches at the Third Congress
of Soviets, a whole series of people have got the idea that a separate
peace with the Germans has been decided on in advance and for
that reason, the voice of the Party, silent for so long, must be heard.
With this in mind, the people in Moscow are suggesting calling a
Party conference*[206]. To speed it up and make it possible to call it
in a week, the leaders of the various regions could possibly be
delegated to it as representatives.

Comrade Zinoviev dwelt on the fact that his speech was not
contrary to the decision taken by the CC and that circumstances
have already changed since the time the Third Congress met because a movement already exists in Austria and Germany, having
begun earlier than we could have predicted. No one, however,
even before these events, thought it possible to conclude or sign a
peace as long as the Germans did not declare *Kuendigung***. He
does not see the sense in calling a conference because, after all, our
group was at the Congress and it was attended by representatives
from the whole of Russia, and the group considered the question
and took a definite decision.

---

*   See p.188.
**   Notice that a peace treaty ceases to operate.

Comrade Lenin asks what sort of conference should be called? In his opinion, we should have it out with the advocates of a revolutionary war since in their *Zwischenrufe** the accusation** may be discerned that one group in the Party suspects the other of being diplomatic on the question of a peace; in reality, there is no diplomacy going on at all because it is stated quite openly in the armistice decision that any side wishing to terminate it must declare its intention seven days before the start of military action. We are delaying the peace on that basis. How was the decision approved at the Third Congress of Soviets[207]? Just as it was proposed by the *TsIK*; the *TsIK* itself passed the decision in agreement with the decision of the group, and the group adopted it in agreement with the decision of the CC. Lenin believes that the best way to dissuade the comrades who advocate a revolutionary war would be for them to go to the front and see there with their own eyes that it would be completely impossible to wage the war. He does not see the sense of a conference for the additional reason that its decisions could not be binding on the CC; to get precise directives from the Party, it is possible that we will find it necessary to call a Party congress***. Dragging out the peace negotiations gives us the chance to continue fraternisation and when we conclude peace we can immediately exchange prisoners of war and so propel a vast mass of people into Germany who have seen our revolution in practice and have been educated by it and it will make it all the easier for them to work to arouse it in Germany. Apart from that, he considers that we should send airmen to Berlin to find out exactly what is going on in Germany for they say this would be perfectly possible.

Comrade Uritsky considers that Trotsky's point of view prevailed at the Congress of Soviets, that is, the same one adopted by the CC. He thinks that a congress needs to be called because the Party's position is not at all definite and it has to be settled through a congress.

---

*   Interjections.
** Crossed out in the original secretarial notes, *l.*13: *of one section.*
*** Crossed out in the original secretarial notes, *l.*13: *at the present moment, under the influence of fraternisation, the position is such that the Germans will not be able to move troops against us as easily as before.*

Comrade Bukharin feels that the Party's attitude to the peace question is extremely uncertain and that the split threatened by the Petersburg Committee* is intolerable. Different groups have formed in the Party and this can be explained by the absence of a definite guiding line. One extreme point of view says that peace cannot be concluded under any circumstances; the other says that two months ago we should have made peace, that now we do not but that if the workers' movement in the West is crushed, then we must make peace. There are others, too, a whole series of points of view, but no definite position in the Party and since one is necessary, a conference has to be called.

Comrade Sverdlov says that the proposed conference cannot be likened to or compared with conferences held in the past because conditions were quite different then. A plenary session of the CC at the present moment does not differ from previous conferences for there are representatives from all the regions in it. The conference we would be able to call would not be a Russia-wide conference and since such a conference could not pass any decisions binding on the CC, its decisions would only have moral significance and could only lead to a situation where the comrades who find themselves in the minority will resign from posts of responsibility. In his view, a congress is necessary to hear the definite opinion of the Party, and especially because we need to change the organisational structure.

Comrade Lenin, on a point of order, suggests that Bukharin should give the facts about the state of affairs in the Petrograd Committee.

Comrade Bukharin reports that, the previous day, a meeting of the Petrograd Committee and active Party workers was held to discuss the war and the peace and that Bukharin's theses**, which did not have at all the same meaning as that contained in the Petrograd Committee's address to the Central Committee, were adopted. The theses were approved unanimously with one abstention.

Comrade Sokolnikov asserts that a congress is needed not so much for the peace question as for general Party questions and he declares himself against a conference because a conference does

*   See p.190.
**   See p.191.

not tell us the opinion of the Party – we can only find that out by means of a referendum. The motive for delaying the peace is the political situation and we must judge this independently of our congress. He personally does not attach great importance to the Petrograd Committee's address since he is sure that the comrades will not take it as far as a split. The movement of which the Petrograd Committee's paper is an expression is not a rank and file movement. He therefore suggests fixing a date to call a congress where we can pass a definite resolution on a peace, and that the report on the peace should be based on the theses about the war representing the CC's view.

Comrade Lomov [Oppokov]* regards the opinion expressed by the Muscovites as extremely important because it is not the opinion of individual comrades but the opinion of the whole Moscow meeting since it carried a corresponding resolution**. We must pay serious attention to the papers reaching the CC since they represent the opinion of the biggest organisations : those of Peter and Moscow. We have the view of a meeting of Party workers in Peter and Moscow. There is undoubtedly some divergence within our ranks which must be resolved by a conference, because a congress which only meets in a month's time has no direct relationship to the peace***.

Comrade Lenin makes a definite proposal. He points out to the people who want a conference organised that it will not heal the rifts which have appeared. A Party congress is necessary whereas a conference is solely to get the opinion of the Party which has to be recorded. For this purpose, he suggests calling a meeting containing all shades of opinion and points of view, each being represented by three people. This meeting would have to work out an agreement.

---

*   There is a beginning to Lomov's speech in the original secretarial notes, *l*.4, which is not in the other versions : *Factual information on the dispatch to the front.* [Then the words are crossed out : *on desertion* and] *abandonment of posts.*

**   See pp. 193 - 194.

***   There are two notes in the original secretarial notes, *l*.4, which do not appear in the other versions : *Krestinsky. The factual side of the matter. Zinoviev. It is not clear why the majority of the CC insists on a conference being called. How much dissatis. in Moscow. And Peter – at the top convocation of a congress necessary.*

Comrade Bubnov does not see the sense in a conference since a congress is the only body with enough competence and legitimacy to express a final opinion binding on the CC. He says that he is against a conference and in favour of a congress. Aside from that, he points out that Lomov [Oppokov] does not speak for the Muscovites and that they have Obolensky [Osinsky] and Stukov as definite spokesmen for their view.

Comrade Stasova points out that a congress cannot be called quickly and that is why she favours the meeting suggested by comrade Lenin.

Comrade Sergeev [Artem] observes that there are two points of view regarding the peace : 1. a peace should not be signed, and 2. it can be signed under certain conditions. An armed insurrection is possible at this moment but without cast-iron arguments*. Some CC members do not seem to understand why we cannot sign a peace and that is why our CC cannot be entrusted with the signature of the peace until the Party's opinion has been clarified. If we want to have the Party's opinion, the discussion should be declared open. A conference will not provide what we need and a congress has to be called anyway, for quite other purposes. He therefore opposes a conference, all the more since it will not reflect rank and file opinion.

Comrade Stalin feels that it has been our Party's whole strength up to now that we have taken a very clear and definite position on all issues. There is no such clarity and precision on the peace question, since various strands exist. We must put an end to this. But the congress is another matter because the peace issue is not connected with a congress. The middle view – Trotsky's position – gave us a way out of a grave situation. Now we face the question, what do we do if the question of a peace becomes pressing? Give the spokesmen for different points of view more chance to be heard and call a meeting to reach a clear position.

Comrade Sverdlov asks how to call a conference and what kind. It does not seem possible to call it in the weeks immediately ahead since there is no point in convening the regional representatives – that is the CC plenum itself and a conference of that sort would not provide the opinion of the masses, the rank and file. He favours a meeting with the regional representatives because a clear

---

*   Thus in the text of the minute notes.

position could be arrived at from such a meeting. The CC will confirm the resolution which comes out of the meeting (or conference, if they want to call it that). But a congress has to be called independently of this meeting*.

Comrade Krestinsky suggests calling a congress for February 15, taking 1 to 5000 people as the norm of representation. Convene the congress by direct wire. Publish theses on the war and the peace. No conference to be called but a meeting of the type proposed by Lenin. No peace to be signed before the congress meets, the peace negotiations to be dragged out.

Comrade Lenin says he is in favour of calling a meeting in two to three days, but not of printing the theses because we do not want to make them Germany's property. The question of a conference should not be decided before the meeting, but it would be senseless to defer the question of the peace until a congress without publishing the theses.

Comrade Lomov suggests calling a meeting for January 20, a conference after (a few days) a week and a congress on February 15.

Comrade Bukharin points out that as soon as we have called a congress, we must work on its agenda to avoid the hasty, last-minute reports we had in July. He suggests adopting Lenin's proposal for the groups to work out an agreement but we need a conference for its own sake and we should agree in advance that its decisions will be binding, and not only in a moral sense. He thinks theses could be contained in a series of articles in the pages of *Pravda*, but in a veiled form. A conference will provide a base for coming to terms with our differences and clarifying our position.

Comrade Krestinsky suggests duplicating the theses and giving them to the members of the Third Congress of Soviets as they disperse.

Comrade Lenin suggests that a meeting be arranged for the members leaving after the Third Congress of Soviets, but that nothing be handed out in writing.

Comrade Zinoviev proposes leaving the question of a conference open until the meeting.

---

*   There is a note in the original secretarial notes, *l.6*, which does not appear in the other versions : *Oppokov – there is no disagreement between Stukov, Obolensky and Smirnov. Bukh[arin] and Opp[okov] – bloc.*

Comrade Lenin points out that it is impossible to get the Party programme ready by February 15 and proposes : a meeting on January 20 composed of : 1. the CC, 2. Spokesmen for the most clearly marked views, namely : Lenin, Sokolnikov, Bukharin, Obolensky, Stukov. If Smirnov, Obolensky, Stukov and Piatakov take differing positions, they should send two representatives, otherwise one. 3. the Petrograd Committee represented by Fenigstein. 4. A Latvian.

Bukharin and Lomov to be authorised to talk it over with the Muscovites and Piatakov. Each group to present its own theses.

This proposal is adopted unanimously.

The meeting is fixed for Sunday, January 21.

The question of a conference is referred to the meeting*.

In favour – 8 votes.

II.   The question of a congress[208].

It is resolved to convene a congress on February 20, using the same representation norm as in October, and to look out the previous announcement for this purpose, giving it to the printers with the corresponding change of date. The agenda is adjourned to the following meeting**.

III.   The *TsIK* delegation abroad.

It is decided that Kollontai is to be sent from the CC but no second candidate is chosen***[209].

IV.   The first session of the *TsIK*.

Object to Dan, Chernov?

Not to object.

V.   Designated for the *TsIK* praesidium : 1. Sverdlov, 2. Mur-

---

*   In the original secretarial notes, *l*.9, this point begins like this : *II. Conference.* Then the beginning of the phrase is crossed out : *After Sunday, theses are communicated to the centres by direct wire.*

**   In the original secretarial notes, *l*.10, this point goes like this : *III. The congress.* [Then, crossed out : *1 from 1000*] *1 from 5000. February 20. Seventh Party Congress Agenda*

***   In the original secretarial notes, *l*.10, this point goes like this : *IV. The TsIK delegation abroad. Natanson and Ustinov from the Left S Rs. (Kamenev), Riazanov and Kollontai. Gnevich to Sverdlov.*

anov, 3. Zinoviev, 4. Lander, 5. Avanesov, 6. Okulov, 7. Peterson, 8. Volodarsky.

VI. Food supply*.

It is decided to replace Shlichter by Briukhanov or Tsiurupa.

Sverdlov is instructed to clear up all the misunderstandings which have arisen in the matter[210].

VII. Allocation of portfolios**.

The Left SRs nominate to finance instead of war, we have to assign a Bolshevik to the railways. Since the railwaymen want all their affairs to be conducted by a collegium, they must elect a Bolshevik as a permanent representative[211].

Document 1
Statement by a group of CC members and People's Commissars about calling an immediate Party conference

To the Central Committee of the Russian Social-Democratic Labour Party.

Since the Central Committee resolved, contrary to the opinion of the comrades who had proposed signing a peace treaty immediately, *not* to sign a 'shameful peace' on January 29; since the Moscow

---

* In the original secretarial notes, *l.11*, this point goes as follows:
VII. Food supply.
1.   The collegium of 28 people elected by the congress on the food supply to be enlarged to 35.
2.   Our own representative in the administration.
3.   Group in charge.
Recognise the congress. A collegium of the congress public, eliminate 9, appoint Briukhanov. Sverdlov to have talks with the food supply Com. and bring the decision to us.

** In the original secretarial notes, *l.12*, this point goes as follows:
VIII. Brilliantov, the Left SRs nominate to finance instead of a military man but with a deliberative vote (instead of Mikhailov) – the railway ministry parity of Bolsheviks in the collegium.
Allocation of the portfolios of labour, trade and industry. Deputy for this session with a deliberative vote – Nevsky, if the group does not object.
The collegium must nominate one Bolshevik commissar.
Bukharin. The commissar is bound by an imperative mandate.
Piatnitsky. The commissar can take no steps without the collegium in the Commissariat's administration of means of communications. The collegium nominates a People's Commissar.

Regional Bureau of the RSDLP, the Petersburg Committee and the January 8 1918 meeting of the Central Committee and Party workers took the same point of view; since the resolution moved at the Congress of Soviets of Workers' and Soldiers' Deputies on behalf of the Bolshevik group does not indicate directly that it is inadmissible to sign a treaty on January 29 and unlimited plenipotentiary powers are simultaneously conferred on the Council of People's Commissars in the matter of concluding a peace, including therefore the right to sign a 'shameful peace'; since this gives rise to a contradiction between decisions of authoritative Party bodies, the possibility that decisions made by the centre of the Party will be violated and a lack of clarity in the Party's political line – the undersigned declare that:

1. they consider that a Party conference must be called immediately (within a week) to resolve finally and clearly this question of historic importance for the international proletariat;

2. in the event of a peace treaty being *signed* on January 29 *without such a conference having been called,* the undersigned find it necessary whatever happens to leave such posts of responsibility in the Party and governmental organs as they may hold.

Member of the CC RSDLP *G. Oppokov (A. Lomov)*
People's Commissar *V. Obolensky (N. Osinsky)*
V. Iakovleva, Sheverdin, N. Krestinsky, V. Smirnov,
M. Vasil'ev, M. Savel'ev
Commissar of the State Bank *Georgii Piatakov*
Member of the CC RSDLP and ed. *Pravda N. Bukharin*
Member of the Urals Regional Committee and the *TsIK*
Preobrazhensky
Petersburg. January 15 1918.

Archives of the IML, *f.*17, *op.*1, *ed.khr.*406, *ll.*17 - 18.

Document 2
Statement from the Executive Commission of the Petersburg Committee to the CC*

RUSSIAN
SOCIAL-DEMOCRATIC
LABOUR PARTY

PETERSBURG COMMITTEE
Liteinyi Prospekt, d.48.
Tel.: 2-08-49.
No. 267

Proletarians of all countries, unite!
Petrograd, January 15 1918.

To the Central Committee RSDLP.

The Executive Commission, in full agreement with the Petersburg Committee resolutions on the policy towards a peace, makes this statement. The political line now pursued by the CC and directed, judging by the resolution from the Bolshevik group in the Congress, at the conclusion of a so-called 'shameful peace', which means at this moment the abdication of our positions in full view of the coming international revolution and the sure death of our Party as the vanguard of the revolution. Since it considers that such a CC policy is in contradiction to the decisions and resolutions of the April Conference and the Sixth Party Congress, the Executive Commission makes a very strong protest on behalf of the Petersburg organisation both against the fundamental direction, already determined in its general features, and against the policy of silence and reserve now being practised in our foreign policy affairs, even in relation to the responsible bodies of the largest Party organisations.

We have very good grounds for asserting that to sign a 'shameful peace' would be in clear contradiction to the opinion of the majority of the Party. This was graphically shown by the January 8 meeting where a huge majority expressed itself against comrade Lenin's point of view and also by the fact that the most influential organisations in our Party – the Petersburg and Moscow regions – stated that they were definitely against an annexationist peace with Germany. If the peace policy is continued in the present spirit, reflected especially characteristically in the Congress resolution, it threatens to split our Party.

---

*   There is a note on the document: *For the CC session 19.1.1918.*

With all this in mind, the Executive Commission demands, in the name of the Petersburg organisation, that a special Party conference be convened immediately, in a week, for with conditions as they are, it alone can resolve the question of our peace policy.

Meanwhile, the Executive Commission declares that we are referring the question of the war and the peace to the highest instances of our Petersburg organisation and also to the district Party organs for consideration.

Executive Commission of the Petersburg Committee,
S. Kosior, G. Boky, Ia. Fenigstein, A. Pluzhnikov, S. Ravich.

Archives of the I M L, *f*.17, *op*.1, *ed.khr*.406, *l*.16 and *ob*.

Document 3
Theses by the Petersburg Committee of the RSDLP(b) on the current situation and the war

[*Adopted at the session of the Petersburg Committee of January 18* [*31*] *1918.*]

1. Revolutionary social-democrats have always seen the question of war as war between certain classes; their sharply negative attitude to the imperialist war being waged by finance capital and to* the slogan of defending the capitalist state belonging to the bourgeoisie by no means excluded a war waged by the proletariat of one country against the bourgeois state of another.

2. The October revolution in Russia and the capture of power by the proletariat and the village poor, with all the consequences flowing from it (the publication and annulment of secret treaties, etc.), completely changed the character of the war from the Russian side; it changed from an imperialist war into a civil war against international capital.

3. Nothing is altered by the fact that English, American and French imperialism figures simultaneously among the forces directed against Germany and Austria. This creates no 'objective connection' with imperialism: 1. because all treaties with them have been torn up and there is no military or any other contact; 2. because the weight of revolutionary Russia on its own is too great for its war to be turned into a simple appendage of the war waged by the imperialist predators of allied capital.

---

* In the text of the document: *on*

4. Thus the issue of concluding a peace on the basis of self-determination and the question of annexations and indemnities is decided according to whether or not it is possible to continue the war.

5. The question of how advisable it is to conclude an unfavourable annexationist peace must be decided with reference to what is best for the development of the international proletarian revolutionary position; [from] this point of view, Europe must be considered as one single territory for the class struggle by the international proletariat, one of whose detachments – the Russian – overpowered a corresponding detachment of the international bourgeoisie.

6. The international proletarian movement is now living through a moment of breakthrough, and at this moment the struggle is inflamed by the peace issue. This is precisely the circumstance which must be taken into account. It will then become clear that to conclude a treaty of 'shameful peace' is to wreck the further development of the proletarian movement in the West for a very long time. A 'shameful' treaty could have been concluded earlier, before the crisis in the West. It cannot be concluded *now* when the crisis is here.

7. Non-conclusion of a treaty and a juridical state of war has no necessary connection with an offensive of any kind nor with a need for universal military service, etc. As to its methods – in the present circumstances of disruption and disorganisation, this state will depend less on the armed might of the Russian revolutionary army than on the demoralisation and impotence of the Austro-German imperialists, who must force their soldiers to march on the socialist detachments. In these conditions, even our defeat on the front will be accompanied by further revolutionising of the troops of the 'opposition'.

8. As for the counter-argument that the fact that there is a peace and that a Soviet republic exists is a thousand times more important than all the rest, and that the conclusion of a peace *ensures* this existence, the answer must be that this is an illusion. International imperialism will not hesitate to violate treaties of any kind once it is in a position to launch an attack on the Soviet republic. It is ridiculous to imagine that we are now 'getting a deferment'. The only kind of deferment we are getting is the deferment of the international revolution.

Archives of the IML, *f*.17, *op*.1, *ed.khr*.406, *ll*.19-20.

Documents 4*
Resolution adopted at a plenary meeting of the Moscow Regional Bureau of the RSDLP (bolsheviks)
December 28 1917 [January 10 1918]

The consolidation and development of the socialist revolution in Russia and the whole world inevitably demands that the imperialist slaughter must first be ended by a democratic peace.

But it is only possible to conclude a democratic peace if the peoples themselves negotiate, after they have overthrown their bourgeois governments. A peace between socialist Russia and imperialist Germany can only be a plundering and coercive peace.

With this in mind, the plenary meeting of the Regional Bureau considers that it is necessary:

1. To halt the peace negotiations with imperialist Germany and also to break off all diplomatic relations with diplomatic robbers of every country.

2. To work energetically to convene the international Zimmerwald socialist congress.

3. To intensify work on organising the Red Guard.

4. To create a Red Socialist Guard among prisoners of war and to organise detachments of agitators to conduct propaganda about the socialist revolution in the ranks of the Austro-German army.

5. To form a volunteer revolutionary army immediately and fight ruthlessly against the whole world's bourgeoisie for the idea of international socialism.

Sotsial-demokrat (Moscow) No.7. January 12 [25] 1918.

Resolution by the Moscow Committee of the RSDLP on the subject of the peace negotiations
(Adopted unanimously at the session of January 11 [24] 1918.)

1. The negotiations in Brest have been helpful up to now in clearly revealing the criminal aims of the war and in radicalising the popular masses in all the countries; at the same time, they have underlined once again that a democratic peace cannot result from diplo-

---

* In this section, decisions made by the Moscow Party organisation on the question of the Brest peace are printed regardless of their dates.

matic negotiations with imperialist governments and will only be attained through the people's mass revolutionary struggle against the imperialists of both groups at war.

2. Acceptance of the conditions dictated by the German imperialists goes contrary to our whole policy of revolutionary socialism, would objectively involve renouncing a consistent line of international socialism in both foreign and internal policy and could lead to opportunism of the worst kind.

3. The revolutionary movement in the West is growing under our eyes, convincing us that we are right to predict that a socialist revolution is inevitable in Europe in the near future.

On the basis of everything that has been said, the Moscow Committee proposes to the Council of People's Commissars that the proposals made by the German delegation should be declared unacceptable and that the peace negotiations should be broken off.

The Moscow Committee simultaneously stresses the need to intensify the work of organising a socialist guard by calling on all comrades to build it up, recruiting an army to repulse the German invaders, an army capable of fighting a holy war for socialism both within the country and against any outside encroachment on the conquests of our revolution, helping the socialist detachments in other countries in their struggle for an international, democratic peace, and to avoid tying our actions in any way at all to the imperialist policy of the powers of the pact.

Sotsial-demokrat (Moscow) No.7. January 12 [25] 1918.

Resolution by the Moscow Area Committee of the RSDLP

After an examination of the international position in connection with the proposal by the Council of People's Commissars to continue peace negotiations with the four-power alliance, the following resolution moved by comrade Solov'ev was adopted.

1. No effective democratic peace on conditions acceptable to the working masses can be concluded with imperialist governments.

2. We consider that there can only be a way out of the blind alley of this three-year war on the plane of a world proletarian revolution.

3. We still consider our previous slogans correct and trust in the support of the Western European proletariat.

4. But for the world socialist revolution to go on to further successes, it is necessary to consolidate socialist power in Russia, necessary

that impregnable trenches be dug here for the international revolution.

5.   For this reason, the Moscow Area Committee approves all the measures of the Council of People's Commissars.

Sotsial-demokrat (Moscow) No.31. February 23 [10] 1918.

Resolution by the Moscow Committee

The Moscow Committee of the RSDLP(bolsheviks), after discussing at a special session on the morning of February 20 the assent by the Council of People's Commissars to a peace with the German government on the conditions proposed by the delegation of the four-power alliance, states:

1.   The Moscow Committee remains committed to the decision passed by the Moscow Committee and the All-City Conference of January 11-13.

2.   The attack by Austro-German forces, which could and should have been foreseen, does not change our attitude to the proletariat's [struggle] for a democratic peace. We consider our previous slogans correct. Our hopes of support from the revolutionary proletariat in the West remain unshaken by this last day's offensive.

3.   The Moscow Committee considers the decision by the Council of People's Commissars harmful to the cause of world revolution. As before, the Moscow Committee appeals to the proletariat to organise the Red Army. Our socialist struggle continues with its former force on all fronts. The Red Army pursues a merciless struggle against the bourgeoisie in its own country. It gives active support to the Western European proletariat in their struggle for a democratic peace.

4.   The Moscow Committee insists that the Council of People's Commissars reviews the decision it has taken and cancels it.

Archives of the IML, *f.*17, *op.*1, *ed.khr.*413, *l.*2.

Resolution by the Moscow Regional Bureau
February 24 1918

After considering the activity of the CC, the Moscow Regional Bureau of the RSDLP declares its lack of confidence in the CC because of its political line and composition and will take the first opportunity to insist on a new election. Moreover, the Moscow Regional Bureau does not consider that it is bound to submit in every case to those CC decisions associated with implementing the conditions of the peace treaty with Austro-Germany. The resolution is approved unanimously.

Document 5
Statement to the CC about calling a Party conference*
To the Central Committee of the RSDLP

Since we consider that a whole series of new factors in the realm of international relations and also the whole course of the peace negotiations urgently demand a review of our international policy, we, on behalf of the Regional Bureau of the Moscow Industrial Region of the RSDLP and a group of comrades, propose to the CC RSDLP that a joint session of the CC and local Party workers be held on January 7 for consideration of the international political situation with reference to the tactics of the proletarian party.

> *A. Lomov,* member of the Moscow Regional Bureau *Stukov*
> *V. Smirnov,* member of the praesidium of the Council of National Economy
> Or for their information – *Ol'minsky, Baryshnikov*
> Member of the Executive Committee of the Saratov Soviet of Workers', Soldiers' and Peasants' Deputies *M. Vasil'ev*
> *V. Iakovleva, M. Savel'ev, Sapronov, Logachev, I. Fokin*
> For consideration and not information – *A. Arosev*

Archives of the IML, *f.*17, *op.*1, *ed.khr.*50, *l.*1.

---

* There are notes on the document. On the right side of the sheet: *January. Moscow.* On the left – *172. 20.1.*

Document 6
Statement to the CC from a group of Urals Party workers about calling a Party conference immediately*
To the Central Committee RSDLP (bolsheviks)

The undersigned members of the former and present Urals Regional Committee of the Party consider it absolutely necessary to call a special Party conference immediately to clarify Party opinion on the question of the war and the peace.

E. Preobrazhensky
A. Beloborodov
N. Krestinsky
On behalf of Spunde and Sosnovsky *E. Preobrazhensky*

Archives of the I M L, *f*.17, *op*.1, *ed.khr*.50, *l*.4.

Instead of Minutes No.39

[The minutes of the CC meeting of January 21 [February 3] 1918 have not been found.

The table of voting (*ed.khr*.51) printed here is from an original document written in ink on one side of a large sheet of writing paper. There is also a hectographed typewritten copy (*ed.khr*.407).

The text of the table is printed from the original, collated with the hectographed copy.]

---

*   On the document are the notes: *Ur. Reg. C. January. For the C C session of* January 19 1918.

Meeting of the CC with Spokesmen for Different Viewpoints on Sunday, January 21 [February 3] 1918[212]

	I. In general, is a peace between socialist and imperialist states admissible?	II. Is it admissible to sign a German annexationist peace now?	III. Drag out the negotiations or not?	IV. Drag them out to the point where the Germans break them off?	V. Break off the negotiations immediately?	VI. Is it admissible to sign a German annexationist peace if they break off negotiations and present an ultimatum?	VII. Is it necessary to sign a peace in that event?	VIII. Is it necessary to sign a peace if Kühlmann, under pressure from the revolutionary movement inside Germany, agrees to our delegation's initial conditions?	IX. Is it necessary to form a Red Army?	X. Are economic treaties between a socialist state and an imperialist one admissible?
Group I Lenin Stalin Muranov Artem [Sergeev] Sokolnikov Zinoviev	+++++ + Left before the vote	+++++ + Left before the vote	+++++	+++++	− − − − −	+++++	+++++	+++++	+++++	+++++
Group II Lomov Krestinsky Bubnov Kosior Bukharin Uritsky	+++ Left before the vote Left before the vote	− − − Left before the vote Left before the vote	++++	++++	− − −	++++	abstained abstained abstained abstained	abstained abstained abstained abstained	++++	++++
Group III Obolensky [Osinsky] Stukov	− −	− −	abstained −	− −	− +	− −	− −	− −	++	− −
Group IV Preobrazhensky Spunde Fenigstein	+++	− − − − −	+ − +	+ abstained +	− − − − −	+++	abstained abstained abstained	− abstained −	+++	+++

Minutes No.40

[The minutes of the CC session of January 24 [February 6] 1918 (*ed.khr.*408) are the original secretarial notes written in ink on both sides of a large sheet of paper torn out of a pad. The second set of minute notes are in the minute book of the secretariat of the CC RSDLP(b).

The text of the minutes is printed from the secretarial notes collated with the text of the minute notes in the CC secretariat book.]

Session of the CC
January 24 [February 6] 1918

Present :
Sverdlov, Lenin, Stalin, Uritsky, Zinoviev, Bukharin, Sokolnikov, Lomov [Oppokov], Bubnov, Stasova.

Agenda :
1. Agenda for the Congress.

Comrade Lenin considers that the Congress agenda should be : the Party programme[213], the peace issue, tactical questions.

Comrade Bukharin considers that the question of the programme must be put first because we are in the awkward position of being governed by an official programme which is out of date. He considers it necessary to put next the question of the different forms of workers' movement (trade unions, factory committees, etc.). And finally, the third point must deal with organisational forms to correspond to the changed political position.

Comrade Sverdlov contemplates the following questions for the Congress agenda : 1. Revision of the programme, 2. the current situation, which he suggests breaking up into the internal situation and the external situation, 3. the forms of the workers' movement and 4. the question of organisation.

Comrade Stalin points out that we have to be guided by the anachronism of our minimum-programme at a time when Soviet power actually exists, which is obviously stupid, so there can be no doubt that we must revise the programme.

Comrade Lenin agrees with everything that has been said

but he is worried by the huge number of October Bolsheviks in the Party, which could prevent the Congress from drawing up a consistent programme.

Comrade Lomov [Oppokov] adds that the current situation should also include a question about the Party's economic position*.

Comrade Lenin feels it is necessary to make it obligatory when registering members to make a note of when they entered the Party : before 25.10 or after it, and that the new entrants must recognise the necessity of the tactics the Party regarded as correct with regard to the October revolution.

Comrade Stasova points out that dual registration of members is practised almost everywhere in Russia and that the members of the organisation who are October Bolsheviks are considered not to have fully equal rights, so there is no reason to fear that the Congress will be overburdened by newly-fledged social-democrats.

Comrade Bukharin suggests going into the detail of the agenda. The proposal is rejected.

Comrade Sokolnikov points out that only those comrades who have been in the Party for more than three months can vote at the Congress.

Adopted.

The Congress agenda is approved as the following:

1. Revision of the programme.
2. The current situation (internal position, external position, economic position).
3. Trade unions, factory committees, etc.
4. Question of organisation.
5. Miscellaneous.

It is decided to form a commission to draw up the programme and Bukharin, Sokolnikov and Lenin are elected to it. In addition, the first two are commissioned to publish a series of articles in *Pravda* on subjects on the Congress agenda, and also to work out reports for the Congress agenda.

---

*   Like this in the text of the minute notes.

Instead of Minutes No.41

[The minutes of the CC session of February 17 1918 have not been found. The table of voting (*ed.khr.*409) printed here is from an original document written in ink on one side of a sheet of writing paper. There is also a hectographed typewritten copy. Footnotes to the first edition of this book of CC minutes refer to alternative readings in Lomov's notes.

The text of the table recorded by Lomov has not been found. The footnotes are taken from the first edition of the book. The text of the table is printed from the original collated with the hectographed copy.

The resolution by the Central Bureau of the Lithuanian Sections printed as an appendix (see p.203) is an original document written in ink on one side of half a sheet of writing paper. The signatures are autographs.]

Voting in the CC RSDLP on February 17 1918 (evening)*214

	Bukharin	Lomov	Trotsky	Uritsky	Ioffe	Krestinsky	Lenin	Stalin	Sverdlov	Sokolnikov	Smilga
For the immediate offer to Germany of new negotiations to sign a peace	−	−	−	−	−	−	+	+	+	+	+
For a revolutionary war No one voted in favour	refuses to vote on the question put in this way.**	the same			the same as Bukharin ***						
In favour of showing every resistance if Germany begins to attack	+	+	+	+	+	+	+	+	+	+	+
In favour of waiting to resume peace negotiations until the German offensive has become quite evident and its influence on the labour movement **** apparent	+	+	+	+	+	+	−	−	−	−	−
If we do not propose peace after the offensive, do we declare a return to the state of war	abstains	abstains	−	−	−	−	abstains	−	−	−	−
Is it admissible in principle to sign a peace with imperialist Germany under certain conditions					all consider it admissible		admissible				
What reply to make to Supreme Command. In favour of resistance and the destruction of all property and war materials useful to Germany in the event of our retreat*****	+	+	+	+	+	abstains	abstains	does not take part in the voting	abstains	abstains	abstains
If the German offensive becomes a fact and there is no revolutionary uprising in Germany and Austria, are we to conclude peace	abstains	abstains	+	abstains	abstains	abstains	+	+	+	+	+

* On the table of voting the words: *Voting in .. (evening)* are written under the table.

** In Lomov's notes, against his and Bukharin's name is written: *refused to take part in the voting, finding the putting of the question incorrect.*

*** In Lomov's notes: *agreed with Bukhar[in], and Lomov.*

**** Lomov's notes add: *of Germany and Austria.*

***** In Lomov's notes: *What to reply to Supreme Command at 10 p.m. on February 17 1918. In favour of using all means to resist the attack and destroying all property and war materials which can be used against us by Germany.*

Document
Resolution by the Central Bureau of
the Lithuanian Sections*

The Central Bureau of the Lithuanian Sections of the RSDLP
(bolsheviks), after hearing information on the course of the peace
negotiations, finds:
1.   that the peace conditions proposed by the Central Powers are unacceptable,
2.   that the CC of the Party does not have the right to go so far as to
compromise with the imperialists of the Central Powers and so the
Central Bureau of the Lithuanian Sections insists on a Party conference being called in a week's time.

Members of the Central Bureau *Stanislav Turlo*
F. Mitskevich
I. Lenkaitis
Secretary *Z. Aleksa*

Archives of the IML, *f.*17, *op.*1, *ed.khr.*413, *l.*1.

Minutes No.42

[Two sessions of the CC were held on February 18 1918 – in the
morning and the evening.

The minutes of the morning CC session (*ed.khr.*410, *ll.*3-5) are
the original secretarial notes written in ink on one side of three large
sheets of paper. Another version of the minutes of the morning CC session of February 18 (*ll.*1-2) is also preserved in the archives. The
minutes are the original ones, written in ordinary pencil on one side of
two medium-size sheets of paper torn out of a pad.

The minutes of the evening CC session (*ll.*6-17) are the original
secretarial notes written in ink on one side of twelve medium-size sheets
of paper torn out of a pad. Minute notes of both sessions are in the
minute book of the secretariat of the CC RSDLP(b) (*ed.khr.*59).

The texts of the minutes are printed from the secretarial notes
(*ll.*3-5, 6-17) collated with the text of the other minute notes.]

---

*   There is a note on the document: *321. 17(4) Feb.*

Session of the CC RSDLP
February 18 1918

Present :
Comrades Lenin, Trotsky, Sverdlov, Smilga, Ioffe, Dzerzhinsky, Zinoviev, Bukharin, Uritsky, Stasova, Lomov [Oppokov], Sokolnikov, Krestinsky.

With a consultative vote, comrade Ravich.

Comrade Trotsky reports some new information ; aeroplanes over Dvinsk ; an attack expected on Reval ; the appearance of four German divisions from the Western front ; the German radio talking about protecting the people from contagion from the East.

Comrade Sverdlov poses the question of whether to have a discussion now or adjourn it.

Comrade Lomov [Oppokov] is in favour of adjournment.

Comrade Lenin is against but in favour of limiting the speakers (opinions of groups with 5 minutes each).

In favour of adjournment – no one. (Vote.)

Speakers representing group opinions :

1.   Trotsky, Bukharin.
2.   Lenin, Zinoviev.

Comrade Bukharin raises the question of whether it is possible to allow more people to speak.

Comrade Lenin says he is against this and suggests restricting the issue to whether or not to send telegrams offering peace and hearing views for and against this.

Lenin's proposal is adopted.

Comrade Trotsky (against sending a telegram offering peace) emphasises that the masses are only just beginning now to digest what is happening ; to sign peace now will only produce confusion in our ranks ; the same applies to the Germans who believe that we are only waiting for an ultimatum. Possibly they are counting on the psychological effect. We have to wait to see what impression all this makes on the German people. The end to the war was greeted with joy in Germany and it is not out of the question that the German offensive will produce a serious outburst in Germany. We have to wait to see the effect and then – we can still offer peace if it doesn't happen.

Comrade Lenin (in favour of offering peace). The vote yesterday was especially characteristic, with everyone recognising the need for a peace if the movement in Germany did not materialise and there was an offensive*. There is the suspicion that the Germans want an offensive to oust the Soviet government. We face a situation where we have to act. If an imperialist attack clearly gets under way, we will all be in favour of defence and this can be explained to the people. If an attack starts now and we explain it to the masses later, we will create more confusion than if we pursue negotiations now to continue the armistice ; there is not an hour to be lost here for the masses will not understand the question put like this. Either we fight a revolutionary war for the socialisation of land, something the masses will understand, or we carry on peace negotiations.

Comrade Bukharin (against). The crux of the matter is not negotiations for a peace but the signing of a peace. The position is uncertain on the other side; it is not known whether they concluded an alliance with the English or not; and then the possibility exists of simple blackmail on the part of the Germans. All this should be clarified in the near future. And if it turns out that the imperialists have concluded an alliance and that the offensive is under way, everyone will understand that there is no other way out for us. We can begin negotiations later on but we have to build up defence now in any case and tell the military so.

Comrade Zinoviev (in favour). The question is not what to say to the military but what to say to the people at large. We must have a clear political position, there is no time to delay. The parties in Germany are fighting. The Germans themselves do not know yet how they should act, they do not know what is going to happen tomorrow. If negotiations are renewed now, the Berlin workers will not be able to reproach us. If the position was already clear in the sense of there being an imperialist attack, we would all be in favour of war, but now we are only playing into the hands of the German butchers. There can only be one decision – to renew negotiations.

It is put to the vote : 1. Make an immediate offer to resume peace negotiations.

For – 6 ; against – 7.

The next session of the CC is fixed for tomorrow at 2 o'clock[215].

---

*   See p.202.

Minutes No.43
Session of the CC RSDLP
February 18 1918 (evening)[216]

Present :
Trotsky, Lenin, Uritsky, Stasova, Sokolnikov, Ioffe, Stalin, Krestinsky, Zinoviev, Sverdlov, Lomov [Oppokov], Bukharin, Smilga. Stuchka attends with a consultative vote.

Comrade Trotsky reports the capture of Dvinsk and rumours of an attack on the Ukraine. If the latter is confirmed, we will be forced to take definite steps, i.e. to send a request to Vienna and Berlin to know what their demands are.

Comrade Uritsky believes that we must act. The CC lacks a decision. A waiting policy is the most damaging ; either we have to count the two votes of the supporters of signing a peace who are absent or, on the other hand, the people in the minority must submit. In any case, the decision must be made today.

Comrade Trotsky considers that the reply to the military is given. The suggestion that we make inquiries of the Germans does not decide the issue in advance and so he maintains his suggestion : to send an inquiry to Vienna and Berlin.

Comrade Sverdlov considers that Uritsky's formal reasoning is correct. It is possible to count the votes of those who are absent since we know their attitude. The question must be decided.

Trotsky's proposal is doubtful because we cannot even wait until tomorrow morning. If a decision is to be taken, it must be taken immediately.

Comrade Stalin. The formal question is superfluous. We want to talk straight, go to the heart of the matter : the Germans are attacking, we have no forces, the time has come to say outright that negotiations must be resumed.

Comrade Lenin. The question is basic. Uritsky's proposal is amazing. The CC voted against a revolutionary war[217] but we have neither war nor peace and we are being drawn into a revolutionary war. War is no joking matter. We are losing railway wagons and our transport is getting worse. Now we can wait no longer because the position has become quite clear. The people will not understand this : since there is a war on, we should not have demobilised. Now the Germans will take everything. Things have reached such an impasse that the revolution is bound to be ruined if the policy of sitting on the fence goes on. Ioffe wrote from Brest that there is not even a beginning of revolution in Germany; if this is so, the Germans will find it rewarding to advance further. Now we cannot possibly wait. This could mean consigning the Russian revolution to the scrapheap. If the Germans were to say that they required the overthrow of Bolshevik power, then of course we would have to fight; further delay is impossible now. It is not a question of the past now but of the present. If we send an inquiry to the Germans, this will only be a piece of paper. It is not a policy. The only thing to do is to offer the Germans the resumption of negotiations. There can be no middle position now. If revolutionary war it is, then it must be declared and demobilisation stopped, but we cannot go on like this. While we write papers, they are taking warehouses and wagons and we are perishing. Now it is on the cards that by playing with war, we are surrendering the revolution to the Germans.

History will say that you surrendered the revolution. We could have signed a peace which did not threaten the revolution at all. We have nothing, we do not even manage to blow things up as we retreat. We have done what we could, we helped the revolution in Finland, but now we can do no more. This is not the time for an exchange of notes and the temporising must stop. It is too late now to 'prod' because it is clear now that the Germans can attack. One cannot argue with the partisans of a revolutionary war but one can and must with those who want to temporise. An offer of peace must be made to the Germans.

Comrade Uritsky. There is no need to 'prod'. If they attack, we must defend ourselves. With the position as it is in the CC now, that is impossible.

Comrade Ioffe. Effectively, it is already too late to prod the German imperialists. But it is not too late to prod the German revolution. We never expected that the very fact of an offensive would produce a revolution. Yesterday I thought the Germans would not attack; once they attack, it means the total triumph of imperialism and the militaristic parties. Now they will not agree to the previous peace but will demand non-intervention in the affairs of Livonia, Estonia, Finland and the Ukraine. We only seem to me obliged to sign peace if our troops run away in panic and feel resentment against us, or if the people demand a peace from us. So long as this does not happen, we must go on striving as before for world revolution. There is not much the Germans can do to us. If they take Reval, etc., it is bad, of course, but it is clear that if there is no revolution in Germany, they will take more and if there is, then everything will come back to us. I stand by my opinion of yesterday.

Comrade Trotsky, apropos the term 'play with war', recalls that the term 'prod' the Germans was Lenin's. There was a plan to 'prod' but it could not be carried out because the Germans presented an ultimatum. No one is playing games with war but moral pressure can be exerted. Everything was built on imponderables. There was no game with the war. It is a question of calculation; an inquiry must be tried. To offer a peace means to invite refusal.

He suggests demanding that the German formulate their demands, with the undertaking to give a reply in a certain time. Now an attack on Kiev is an attack on Soviet power. 'The game with the war' was that for two months, with no military force, we spun out the negotiations, provoked a movement in Berlin and Vienna and antagonised the Germans.

Comrade Stalin. The Germans may say they do not recognise us but even in this worst case, we will find ourselves in a more disadvantageous position*. Five minutes after firing starts, we will not have a single soldier left on the front. There must be an end to this confusion. He disagrees with Trotsky; such a question can only be posed in literature. Now we have to weigh everything and say that we are in favour of resuming peace negotiations. They will take notice of a political act like that but we cannot confine ourselves to putting a question.

Comrade Bukharin. This talk of a 'game' is astonishing, nothing can be further from the truth. On the contrary, events have developed as they had to. There are signs of panic and bewilderment here. We foresaw everything that is happening now. We said that either the Russian revolution would spread or it would perish under the pressure of imperialism. It has been said here that earlier the militarists aimed at a peace; it is true, but now new facts are involved : the Ukraine[218] and the agreement between

---

* Like this in the text of the minute notes. Obviously, it should be : more advantageous.

the imperialists. And in this sense our prodding has already had results. The second result is that the Germans are no longer aiming at trade treaties but it is quite clear that they are waging a class war. This is the iron logic of events, things happen as they were bound to. Earlier there was that chink* of which Lenin spoke and now it is there no longer. We underestimate the social forces of the revolution just as we did before the insurrection. At the time of the insurrection, we were victorious although we were in confusion and they were organised. We have been triumphant in every province up to now. There is no sense in the German imperialists adopting peace now they are going *va banque*. Now there is no chance of postponing the fight. United imperialism is marching against the revolution. Even if they take Peter, the workers will react as they did in Riga. All our social possibilities are not exhausted even now. We can also set the muzhiks on the Germans. Only our old tactics remain, the tactics of world revolution. The Germans are now demanding the surrender of all our social and revolutionary positions.

Comrade Lenin. Bukharin did not notice how he has gone over to the position of a revolutionary war. The peasants do not want war and will not go to war. Can we now tell the peasants to fight a revolutionary war? But if that is what is wanted, the army should not have been demobilised. A permanent peasant war is a utopia. Revolutionary war should not be a mere phrase. If we are not ready, we must sign a peace. Since we have demobilised the army, it is ridiculous to talk of a permanent war. A civil war is no comparison. The muzhik will not fight a revolutionary war – and he will overthrow anyone who calls for one openly. The revolution in Germany has not yet begun and we know that here, too, our revolution was not successful all at once. It has been said here that they will take Livonia and Estonia, but we can give them up for the sake of the revolution. If they demand that our troops withdraw from Finland – well, let them take revolutionary Finland. If we cede Finland, Livonia and Estonia – the revolution is not lost. These prospects which comrade Ioffe frightened us with yesterday do nothing to destroy the revolution.

I propose a statement that we are signing the peace the Germans offered us yesterday; if they add on non-intervention in the

---

* In the minute book of the CC secretariat, *l.*203 : *aim.*

affairs of the Ukraine, Finland, Livonia and Estonia, then we should unconditionally accept this, too. Our soldiers are in a bad state; the Germans want grain – they will take it and go back, having made Soviet power impossible. To say that demobilisation has been stopped is to be overthrown.

Comrade Lomov [Oppokov]. The peasant army had to be demobilised but tomorrow we must issue an order summoning everyone to the revolutionary banner. We did not just say we had to wait; we said we had to wait until the influence on the German workers had taken shape. We have still not waited it out. And if we give in now, there was no need for all the trouble. Once having embarked on this line, we must pursue it; nothing is changed by the fact that they will take a number of towns from us, I envisaged that events might develop like this. Now we must put maximum energy into developing our tactics of unleashing revolution.

Comrade Zinoviev. If you look back, it is clear that a peace should have been concluded in November. The more successful we were in the civil war, the more obvious it became that the only military force we had to reckon with was the German army. The condition, in my view, was this : if they take us by the throat, we will sign a peace. Of course, the strikes in Vienna and Berlin beguiled us too much and we let the moment pass. Now I, too, am afraid that they will not sign that peace. V.I. [Lenin] says that if they demand non-intervention in Ukrainian [affairs] we must accept, but the question is what kind of non-intervention they require. If comrade Trotsky meant that he wants to give more by his telegram then we must adopt it. It must be said, in any case, that we want to sign a peace but if they require that we turn over the Ukrainian workers, for example, we cannot do it and we will have to consider again. We must send a telegram to the Germans today. We have to know what they demand. If it is only Livonia, I would be in favour, but if we have to hand over the Ukrainian workers, that is difficult.

The discussion is closed.

Trotsky formulates his proposal.

Not to demand an armistice but to ask what their demands are.

The question is tabled : *Should we send the German government an offer straight away to conclude peace immediately?*

For – 7 : Lenin, Smilga, Stalin, Sverdlov, Sokolnikov, Trotsky, Zinoviev.

Against – 5 : Uritsky, Ioffe, Lomov [Oppokov], Bukharin, Krestinsky (supported by Dzerzhinsky).

Abstains 1 – Stasova.

The suggestion is made to formulate the adopted decision in detail straight away. It is proposed that the text of the address to the German government be drawn up immediately.

Comrade Krestinsky suggests starting with a protest and ending with a statement that we are forced to sign the previous peace offer.

Comrade Stalin endorses this.

Comrade Lenin, too, but with a question* added about their demands.

Comrade Uritsky considers the addition unnecessary.

Comrade Bukharin. We ask to be informed of your final conditions.

Comrade Stuchka. A reference to the German proletariat, since it did not protest, then we must sign.

Comrade Zinoviev. The telegram – three parts : 1. protest, 2. readiness to sign the peace conditions, 3. offer to meet somewhere and reply within a certain time.

Comrade Sokolnikov 1. protest, 2. inquiry as to the reason for the offensive and 3. agreement to sign a peace.

Comrade Lenin proposes a vote on all three sections of the proposals.

Comrade Trotsky suggests voting on the whole text and not the theses.

For the protest – everyone. 2 abstained.

Agree that we are compelled to sign a peace – everyone, 2 abstained.

Readiness to sign the old conditions while indicating that we are not refusing to accept a worse offer, for – 7; 4 against; 2 abstained.

Comrade Lenin and comrade Trotsky are charged with drawing up the text itself[219].

A suggestion is made to add Ioffe – rejected.

A proposal is made to adopt the decision of the two CCs[220] as a decision of the Council of People's Commissars.

---

*   The word : *question* is taken from the minute book of the CC
      secretariat, *l.*209. The original secretarial notes, *l.*15 have : *inquiry*.

The proposal is approved to send a wireless message straight away.

The Left SRs are to be informed of our decision (send comrade Sverdlov).

Minutes No.44

[The minutes of the CC session of February 22 1918 (*ed.khr.*411) are the original secretarial notes written in ink on one side of two large sheets of writing paper. The second set of minute notes are in the minute book of the secretariat of the CC RSDLP(b) (*ed.khr.*59).

The text of the minutes is printed from the secretarial notes collated with the text of the minute notes in the CC secretariat book.

The following documents are appended to the minutes: 1. A typewritten copy of V.I.Lenin's note to the CC written in the old orthography (see p.215). The original copy is preserved in *f.*2, *op.*1, *ed.khr.* 5368. 2. Bukharin's original statement to the CC RSDLP (see p.215). 3. The statement to the CC RSDLP(b) from a group of its members and People's Commissars (see pp.215-217). The text is in handwriting, the signatures are autographs.]

Session of the CC RSDLP
February 22 1918

Present :
Comrades Trotsky, Lomov [Oppokov], Krestinsky, Dzerzhinsky, Smilga, Ioffe, Sokolnikov, Bubnov, Bukharin, Sverdlov, later Uritsky.
Comrade Piatakov attends with a consultative vote.

Comrade Trotsky reports on the offer by the French and the English to help us in the war against the Germans and reads out the note from the French military mission.

Comrade Sverdlov moves the rejection of the note without further discussion.

This is rejected.

Comrade Bukharin believes that the 'allies' have a plan here to turn Russia into one of their colonies. He points out that it is unthinkable to accept support from imperialists of any sort.

Comrade Ioffe considers that from the point of view of the 'struggle for peace' we must not put ourselves at the mercy of the German imperialists and to this end resistance to the Germans is important, but there is no point in taking this to extremes. If we were to declare a 'holy war' then it would* even be necessary to reject the support of the Russian officers and capitalists ; we would have to accept everything which helped our resistance and this could not change the character of the revolutionary war.

Comrade Lomov [Oppokov] objects that we will get no help in practice and that support from imperialists** is unacceptable.

Comrade Krestinsky considers that the proposal must be rejected but we must take advantage of French and English help in each particular case.

Comrade Bubnov proposes closing the debate (rejected).

Comrade Trotsky asserts that Bukharin's arguments do not stand up to criticism. The state is forced to do what the Party would not do. Of course the imperialists want to take advantage of us and if we are weak, they will do so ; if we are strong, we will not allow it. If we wage a revolutionary war, we must accept support from France and England.

Comrade Dzerzhinsky declares that he is against a peace being signed but very positively against Bukharin's point of view.

Comrade Sverdlov looks at the matter from the angles of principle and expediency ; from the first point of view, there are no objections to accepting the proposal but from the second point of view, it is inadvisable to accept support from the English and French because they are already discredited in the eyes of the broad masses of Russia.

Comrade Smilga considers that if something can be taken, it should be taken, but he agrees with comrade Sverdlov that it is not advisable to give the French and English any privileges whatsoever.

---

*   Obviously left out : not.

**   The word : *imperialists* is taken from the CC secretariat minute book, *l.*213. In the original secretarial notes, *l.*1 : *imper. nationalists.*

Comrade Bukharin defends his view that it is inadmissible to use imperialist support.

Comrade Sokolnikov demonstrates that all comrade Bukharin's arguments are arguments against a revolutionary war. Help received from imperialists does not commit us to anything. One must always bear in mind the political consequences. The issue must be decided according to each individual case : accepting one, rejecting another.

Comrade Uritsky believes that once we had taken power, we forgot about the world revolution. This proposal envisages a long defensive war and we aim at influencing the German proletariat very quickly. That is why the proposal is unacceptable.

Comrade Bubnov. The general proposition that once we defend ourselves, we have to take everything we can to help is correct, but the time and circumstances must be taken into account. You will not get guns without instructors. Aid is offered in their own interests. Here we have a direct plan to use us in their own interests. It will get us into a position where our internationalism goes to pot.

Comrade Trotsky. We have always said that it is when a socialist comes to power that he gets the right to defend his homeland. By fighting* against the Germans, we are indirectly helping English imperialism. If we fight, we will have to defend ourselves well. All the arguments go against a revolutionary war. Bubnov is frightened of instructors but a penny-farthing for our dictatorship if we are frightened of that. In conclusion, he makes a formal announcement that he is resigning the title of People's Commissar for Foreign Affairs.

Comrade Bukharin moves a concrete proposal. No agreements to be entered into which concern buying weapons or the use** of the services of officers and engineers with French, English and American missions.

Comrade Trotsky. As the party of the socialist proletariat which is in power and conducting a war against Germany, we mobilise every means through state institutions to arm and supply our revolutionary army in the best way possible with all necessary

---

*   In the minute book of the C C secretariat, *l.*216 : *trying.*
**   In the minute book of the C C secretariat, *l.*217 : *non-use.*

resources and, for that purpose, we obtain them where we can, including therefore from capitalist governments. In doing this, the Russian Social-Democratic Labour Party retains full independence in its external policy, gives no political undertakings to capitalist governments and examines their proposals in each separate case according to what is expedient.

Trotsky's motion is approved : for – 6 votes, against – 5.

TO THE CC RSDLP*

Please add my vote *in favour* of taking potatoes and weapons from the Anglo-French imperialist robbers.

Lenin.

TO THE CC RSDLP

Dear comrades,

I declare herewith that I am leaving the CC and resigning the post of editor of *Pravda*.

N.Bukharin.

Document

Statement to the CC from a group of its members and People's Commissars

For the session of February 22 1918.
To the Central Committee of the RSDLP (bolsheviks).

Dear comrades !

The response of the Party CC to the attack by the German imperialists, who have openly declared that they aim to suppress the proletarian revolution in Russia, was an agreement to conclude peace on the conditions which the Russian delegation in Brest had rejected a

---

*   The statements by Lenin and Bukharin are written into the minute book of the CC secretariat at the end of February 22 session.

few days before. This agreement, given as soon as the enemies of the proletariat made their first attack, means that the advance contingent of the international proletariat has capitulated to the international bourgeoisie. By demonstrating to the whole world the weakness of the dictatorship of the proletariat in Russia, it strikes a blow at the cause of the international proletariat which is especially cruel at a moment of revolutionary crisis in Western Europe, and at the same time it cuts off the Russian revolution from the international movement. The decision to conclude peace no matter what, taken under the pressure of petty-bourgeois elements and petty-bourgeois attitudes, will inevitably result in the proletariat losing its guiding role inside Russia, too. The restrictions we will be forced to make, if we conclude a peace, in the sphere of action of the Soviet authorities' economic programme to make way for capital of German origin will mean that the work the proletariat has done since the October revolution to build socialism will be brought to nothing. The surrender of the proletariat's positions abroad inevitably prepares the way for surrender internally, too.

We consider that after power has been seized, after the last strongholds of the bourgeoisie have been completely destroyed, the proletariat unavoidably confronts the task of developing civil war on an international scale, a task it must face any dangers to fulfil. If it renounces the task, the result will be the ruin of the proletariat from internal demoralisation equivalent to suicide.

We scornfully reject the attacks on Soviet power made by conciliating elements who see the struggle against the German imperialists as merely a pretext to establish civil peace and who, instead of a civil war with the international bourgeoisie, want to wage a national war with Germany based on the unity of classes and an alliance with the Anglo-French coalition. To renounce the dictatorship of the proletariat in the name of war is just as unacceptable to us as to renounce it in the name of peace. At a moment when imperialist bands are not only seizing new territory but also throttling the proletariat and its organisations, it is the Party's duty to call for the defence of the dictatorship of the proletariat, weapons in hands, and to organise that defence. By a tiny majority, responsible Party leaders took another decision, contrary to the interests of the proletariat and not corresponding to the Party's attitude. Maintaining organisational unity, therefore, we consider it our fundamental task to agitate widely in Party circles against the policy of the Party centre as it has appeared recently and to prepare for a Party congress where the question of a peace must be discussed in its full breadth.

Members of the CC RSDLP $\Bigg\{$

G.I.Oppokov – A.Lomov
M.Uritsky
N.Bukharin
A.Bubnov
V.Smirnov
In.Stukov
M.Bronsky
V.Iakovleva
Spunde
M.Pokrovsky
Georgii Piatakov

While we consider that the decision adopted by the majority of the CC to offer a peace immediately is wrong, we nevertheless cannot associate ourselves with this statement since we believe that to agitate widely in Party circles against the policy of a majority of the CC at the present time could lead to a split which we would consider inadmissible.

A.Ioffe
N.Krestinsky
F.Dzerzhinsky

Archives of the I M L, *f.*17, *op.*1, *ed.khr.*411, *ll.*5 -6.

Minutes No.45

[The minutes of the CC session of February 23 1918 (*ed.khr.*412, *ll.*5 - 12) are original secretarial notes written in ink on eight sheets of paper of various sizes and in two handwritings. The beginning of the minutes is written on both sides of three large sheets of paper with an insertion (of a half-sheet) on the back of the second page of the minutes. The minute notes continue in another handwriting on four sheets of paper; the first two sheets are large and written in ink on one side, the next two sheets are small and written in ink on both sides.

The archives contain yet another version of the minutes (*ll.*1 -3), original minute notes written on three sheets of medium-size paper torn out of a pad. The first sheet is written on one side with an ordinary pencil, the second on both sides with an ordinary pencil, the third on both sides in ink. The third set of minute notes is in the minute book of the secretariat of the CC RSDLP(b) (*ed.khr.*59).

The text of the minutes is printed from the secretarial notes (*ll.*5 - 12) collated with the text of the other minute notes.]

Session of the CC RSDLP
February 23 1918

Present :
Bubnov, Krestinsky, Dzerzhinsky, Ioffe, Stasova, Uritsky, Zino-viev, Sverdlov, Bukharin, Stalin, Trotsky, Lomov [Oppokov], Lenin, Sokolnikov, Smilga.
Guests : Fenigstein, Smirnov, Shotman and Piatakov.

Comrade Sverdlov reads out the German terms[221].

Trotsky explains that 48 hours is evidently counted up to 7 o'clock tomorrow morning.

Comrade Lenin considers that this is where the policy of revolutionary phrase-making ends. If this policy continues now, he is leaving both the government and the CC. You need an army for a revolutionary war and there isn't one. That means that the terms must be accepted.

Comrade Trotsky. We cannot fight a revolutionary war when the Party is split. It is not only international relations that has to be taken into account but with conditions as they are, our Party is in no position to lead a war, especially as some of the supporters of a war do not want the material means to wage it with[222]. The arguments of V.I. [Lenin] are far from convincing; if we had all been of the same mind, we could have tackled the task of organising defence and we could have managed it. Our role would not have been a bad one even if we had been forced to surrender Peter and Moscow. We would have held the whole world in tension. If we sign the German ultimatum today, we may have a new ultimatum tomorrow. Everything is formulated in such a way as to leave an opportunity for further ultimatums. We may sign a peace;

and lose support among the advanced elements of the proletariat, in any case demoralise them. Where internal policy is concerned, the dilemma Lenin describes does not exist but from an international point of view, much could have been gained. But maximum unanimity would have been needed; as it is not there, I for one will not take the responsibility of voting for a war.

Comrade Zinoviev declares that going by the experience of the last few days, it is clear that there is no enthusiasm and nothing can be done; only a general weariness is noticeable. We have now reached the point where we must accept the offer. It should have been signed earlier; since we missed that, it has to be signed now. We are all obliged to do everything we can to avoid a split in the Party.

Comrade Bukharin. The terms presented did not bear out Lenin's prognosis at all. (He criticises the German proposals themselves.) There is no way out through delay. Are we to accept the demands to disarm Soviet troops? That is the key question now.

Comrade Stalin. It is possible not to sign but to start peace negotiations. No demands have been made to disarm Soviet troops inside Russia; the Germans are provoking us into a refusal. This is the alternative : either our revolution is defeated and the revolution in Europe checked, or we get a breathing space and strengthen ourselves. This will not hold back the revolution in the West. Since we have not the resources to stop the German offensive by armed force, we must adopt other methods. If Petrograd has to be surrendered, this will not just be a surrender but the decay of the revolution. Either a breathing space or the revolution perishes – there is no other outcome.

Comrade Dzerzhinsky. There will be no breathing space, on the contrary, our signature will reinforce German imperialism. Signing the conditions will not guarantee us against new ultimatums. We are saving nothing by signing this peace. But he agrees with Trotsky that if the Party had been strong enough to stand disintegration* and Lenin's resignation, then it would have been possible to adopt the decision, but now – no.

Comrade Lenin. I have been reproached by some for the ultimatum. I am presenting it in an extreme case. If our CC mem-

---

*   Like this in the text of the minute notes.

bers talk of an international civil war, they are taunting us. There is a civil war in Russia but there isn't one in Germany. Our propaganda will remain. We campaign not with words but with revolution. And this will last. Stalin is wrong when he says it is possible not to sign. These terms must be signed. If you do not sign them, you will be signing the death sentence of Soviet power in three weeks. These terms do not touch Soviet power. I have not the least shadow of hesitation. I am not presenting the ultimatum in order to withdraw it. I do not want revolutionary phrase-making. The German revolution has not yet ripened. This requires months. The terms must be accepted. If there is a new ultimatum after that, it will be in a new situation.

Comrade Ioffe declines to speak.

Comrade Uritsky protests to Stalin that the terms must either be accepted or not but there can be no more negotiations now. Our capitulation to German imperialism will hold back the awakening revolution in the West. If we sign the peace, we will have Miliukov without Chernov, with the aid of the German imperialists. Soviet power will not be saved by signing this peace.

Comrade Sverdlov considers it necessary to accept this peace. He cites as proof the experience of the last few days.

Comrade Bukharin. The central point is a breathing space and arms. Therefore the breathing space must be used to organise armed force; in their demand for demobilisation, the Germans say nothing about the front-line area. If we are going to continue organising the Red Army, it will turn out that we are only signing a piece of paper. The civil war must not at all be only in one country. There is no breathing space.

Comrade Stalin objects to the assertion that it is not a national war going on against Germany but a civil war. It is not true that the treaty denies the Russian population the right to insurrection. Everything comes to the fact that we must sign these terms immediately. To assume that there will be no breathing space and that there will be constant ultimatums means to believe that there is no movement in the West at all. We believe the Germans cannot do everything. We also put our stake on the revolution but you calculate* in weeks, but in months.**

---

*   In the minutes book of the CC secretariat, *l.*227 : *sort things out.*
**   Like this in the text of the minute notes.

Comrade Lomov [Oppokov]. The outcome which Lenin suggests, and therefore I will not take that path.* The panic described here also does not exist. We can do a lot. There is certain to be demoralisation among the German troops. If Lenin threatens resignation, there is no reason to be frightened. We have to take power without V.I.[Lenin]. We have to go to the front and do everything we can.

Comrade Dzerzhinsky (on a point of order). 2,000 workers are embarking in Walk. The information about defence is not so pessimistic at all. He proposes a break of 15 minutes.

Comrade Uritsky is against a break since the new information will not convince anyone.

The proposal is rejected.

Comrade Trotsky finds that Lenin's evaluation of the ultimatum is different now from before. The terms offered us are worse now than they were at Brest and, of course, they were best of all when Kamenev made the first trip and it would have been better if Kamenev and Ioffe had signed a peace. We put it off because we needed to be clear about our reasons for concluding it, everyone had to be clear. From the international point of view, we would have lost if we had signed a peace at Brest. Now things are quite clear and no one can have any doubt of Germany's imperialist ambitions in this war. The concrete terms of the peace are not so colossally significant as Bukharin thinks. Of course, certain of them are significant but, in any case, they do not hold the key to the true motives. History will correct everything. The material character of the relationship is such that the Germans will take what they can; will they be able to attack again after a peace has been concluded? Yes, of course. The tempo of life is different now from 1871 because now every side is acting on two fronts. If the French start to attack now, what the Germans do next will be different. He does not agree that an ultimatum means you can shed responsibility. Il'ich stood aside and did not defend my position when it went through. He does not think we are threatened by destruction but there is danger along both paths, i.e. the path of peace and the path of revolutionary war. It is not true that the situation can only turn out one way. Facts intermesh and so there

---

*   Like this in the text of the minute notes.

may be a middle position. There is a lot of subjectivity in Lenin's position. I am not convinced that his position is right but I do not want to do anything to interfere with Party unity – on the contrary, I will help as far as I can, but I cannot stay and carry personal responsibility for foreign affairs.

Comrade Sokolnikov considers that the terms presented to-day show that the respite offered now can be measured in weeks, at best in months. The war party in Germany has a well-defined plan – to suffocate us. We need a certain breathing space to be able to progress further. In practice, it is now that preparations for a revolutionary war begin. We are signing these terms as a definite respite to make ready for a revolutionary war. Then I will vote to sign the peace.

Comrade Lenin. I, too, think it is necessary to prepare for a revolutionary war. The treaty can be interpreted, and we will inter-pret it. Demobilisation is meant here in a purely military sense. Before the war, we also had an army. We must make serious pre-parations for a revolutionary war. I do not doubt for a moment that the masses want peace.

Comrade Zinoviev declares that the Dzerzhinsky's inti-mate facts* are not so at all. The mood as before is completely pessimistic. (He interprets the section on demobilisation.) The sec-tion about the Ukraine is far worse. None the less, the ultimatum must be accepted unconditionally. There is no choice and if we have wronged the Party, it is only by our delay.

Comrade Bukharin discusses the German proposals in more detail.

Lenin proposes putting to the vote :

1. Should the German proposals be accepted immediately?
2. Should there be immediate preparations for a revolutionary war?
3. Should an immediate referendum be held among the electors to the Petrograd and Moscow Soviets?

---

* Like this in the text of the minute notes.

	Should the German proposals be accepted immediately	Should there be immediate preparations for a revolutionary war?	Should an immediate referendum be held among the electors to the Petrograd and Moscow Soviets?
	No. 1	No. 2	No. 3
Trotsky	abstained		
Lenin	in favour		
Bubnov	against		
Krestinsky	abstained		
Dzerzhinsky	abstained		
Ioffe	abstained		
Stasova	in favour		in favour 11,
Uritsky	against	unanimous	abstained 4
Zinoviev	in favour		
Sverdlov	in favour		
Bukharin	against		
Stalin	in favour		
Lomov	against		
Sokolnikov	in favour		
Smilga	in favour		
	in favour 7, against 4 abstained 4		

After the vote, comrade Krestinsky reads out a statement signed by Ioffe, Dzerzhinsky and himself, containing the following:

TO THE CC RSDLP(bolsheviks)

Just as on February 17, we consider it is impossible to sign a peace now with Germany. But we believe that only a united Bolshevik Party can measure up to the enormous tasks which the proletarian revolution faced in Russia after the German offensive and which will arise all the more after a rejection of the German ultimatum. If the split heralded by Lenin's ultimatum actually comes about and we have to wage a revolutionary war against German imperialism, the Russian bourgeoisie and a section of the proletariat headed by Lenin, then the Russian revolution will find itself in an even more dangerous position than if a peace is signed.

Because we do not want to help bring about such a situation by voting against the signature of a peace and *not being in a position to vote for a peace,* we are abstaining from voting on this question.

February 23 1918

N. Krestinsky
A. Ioffe
F. Dzerzhinsky

Then comrade Uritsky reads out the following statement :

On behalf of CC members Bukharin, Lomov and Bubnov, candidate member of the CC Iakovleva, Piatakov and Smirnov attending the session and myself, I state that, not wishing to bear responsibility for the decision adopted, which we consider deeply mistaken and fatal to the Russian and the international revolution, particularly as this decision was passed by a minority of the CC – because it is clear from the reasoning of the four who abstained that they share our position – we declare that we are resigning from all responsible Party and Soviet posts and retaining complete freedom to campaign both within the Party and outside it for what we consider to be the only correct positions.

February 23

M. Uritsky

Comrade Trotsky explains his abstention by the need to find a way out of the position which had arisen ; the only way out was to arrive at a single line by doing nothing to hinder the formation of a majority.

Comrade Lomov [Oppokov] poses the question : would Vlad[imir] I[l'ich] allow tacit or open agitation against the signature of the peace.

Comrade Lenin answers in the affirmative.

Comrade Sverdlov proposes that in the current situation, CC members should remain in the CC and in their places in general until the congress and carry on their agitation in Party circles.

Comrade Lenin is in favour of considering Sverdlov's suggestion because, first, there is an interval of three days before the signature and, second, 12 days for ratification so it is possible to get the Party's opinion and if it is against signing, no ratification will follow, but as we are pressed for time today, he suggests adjourning the matter until tomorrow.

Comrade Sverdlov puts the question of whether the comrades would agree to postpone their resignation until tomorrow and if they would, we will adjourn the discussion until tomorrow.

Comrade Uritsky asserts that the suggestion is only acceptable if there is full freedom to agitate. We are loyal and do not see it as possible to campaign while we are still members of an institution ; since we cannot be loyal, we must leave.

Comrade Stalin raises the issue of whether leaving a post does not in practice mean leaving the Party ? Do the comrades realise that their resignation from their posts is desperate for the Party and are they not obliged to submit to Party decisions? The Brest decision was also adopted by a majority of one vote.

Comrade Lenin indicates that resigning from the CC does not mean leaving the Party.

Comrade Uritsky declares that in the first place, there was no discussion on the rationale when the Brest decision was taken, and in the second place, the majority of the CC does not share Lenin's point of view. The comrades are resigning from posts of responsibility but not from the Party. The Congress will decide the question of who speaks for the Party.

Comrade Lomov [Oppokov] considers that the situation needs analysing : comrade Lenin considers that we will strengthen Soviet power by signing the peace and we consider that we will undermine it.

Comrade Trotsky objects, pointing out that the value of the adopted decision lies in the fact that we were supporting the resolution by abstaining from voting. He indicates that he would perhaps have voted differently if he had known that his abstention would lead to comrades resigning. He considers Stalin's opinion mistaken.

Comrade Stalin says that he is accusing no one and considers they have the right to act in the way they think best, but he points out that there is absolutely no one to replace Lomov, Smirnov and Piatakov. Do the comrades realise that their conduct is leading* to a split ? If they want a clear position and not a split,

---

*   In the minutes book of the CC secretariat, *l*.239 : *will lead*.

he asks them to postpone their statement until tomorrow or until the Congress in a few days time.

Comrade Trotsky suggests that the session be considered suspended.

Comrade Uritsky says that they regard the statement as made and they have given up their responsible posts, but they will come to the discussion tomorrow.

Comrade Lomov [Oppokov] says that they cannot postpone the statement because the answer to the Germans is not to be post-poned but sent straight away*.

Comrade Krestinsky suggests that since the Congress is so close and there will be a referendum of Moscow and Peter workers before the peace is signed, and also since many people may perhaps change their vote by that time, freedom to agitate and permission not to vote in the Council of People's Commissars should be given to these comrades.

Comrade Lomov [Oppokov] disagrees with the suggestion, pointing out that today's decision may be annulled in two weeks and recognised as mistaken. They consider today's decision mistaken and that is why they cannot associate themselves with it.

Comrade Uritsky says that even though they are getting freedom to agitate, the peace will be signed. We are not leaving the Party. If you give us freedom to campaign and a free vote in the $TsIK$[223] – we postpone our decision.

Comrade Sverdlov points out that one can vote against or abstain and he asks what they are thinking of doing?

Comrade Uritsky says since he is not forbidden to act as he thinks fit, he will leave the hall when the vote is taken. He goes on to assert that he is not leaving in practice but considers that their statement stands.

Comrade Smirnov says that this is also unacceptable for him, that he cannot take responsibility for something he does not agree with and so he is not postponing his decision.

Comrade Lenin suggests to the comrades that they leave sessions during the voting and do not sign any documents so as

---

*   In the original secretarial notes, *l.3 ob.*, written between the speeches of Lomov and Krestinsky: *Lenin.* Lenin's speech is also left out of the original secretarial notes.

not to take responsibility but that they should not abandon work in the Council.

Comrade Sverdlov considers that for the time being the comrades should remain in their places and should not leave the CC and the commissariats and he suggests planning the work for the rest of the day.

1. Joint session of our CC and the CC of the Left SRs.
2. Sessions of the groups.
3. Session of the *TsIK* jointly with the Petrograd Soviet but voting separately. The session is suspended until tomorrow, keeping a note of the speakers : Dzerzhinsky, Uritsky, Sverdlov and Stalin.

Minutes No.46

[The minutes of the CC session of February 24 1918 (*ed.khr.* 412, *ll.*12-17) are the original secretarial notes written in ink on both sides of six half-sheets of paper. In addition, the archives contain yet another set of minute notes, written in the same handwriting on one side of seven medium-size sheets of paper torn out of a pad (*ll.*20-27). Alternative readings from the minute notes are given in the footnotes. The third set of minute notes is in the minute book of the secretariat of the CC RSDLP(b) (*ed.khr.*59).

The minutes are printed from the secretarial notes (*ll.*12-17) collated with both sets of minute notes.

The following documents are appended to the minutes: 1. The original statement to the Council of People's Commissars from Lomov, Smirnov and others (see p.232), 2. The original note of Trotsky's proposal, also included in the text (see p.236); 3. The original statement to the CC by Ioffe (see attached, p.237); 4. The original statement by Uritsky, Lomov and Smirnov to the CC RSDLP(b), apparently given later – the date is not marked on the document (see p.238).]

Session of the CC
February 24 [1918]

Present :
Sverdlov, Trotsky, Krestinsky, Dzerzhinsky, Uritsky, Smilga,
Zinoviev, Ioffe, Stalin, Lenin, Sokolnikov, Stasova.
Attending as guests : A. Smirnov, Latsis, Petrovsky.

First, the question of the delegation is tabled[224].

Comrade Lenin considers it necessary to preserve continuity
with the previous delegation and since comrade Karakhan is not
enough on his own, it would be very desirable for comrades Ioffe
and Zinoviev to go.

Comrade Sverdlov* says he is against Zinoviev making the
trip for internal Party considerations. Sokolnikov, Karakhan and
Chicherin (from the Commissariat of Foreign Affairs) should go.
Ioffe would have been best of all but he regards such a demand as
coercion and it may have undesirable consequences.

Comrade Ioffe points out that there is no need for the practical information possessed by the old peace delegation representatives since the new delegation is only going to sign the peace treaty
and not to discuss it, as can be clearly seen from the wording of the
text the Germans sent. It may be that my presence will become
necessary after the signature in some commission or another and
then I will not refuse to go. But now it is unthinkable because the
signature of the peace is the death of the whole Brest policy.

Comrade Lenin says that he does not insist that Ioffe go as a
plenipotentiary to sign the treaty but considers that comrade Ioffe
must make the trip as a consultant. The Germans undoubtedly
sent their reply in the form of an ultimatum because they feared
opposition on our part and when they see that we agree to sign the
peace, they may also agree to negotiations. This makes it essential
to have a consultant who knows all about the matter. If it turns
out that only a signature is needed, then of course there is nothing
to talk about and the consultant will not even appear at the session.

---

*   Sverdlov's speech is set out in the secretarial notes, *l.*20, like this:
*Sverdlov – it cannot be Zinoviev. Clarity for Moscow. Zinoviev and
Sverdlov. Sokolnikov, Karakhan and Chicherin in the delegation.*

Comrade Sverdlov acknowledges that the answer to the question must depend on comrade Ioffe's reply and that there can be no kind of pressure.

Comrade Zinoviev says that Ioffe ought not to refuse and that he can explain his position in an interview before he starts out, there being nothing unacceptable in that since exact figures of the voting in the CC have appeared in *Nash vek*[225].

Comrade Ioffe says that he sees no need for the trip since there is to be no discussion at Brest and the Germans will conduct everything in the spirit of an ultimatum. If information is needed, he can give it in a couple of hours and he would even agree to go as far as Dvinsk, but he refuses to be included in the delegation.

Comrade Lenin says that although Radek was against concluding a peace, he agreed to go nevertheless, but the Poles forbade it.

Comrade Sokolnikov points out that we sent an agreement by radio to conclude a peace and that the exact text has to be presented in Brest because it is not the ultimatum we are signing but the peace treaty itself. This being so, it is very likely that someone from the old delegation will have to be summoned from Peter to explain things. For this reason, he thinks it very desirable for Ioffe to make the trip.

Comrade Trotsky feels that those present do not realise what the delegation has to do in Brest, either in essence or in form. The German reply covers the most important questions : 1. the territorial question, 2. the trade question, 3. precise figures on the question of rights. In sum, everything important is there and only details are missing, to be clarified in the commissions only after the treaty is signed. The word 'ultimatum' does not appear in the German reply, though this is what it really is.

Comrade Lenin thinks he is wrong because specialists are undoubtedly needed at the signing of the treaty and we have none, even for a trade treaty. Krasin could have gone but he has left to spend some time in Stockholm. We are signing the treaty with clenched teeth, as the delegation states, but we do not know the situation, we do not know what may happen by the time the delegation arrives in Brest and that is why Ioffe is needed as a consultant. In general we must bear it in mind that we are authorising the delegation to enter into negotiations if there is any chance of it.

Comrade Sokolnikov points out that if the delegation is going just for a signature, there is no need for it at all and it is enough to send one man with batmen ; since we are sending a delegation, it means that we envisage the possibility of negotiations, and so comrade Ioffe's trip is necessary.

Comrade Trotsky says that our whole conduct in Brest was pressure on the German government ; now the position is different. We have had a split. It is not in our interest that Germany should not appreciate the break in our policy and that our previous policy has suffered an *échec**. We cannot send a batman, we must send an expert but we must do it in such a way as to make a political impact. For this purpose, we have to send people who, by their position, have the right to sign a peace. Ioffe's presence as a consultant has such political impact. He was the head of the previous delegation and now he is only a consultant. This way, we are clearly demonstrating that we are forced to pursue a different policy. Sokolnikov's point of view is radically wrong.

Comrade Zinoviev points out that effectively there has been a break in our policy but it must be demonstrated by arranging something bigger than a change of personnel. We need a man who would not let anything big slip by, who is up with the whole affair, and comrade Ioffe as a consultant is just the man.

Comrade Ioffe considers that the best political gesture of all would be for no one to go. The German functionary will not understand that my presence is symbolic, he will just see it as a come-down. There is no practical sense in my attending. Trotsky was right in saying that everything important has been clearly set out in the German reply, and it only needs an hour to read through the text of the reply together. The Germans will certainly refuse to talk and they will be quite right. As far as the gesture goes, there will be one even without him because all the members going are new and consequently we are showing that both the majority and the minority in the CC considers the previous Brest line abandoned.

Comrade Ioffe asks whether, in the event of his going, the statement he signed with Dzerzhinsky and Krestinsky will be published.

---

*   – blow, failure.

Comrade Sverdlov says that the statement will be published whether he goes or not. The offer has even been made to comrade Ioffe to publish an explanatory statement that he is taking on the role of consultant but pointing out his position in doing so*. Comrade Sverdlov proposes that comrade Sokolnikov head the delegation.

Comrade Sokolnikov suggests that since Karakhan and Ioffe are making the trip, Zinoviev should go.

Comrade Sverdlov says that the decision has already been made with regard to comrade Sokolnikov. Zinoviev is needed in Peter to make appearances; there is no one apart from him and Sokolnikov but Zinoviev is very valuable for public appearances since he is Chairman of the Petrograd Soviet and he will probably have to go to Moscow instead of Lenin.

Comrade Zinoviev states that he does not refuse to go but looking at the question from the point of view of usefulness, he thinks that Sokolnikov is more useful in the delegation and he here. The Left SRs are sending Alekseev who, it seems, does not know very much about the matter and for that reason the person who goes from us must be more knowledgeable than he – Zinoviev.

Comrade Sokolnikov points out that they were dissatisfied at the time of his first trip, that while Zinoviev is needed in the Soviet, he is needed in *Pravda* and the banks and that it is better to send Zinoviev just because he is Chairman of the Soviet.

Comrade Lenin feels it necessary to send both and that if it is only a question of signing a peace, they could both leave straight away after settling further developments with Chicherin.

Comrade Zinoviev asserts that there is no reason for the two of them to go and that it is better if Sokolnikov goes.

Comrade Sokolnikov states that because his conduct aroused disapproval on the first journey, he will not go and if it is insisted on, he will leave the CC.

Comrade Trotsky makes ironic remarks about comrade Sokolnikov's ultimatum.

Comrade Lenin asks the comrades not to get overstrung and points out that as a People's Commissar, comrade Petrovsky can go in the delegation.

---

*   See p.237.

Comrade Sverdlov supports this suggestion but feels that Petrovsky should only go as a second.

It is decided that comrades Sokolnikov, Petrovsky, Karakhan and Chicherin* are to go.

A vote is taken on the issue of whether comrade Ioffe's journey is desirable and necessary but without this decision being binding on him, and the majority answered in the affirmative.

The statement by Lomov, V. Smirnov, Spunde, Uritsky** and Bogolepov is discussed.

To the Council of People's Commissars

Finding it impossible to take responsibility for accepting the German ultimatum, we resign the posts we hold in the Council of People's Commissars.

> *A. Lomov (G. Oppokov),*
> *V. Smirnov, M. Uritsky,*
> *G. Piatakov, D. Bogolepov, A. Spunde.*

Comrade Uritsky says that this is a statement for the Council which is being transmitted through the CC. Comrade Lomov is carrying on with practical work for the time being, comrade Smirnov, too, comrade Uritsky is leaving the small Council of Commissars but staying at work in the Supreme Council of National Economy and giving up everything to do with the dissolution of the Constituent Assembly, comrade Spunde is abandoning the lot and leaving for the Urals, comrade Piatakov is leaving for Kiev, comrade Bogolepov, it seems, is leaving for Moscow. This is a collegial not a personal decision.

Comrade Trotsky, too, refers to the statement he made about five days ago[226].

Comrade Krestinsky suggests putting the following proposal up for discussion : The CC suggests that the comrades who issued the statement should remain at their posts for the time being without taking any political responsibility and enjoying complete freedom to defend their point of view in the Party, the press and at meetings.

---

*   In the secretarial notes, *l.23* : *as secretary Chicherin. Trotsky's statement.*
**   In the secretarial notes, *l.23*, there is the name : *Piatakov.*

Comrade Sverdlov suggests not discussing the question of Trotsky for the moment.

Comrade Trotsky objects to this, saying that he has not caused trouble with his statement up to now and has done nothing to hamper the work in hand but he considers that he can no longer speak in the CC's name in the future because he cannot defend its positions.

Comrade Zinoviev tries to persuade him to stay until the peace treaty is signed because the crisis is not yet over.

Comrade Trotsky points out that it is just when the peace is being signed that he finds it unacceptable to stay because he is forced to defend a position he does not agree with.

Comrade Stalin proposes nothing but talks of the pain his comrades are causing him. He is shattered by their hurry and attack when they know very well there is no one to replace them and he asks why they do it.

Comrade Trotsky feels that he is quite able to leave since all the practical work is done without him, the direction of external affairs included. He is not refusing practical help where it is needed but he does not want to be responsible any more*.

Comrade Uritsky expresses astonishment at Stalin's words. Apart from those going away, they are all staying at their posts but they are shedding political responsibility and carrying on the campaign which they consider their primary work. Yesterday Stalin suggested they leave the Party but they are not thinking of leaving the Party**.

Comrade Zinoviev understands that comrade Trotsky's position is very difficult and that this is a sacrifice but everyone still considers that at such a grave moment of crisis he cannot leave and he asks him to put off going for two or three days.

Comrade Stalin says that he is not reproaching Trotsky in the least and he also sees this situation as a crisis of power, as solidarity with the Left SRs, but nevertheless he asks him to wait for a couple of days; to comrade Uritsky, he says that he was only trying to get things clear the day before and did not want them to

---

*   There is an addition to Trotsky's speech in the secretarial notes, *l.24*: *he suggests to all comrades who do not agree to continue to fulfil their obligations.*

**   In the secretarial notes, *l.24* there is the following phrase in Uritsky's speech: *he cannot take responsibility but only work.*

leave the Party at all but wanted them to say openly whether this was a split or not. The provinces will take this as a split in practice. If their decision is subjective, he asks them to wait a bit for the effect is to open a new way to a split and this strikes a very serious blow at the whole apparatus of Soviet power. He considers that they must find themselves deputies; their conduct is placing both the apparatus and the Party in a position where all the Party comrades will have to leave.

Comrade Trotsky cites the article by Lenin which first introduced a split. He points out that there are now two wings in the Party very sharply differentiated from each other. If you look at it from a parliamentary angle, we have two parties among us and in a parliamentary sense the minority would have had to yield but this is not so with us because we have a struggle going on between groups. We cannot surrender our position to the Left SRs. The differences which exist in the Party are on a world scale and the groups articulating them take responsibility for them. Lenin put the question clearly. As for Trotsky himself, he must set a minimum of reservations* because he does not want to split the Party. He points out that Chicherin can take charge of current work and Lenin should take over political direction. He agrees to make his

---

*   There is no text of the end of Trotsky's speech in the secretarial notes, *ll.24-25*. The following speeches go like this:

Sverdlov — about the four seeking deputies, clarify. Change the official title. Where Trotsky is concerned.

Trotsky. Curr[ent matters] — to Chicherin, but Lenin must take on the political. Let us arrange one more session before the signature.

Trotsky. Statement about resigning in an unobtrusive way so that I could tell people whom to approach.

Lenin — unacceptable. Disagreement.

Trotsky — physically impossible.

Change of policy even raised by Lenin himself.

Lenin — change of policy is a crisis. The questionnaire has been sent off, a little polemic won't hurt.

Practical suggestions.

Ask Trotsky to put it off until the next CC session, until Tuesday.

Amendment: until the delegation returns from Brest.

Trotsky — I resign, I am not making it public, I will take no part in official bodies, i.e. the Council of People's Commissars and the TsIK.

statement resigning full powers in the most unobtrusive way, but he must be able to direct people to someone if they come with problems.

Comrade Lenin points out that this is unacceptable, that the change of policy is a crisis. A policy questionnaire has been sent round the provinces[227] and it will do no harm to polemicise a little.

He moves a practical proposal: the CC requests comrade Trotsky to postpone his statement until the next CC session, until Tuesday. (Amendment – until the delegation returns from Brest.)

Comrade Trotsky states that he is resigning the title of commissar, is not publicising it, but he is taking no part in official bodies, i.e. the Council of People's Commissars and the *TsIK*.

Comrade Lenin suggests putting the following statement to the vote: the CC, considering it impossible to accept comrade Trotsky's resignation at the present moment, asks him to defer this decision of his until the delegation returns from Brest or until there is a change in the current state of affairs.

It is approved with 3 abstentions.

Comrade Trotsky considers that he has made his statement and that it was not accepted, and so he is forced to abstain from appearances in official bodies.

Comrade Lenin moves a vote: The CC, having heard comrade Trotsky's statement and being fully reconciled to comrade Trotsky's absence when the Council of People's Commissars is taking decisions on foreign affairs, requests comrade Trotsky not to stay away when other decisions are being taken.

Approved.

Comrade Uritsky hopes that their statement resigning from the CC and posts of responsibility will be published.

Comrade Lenin proposes the adoption of the following: the CC asks the comrades who submitted the statement to put off their* decision until the delegation returns from Brest and to discuss this CC decision in the group.

Comrade Uritsky considers himself obliged to declare that they regard themselves as having already left the CC and responsible posts.

Comrade Dzerzhinsky points out that we must reckon with

---

* In the secretarial notes, *l.*25, is the word: *final.*

this fact but he supports Lenin's proposal and says that we are asking the comrades not to sabotage and wreck the work. He asks them to grant a postponement, observing that Uritsky is not the holy spirit and cannot foresee every circumstance which may oblige the comrades to agree with the CC proposal.

Comrade Krestinsky again proposes putting his motion to the vote*.

Comrade Lenin moves two proposals :

1.   While acknowledging that the demand made by the four is legitimate, the CC requests them to discuss the CC proposal and to postpone their statement in view of the nearness of the Congress and the complexity of the political situation**.

2.   Guaranteeing to the comrades that their statements will be published in *Pravda*, the CC asks them to reconsider their decision and to discuss whether they do not find it possible to remain both in responsible posts and in the CC***.

Comrade Trotsky also moves a proposal : since the situation created by the resignation of the four CC members from responsible *political* functions would not necessarily entail their resignation from the CC and since this latter threatens to start a split in the Party, the CC suggests that they remain members of the leading Party body, retaining the right to campaign freely against the decision adopted by the CC.

All four proposals are put to the vote :

Comrade Krestinsky's**** resolution : all in favour.

Comrade Lenin's first resolution : 5 in favour, 1 against, 3 abstained.

---

*   In the secretarial notes, *l.*25, Krestinsky's speech goes like this: *Krestinsky — Lenin's resolution is wrong. It is impossible. Having adopted their statement in the CC.*

**   In the secretarial notes, *l.*25, it continues: *1 against — 3 abst. Do we ask for an announcement in the press? Does the CC recognise it. We recognise it : on the basis of Lenin's intervention.*

***   In the secretarial notes, *l.*27, it continues: *5-3 abst. — 1 against. To Bukharin — collegium to discuss it.*
      The CC sees no grounds for leaving the CC, considering it possible for them to carry on the struggle.
      The CC proposes no departure from the CC 1 against 1 [then crossed-out: *abst.*]. (*Ur.*)
      In view of the outlined compromise decision.

**** See p.232.

Comrade Lenin's second resolution : 5 in favour, 1 against, 3 abstained.

Comrade Trotsky's resolution : all in favour.

TO THE CC RSDLP*

Until the time when the CC and the Council of People's Commissars are forced to take the line of defence, we postpone implementation of our decision.

In the name of a group of comrades :

M.Uritsky
A.Lomov
V.Smirnov

February 25.

Document 1
Ioffe's statement to the CC
TO THE CC RSDLP(bolsheviks)

Dear comrades!

As you know, I was resolutely opposed from the very beginning to the foreign policy pursued for the last week by the majority of the Soviet government and I did what I could to fight inside the CC against the acceptance of the German peace proposals. Because there was a serious danger of a split in our Party, I did not feel I had the right to come out publicly against the CC's majority line, but it goes without saying that I cannot implement that line. For that reason, I absolutely refused to take any part in the peace delegation now setting out for Brest-Litovsk.

But in view of the CC's categorical resolution that it considers my participation in the peace delegation obligatory, if only as a consultant, I am forced to submit to this decision in order to safeguard all possible unity in the Party and I go to Brest-Litovsk merely as a consultant, bearing no political responsibility whatsoever.

With comradely greetings, *A.Ioffe (V.Krymsky)*
Member of the CC RSDLP and former chairman of the
Russian peace delegation

24.2-1918.

Archives of the IML, *f*.17, *op*.1, *ed.khr*.412, *l*.29.

---

*　This statement signed by three is written in the minute book of the CC secretariat, *l*.264, directly after the February 24 minutes.

Document 2
To the CC RSDLP (bolsheviks)

In view of the fact that the peace is signed, we withdraw our statement*
deferring the implementation of our decision, resign from the CC
and responsible Soviet posts and insist on the publication of all our
statements in *Pravda*.

In the name of a group of comrades
M.Uritsky
G.Oppokov (A.Lomov)
V.Smirnov

Archives of the IML, *f*.17, *op*.1, *ed.khr*.412, *l*.4.
Published for the first time.

**The position of the CC RSDLP (bolsheviks) on the
question of the separate and annexationist peace**

Dear comrades !
The Organisational Bureau of the CC considers it necessary to explain to
you the reasons which impelled the CC to agree to the peace
terms proposed by the German government. The Organisational
Bureau submits this explanation to you, comrades, so that all Party
members will be fully informed of the view taken by the CC,
which represents the whole Party in the period between congresses.
The Organisational Bureau feels it necessary to point out that the
CC was not unanimous on the question of signing the peace terms.
But since the decision has been taken, it must be supported by the
whole Party. A Party congress is due to take place in a few days and
only there will it be possible to tell how accurately the CC expressed the real position of the whole Party. Until the congress, all
Party members in the name of Party duty and for the sake of keeping our ranks united carry out the decision of their central leading
body, the Party's CC.
The indisputable necessity of signing at this moment (February 24 1918)
a grasping, unbelievably severe peace with Germany is due primarily to the fact that we have no army, that we cannot defend
ourselves.

---

*   For statements made by them earlier, see pp. 232 and 237 of the
present edition.

Everyone knows the reason why, after October 25 1917, after the victory of the dictatorship of the proletariat and the poor peasantry, we all became defensists, why we favoured defence of the fatherland.

From the point of view of defending the fatherland, it is unthinkable to allow yourself to be drawn into a military conflict when you have no army and the enemy is armed to the teeth and magnificently prepared.

It is impossible for the Soviet socialist republic to fight a war while an obviously enormous majority of the worker, peasant and soldier masses who elect the Soviets are against the war. This would be adventurism. It will be another matter if this war ends, harsh though the peace may be, and then German imperialism wants to start an aggressive war against Russia again. Then the majority of the Soviets would certainly favour war.

Fighting a war now would objectively be to fall for the provocation of the Russian bourgeoisie. It knows very well that Russia cannot be defended now and that even insignificant German forces could crush us, for they have only to cut the main railway lines to take Peter and Moscow by starvation. The bourgeoisie want war because they want the overthrow of Soviet power and an understanding with the German bourgeoisie. The jubilation of the bourgeoisie in Dvinsk and Rezhitsa, in Wenden and Hapsal, in Minsk and Drissa, when the Germans came confirms this clear as can be.

To advocate a revolutionary war at this moment is inevitably just a revolutionary phrase. For it is impossible for a ruined peasant army to fight a modern war against advanced imperialism without an army and very serious economic preparation. There is no doubt that it is essential to resist German imperialism, which will imprison and crush us. But it would be a mere phrase to demand that resistance must take the form of an armed uprising and must be now, when *this kind* of resistance is obviously hopeless for us and obviously profitable to both the German and the Russian bourgeoisie.

To use the argument about supporting the international socialist movement in advocating a revolutionary war is, at this moment, just such a phrase. If we make it easier for German imperialism to destroy the Soviet republic by deciding to fight at the wrong time, we will be harming and not helping the German and international workers' movement and the cause of socialism. All-round, dogged, systematic work is needed to help only the revolutionary internationalists inside every country but it is unworthy of a Marxist to gamble on an armed uprising when it obviously is a gamble.

If Liebknecht wins in two or three weeks (which is possible) he will, of course, get us out of all our difficulties. But it would be simply stupid and it would turn the great slogan of the solidarity of the workers of all countries into a mockery if we were to take it into our heads to guarantee to the people that Liebknecht is unfailingly bound to triumph in the next few weeks. It is just by reasoning like this that they are turning the great slogan, 'We bank on the world revolution' into an empty phrase.

Objectively, the situation is similar to the summer of 1907. Then it was the Russian monarchist Stolypin who crushed and imprisoned us, now it is the German imperialist. Then the slogan of an immediate insurrection, turned out to be an empty phrase unfortunately taken up by the whole S R Party. Now, this moment, the slogan of a revolutionary war is clearly a phrase which has caught the enthusiasm of the Left S Rs as they repeat the arguments of the Right S Rs. We are the prisoners of German imperialism and we have a long and difficult struggle ahead of us to overthrow this leader of world imperialism; this struggle is undoubtedly the last and final battle for socialism but it is adventurism to begin this struggle with an armed rising against the leader of imperialism at this moment and no Marxist would ever do it.

To systematically, unflinchingly, comprehensively build up the defence capacity of the country, develop self-discipline everywhere, use the grave defeat to raise discipline in every sphere of life in the interest of the country's economic progress and the consolidation of Soviet power – this is the task of the moment, this is how to prepare a revolutionary war in deeds not words.

In conclusion, the Organisational Bureau considers it essential to point out that as the German imperialist offensive has not yet been halted, all Party members must organise concerted resistance. If we cannot gain time by signing a peace, even an extremely onerous one, so that we can prepare for new battles, our Party must emphasise the need to strain every resource for all-out resistance.

If we can gain time, get even a short breathing space for the work of organisation, we are obliged to try for it. If we are not given a respite, our Party must appeal to the masses to fight, to defend themselves vigorously. We are convinced that all Party members will fulfil their obligations to the Party, to their country's working class, to the people and the proletariat. By preserving Soviet power, we are giving the very best and strongest support to the proletariat of all countries in their incredibly difficult and tough struggle against their own bourgeoisie. There is and can be no greater blow to the cause of socialism now than the collapse of Soviet power in Russia. With comradely greetings

Organisational Bureau of the CC RSDLP(bolsheviks)

Written on February 24 1918
V.I.Lenin, *Sochineniia,* 4th ed., vol. 27, pp.37-40.

Appendix
Bulletins of the CC RSDLP(bolsheviks)[228]

BULLETIN OF THE CC RSDLP(bolsheviks) No.1.

Because newspapers are not getting through and telegrams are not being transmitted, the CC has decided to send out short bulletins giving information on the situation.

The democracy, represented by the workers and the soldiers, is supporting us and so we have strength at our disposal, but the petty bourgeoisie and the bureaucracy are opposing us and are sabotaging and boycotting the Military Revolutionary Committee and the Commissars in such a way that we do not really control the technical apparatus. The telegraphists, too, are similarly sabotaging us and are not transmitting our telegrams. Part of the garrison in Gatchina is against us and this has already caused a clash and it must be considered that the approaches to the capital will have to be defended by armed force. A strong and organised bourgeois guard has been formed in Finland. *Rumcherod*[229] is against us. In Petersburg, on the night of the 29th, junkers and a section of the cossacks went into action against the Revolutionary Committee. They managed to seize the telephone and two armoured cars; measures have been taken against them. The Petersburg garrison is on the side of the Revolutionary Committee. Kerensky and several echelons of cossacks continue to move towards Petrograd. The town is guarded by the garrison and the Red Guard. Forces committed to support the Revolutionary Committee are marching in Kerensky's rear. The Northern front is on the side of the Revolutionary Committee. In Moscow[230], Minsk, Vitebsk, Ufa, Samara and Mogilev, power has passed into the hands of the Soviets.

October 29 1917.

BULLETIN OF THE CC RSDLP(bolsheviks) No.2.

On October 29th, the CC decided the question of supplementing the *TsIK**. What was decided was that the *TsIK* should be supplemented on a proportional basis by representatives of the parties which left the Congress of Soviets and also by representatives of those Soviets which were absent; taking a norm of approximately 1 to 125 thous. The government is formed by the *TsIK* and is responsible to it. All parties represented in the Soviet can enter the government. All the decrees issued up to the time of the agreement are confirmed. The All-Russian Union of Railwaymen demanded the formation of a coalition socialist ministry; the rail-

---

*   See pp.127-128 of the present edition.

waymen are threatening a general strike if the sides in the conflict refuse to fulfil this demand. A conciliation commission has been formed with representatives from the *TsIK,* the CCs of all parties, the Committee to Save the Revolution, the Union of Railwaymen, the Union of Post and Telegraph Employees. A *junker movement has been suppressed* in Petersburg.

There were many casualties. It is quiet in the town. A session of the Committee to Save the Revolution in the City Duma issued an order to arrest members of the Revolutionary Committee. In Moscow, junkers and French troops revolted again and there is fighting in the streets. According to rumours, Kerensky is surrounded by Revolutionary Committee troops. Kornilov is with Kerensky[231]. Kerensky is in telephone contact with Mikhail Aleksandrovich. *All power has passed to the Soviets in the Crimea (Sevastopol', Eupatoriia, Feodosiia).* A parallel Committee to Save the Revolution has been formed in Simferopol'. The junction stations of Orsha, Molodechno and Minsk are in our hands. Newspapers from the capital are not reaching the provinces. Peter is badly informed about the provinces. Please spread the information you receive from us round your region and tell us by direct letter what the position is where you are.

October 30 1917.

BULLETIN of the CC (bolsheviks) No.3.

The conciliation commission consisting of representatives of the *TsIK,* the CCs of all parties, the CC of the union of railwaymen and the post and telegraph employees has not arrived at any result. The defensists made the following conditions for agreement: 1. The Bolsheviks must declare that all regiments are to be transferred from the Military Revolutionary Committee and put at the disposal of the City Duma. 2. The workers must disarm and not oppose Kerensky's troops when they arrive. 3. Those arrested by the Military Revolutionary Committee to be freed. 4. The Military Revolutionary Committee to be disbanded. These conditions were not acceptable to the Bolsheviks, the Left SRs, the Internationalist Mensheviks and United Internationalist Mensheviks. The railwaymen's CC (*Vikzhel'*) and the post and telegraph employees are wavering. A general meeting of railway employees at the Zvanka station resolved: not to form a strike committee and not to join a strike if *Vikzhel'* declares one. Similar information has been received from other points. It is quiet in the town. The staff of higher telegraph employees will be removed and it is possible the telegraph will temporarily stop work. Postal services are functioning. Officers from the air school in Lesnoi tried to disarm the Red

Guard. Our troops are in Tsarskoe and Pavlovsk. Three Lettish regiments have occupied Gatchina. According to rumours, Voitinsky and Savinkov are at Kerensky's headquarters. In Moscow, fighting in the streets continues. There is news that troops are going to Moscow's aid from nearby towns. In the Urals, power has passed to the Soviets. According to rumours, Kaledin has occupied Kharkov.

Telegraph communication between Reval and Petrograd has broken down because of damage to the lines. Reval makes contact through Helsingfors. In Finland, the mood is cheerful. A district Military Revolutionary Committee has been formed in Schluesselburg. The head of the garrison has been chosen.

October 31 1917.

BULLETIN CC RSDLP(bolsheviks) No.4.

The CC of the United Mensheviks has asserted that the only way out of the current situation is to form a homogenous ministry of socialists, from SRs to Bolsheviks. A Petrograd city conference of SRs has been held. It was attended by 99 Left SRs and 4 Right SRs. The conference is appealing for full submission and assistance to the committee of the Council of People's Commissars. The SR group in the *TsIK* adopted a similar resolution. The Left SRs officially declared that they are joining in all the Revolutionary Committee's work. After the occupation of Tsarskoe Selo, Kerensky has 700 cossacks left in all. Heavy artillery and one shuttered train have fallen into our hands. Help in the form of cossacks and SRs has been sent to Kerensky from Luga. Delegates from the Luga garrison declared in the Revolutionary Committee that they are opposing their Soviet and when they return home, they will immediately hold new elections and throw all the defensists out of the Soviet. During yesterday, delegates came to the Military Revolutionary Committee from the 5th, 1st, 12th, 10th, 2nd, 3rd and 8th armies announcing that their armies are supporting the Petrograd Soviet and corresponding resolutions have been carried everywhere. Information is coming from all over that the mood is cheerful. Things are quietening down in Moscow. Troops have arrived from the provinces, among them artillery from Rostov-Iaroslav, which helps the Moscow garrison to cope with the enemy. In Petrograd, there are provisions for seven days. The sailors are making searches of stores everywhere in the town and they have already brought to light 80,000 poods of flour, 50,000 poods of sugar, 30,000 poods of cabbages. At 6 o'clock this morning, a delegation from Petrograd regiments and the men at the front is going to the cossacks to suggest they surrender and give up the struggle.

In Minsk, the Soviet after the first days of its victory, suffered defeat and had to concede supremacy to the counter-revolutionary front committee, which has already been partly re-elected but is not giving up its powers. Because of the situation which has arisen, the armies which have already held new elections of their representatives are sending units to Minsk to displace the committee and transfer power to the Soviet. The front committee has managed to carry off the equipment and give it to the cossacks surrounding Minsk but the Soviet has the arms. The position will change immediately the men arrive from the front. There is a similar position in Smolensk. In Orsha, there is a Military Revolutionary Committee and a Committee to Save the Revolution and power is controlled by the first. When the regiment Kerensky summoned from the front learnt of the state of affairs in Orsha, it stayed in Orsha and is mounting guard on the station, not letting counter-revolutionaries through. The cossacks in Orsha are wavering. In Saratov, the garrison clashed with the junkers and the officers (only two officers remained with the garrison). Victory for the Soviet. In Tambov, the Soviet holds power but Kadets are spreading false rumours about Peter and a conflict is possible. The cavalry persisted longest of all but the infantrymen surrounded them and forced them to surrender. The cossacks in Villmanstrand in Finland are uneasy, stirred up by spokesmen from the cossack troops. Delegates have been sent from the Vyborg Soviet, the army committee and the cossack units in Vyborg to settle them down. In Gomel, the Soviet has passed a resolution in support of the Petrograd Soviet but the Executive Committee, elected on a proportional basis, is not implementing this decision. Up to Sunday evening, Kharkov had heard nothing of Kaledin. Our garrison is very strong. From the Western front, they report a de facto ceasefire: soldiers from both sides are going out to mow the autumn sedge. There is no fraternisation.

November 1 1917.

BULLETIN OF THE CC RSDLP(bolsheviks) No.5

The cossacks in Gatchina have gone over to the Soviet side after talks with People's Commissar Dybenko and a spokesman from the Fifth Army. The cossack divisional committee passed a decision to end the civil war quickly, to arrest Kerensky and to hand him over to the discretion of the Military Revolutionary Committee to be brought before a public people's court. Kerensky fled in disguise. The cossacks have taken vigorous measures to detain him. The headquarters staff of Kerensky, Krasnov and Voitinsky has been arrested. Gatchina is occupied by the Finnish regiment and there is complete order there. The Finnish regiment and the cossacks are keeping guard. A Military Revolutionary Committee was organised in Gatchina on November 1st, including Ussur cossacks taking a stand on the transfer of power to the Soviets. On November 8, the Petersburg Duma is summoning an assembly of representatives from the city and *zemstvo* local governments and the Executive Committee of the Soviet of Peasants', Workers' and Soldiers' Deputies to reconstitute a state power. Information has been received from the Urals that everything is quiet there. The *TsIK* approved a resolution moved by the Bolshevik group (40 to 30) about an agreement between the socialist parties: 'While it considers an agreement between socialist parties desirable, the *TsIK* states that an agreement can only be reached on the following conditions: 1. Recognition of the Soviet government's programme expressed in the decrees on land, peace, and both drafts on workers' control. 2. Recognition of the need for a merciless fight against counter-revolution (Kerensky, Kornilov, Kaledin). 3. Recognition that the Second All-Russian Congress of Soviets of Workers' and Soldiers' Deputies, with the peasants participating, is the sole source of power. 4. The government to be responsible to the *TsIK*. 5. Total rejection of representation in the *TsIK* for organisations not represented in the Soviets. 6. The *TsIK* to be supplemented by representatives from the Soviets of Workers', Soldiers' and Peasants' Deputies not represented in it and from all-Russian trade unions, such as: the Council of Trade Unions, the Council of Factory Committees, *Vikzhel'* and the Post and Telegraph Union, provided that and only after there are new elections for the All-Russian Soviet of Peasants' Deputies and those forces' organisations which have not had elections in the last three months.'

Telegrams have gone out from the *TsIK,* the Military Revolutionary Committee and the Council of People's Commissars to detain Kerensky. A general strike began in Finland at 12 o'clock midnight on November 1st: the implementation of bills adopted by the seim in June-July.

November 2 1917.

BULLETIN OF THE CC RSDLP(bolsheviks) No.6

The Mensheviks have split: Liber, Skobelev and others have left the CC. According to rumours, the SRs are also splitting. The *TsIK* adopted the following resolution on the subject of an agreement: the *TsIK* considers it desirable that the government should include representatives of those socialist parties in the Soviets of Workers', Soldiers' and Peasants' Deputies who recognise the achievements of the revolution of October 24-25, that is the power of the Soviets, the decrees on land, peace and workers' control, and the arming of the workers. The *TsIK* decides therefore to continue talks on power with all the Soviet parties and insists on the following conditions for an agreement. The government to be responsible to the *TsIK*. The *TsIK* to be enlarged to 150 people. To these 150 delegates from the Soviet of Workers' and Soldiers' Deputies are to be added 75 delegates from the provincial peasants' Soviets, 80 from units of the forces and the navy, 40 from the trade unions (25 from all-Russian trade associations, 10 from *Vikzhel'* and 5 from the post and telegraph employees) and 50 delegates from the socialist [parties] in the Petrograd City Duma. The Bolsheviks must be given at least half the places in the government. The Ministries of Labour, Internal Affairs and Foreign Affairs must go to the Bolshevik Party in any case. Control over the troops in the Moscow and Petrograd districts will belong to those authorised by the Moscow and Petrograd Soviets of Workers' and Soldiers' Deputies. The government makes it its task to systematically arm the workers in the whole of Russia. A decision is made to insist on the candidatures of comrades Lenin and Trotsky. The resolution is adopted by a vote with six against and one abstention. The People's Commissar for Posts and Telegraphs is dismissing all counter-revolutionaries in the telegraph, who, when they receive notice, are obliged to report to the military commander. Their vacancies are filled by comrades from the trade unions who have some knowledge of telegraph work. In Ivanovo-Voznesensk, all striking post and telegraph employees gave an assurance after five hours of arrest that they would do their work meticulously. The Finnish railways have gone on strike right up to Petrograd and in this way Russia is cut off from Europe. In Petrograd, 300,000 poods of grain have been confiscated. Employees and workers of the Nikolaev railway, without the knowledge of their committee, sent four military trains to Moscow's aid, including one train of sailors and one shuttered train. In Moscow, the Soviet has taken over power. The junkers have surrendered. The Novgorod Soviet is defensist but it is only supported by one shock battalion, which was told by the Military Revolutionary Committee elected by the cavalry units that it would not release it but would wipe it all out to the last man. However, the Military Revolutionary Committee is operating in contact with the Soviet and the railwaymen, who do not want to give wagons to either side. Shock troops advanced on Gatchina on November 3 and skirmishes occurred but then they sent a delegation to Petrograd, to Smolny, and the delegation left there with a decision to persuade their unit to go back to its position. On November 2nd, the CC RSDLP adopted the following resolution*.

---

*   See pp.136-138 of the present edition.

1. The Central Committee affirms that if the slogan of rule by the Soviets of Workers', Soldiers' and Peasants' Deputies is not to be betrayed, there can be no resort to petty bargaining over the affiliation to the Soviets of organisations which are not of the Soviet type, that is of organisations which are not voluntary associations of the revolutionary vanguard of the masses fighting to overthrow the landowners and the capitalists.

2. The Central Committee affirms that to concede to ultimatums and threats from the minority in the Soviets amounts to a complete renunciation not only of Soviet power but of democracy, too, for such concessions add up to a fear of the majority to use its majority, inviting anarchy and new ultimatums from any minority.

3. The Central Committee affirms that, not having excluded anyone from the Second All-Russian Congress of Soviets, it is fully prepared even now to reinstate those who walked out and to agree to a coalition within the Soviets with those who left, so that the claim that the Bolsheviks do not want to share power with anyone is absolutely false.

4. The Central Committee affirms that on the day the present government was formed, some hours before that formation, the CC invited three representatives of the Left Socialist-Revolutionaries to its meeting[174] and formally proposed that they join the government. The Left SRs' refusal, though temporary and conditional, means that all responsibility for the failure to reach an agreement with them must be put fairly and squarely on these Left SRs.

5. The Central Committee recalls that the Second All-Russian Congress of Soviets adopted a resolution moved by the Bolshevik group which said that it was prepared to supplement the Soviet with soldiers from the trenches and peasants from the localities and villages – and therefore the assertion that the Bolshevik government is against a coalition with the peasants is completely false. On the contrary, the CC declares that our government's land law, embodying the SR mandate, has proved in practice that the Bolsheviks are completely and very sincerely ready to establish a coalition with the vast majority of Russia's population.

6. The Central Committee affirms, finally, that no matter what the difficulties, the policy of the present government must be continued unswervingly if the victory of socialism both in Russia and in Europe is to be ensured. The Central Committee expresses its complete faith in the victory of this socialist revolution and invites all sceptics and waverers to abandon their hesitations and give wholehearted and energetic support to the activity of this government.

November 4 1917.

BULLETIN OF THE CC RSDLP(bolsheviks) No.7

In the *TsIK,* Lenin's and Trotsky's resolution against the freedom of the press[232] has been approved by 34 to 24. People's Commissars Nogin, Rykov, Miliutin, Teodorovich, Riazanov and Derbyshev have resigned as People's Commissars. They gave the following statement* to the *TsIK* of the Soviet of Workers' and Soldiers' Deputies and to the Council of People's Commissars: It is our view that a socialist government must be formed from all the parties in the Soviet. We consider that only if such a government is formed will there be an opportunity for the fruits of the heroic struggle waged by the working class and the revolutionary army in the October and November days to be made secure.

We believe that, apart from this, there is only one other path: the retention of a purely Bolshevik government by means of political terror. The Council of People's Commissars has embarked on that path. We cannot and will not take it. We see that it leads to the mass proletarian organisations being cut off from the leadership of political life, to the establishment of an unaccountable regime and to the destruction of the revolution and the country. We cannot be responsible for this policy and so, before the *TsIK,* we relinquish our titles of People's Commissars. Commissar Shliapnikov, while endorsing the overall assessment of the political situation, regards it as inadmissible to resign his responsibility and obligations.

Kamenev, Rykov, Miliutin, Zinoviev and Nogin have left the Bolshevik CC**. German and Austrian socialists welcome the Russian revolution. The Viennese proletariat is demanding an immediate cease-fire. The French internationalists welcome the Bolsheviks. In Kharkov, power is in the hands of the Revolutionary Committee. The cossacks did not advance on Kharkov. In Krasnoiarsk, the Soviet holds power; they have no news from Petrograd and the rest of Russia and ask to be told how they can help the Petersburg movement and what is needed. In Cheliabinsk, 500 men have been killed and a large number injured[233]. *Vikzhel'* is taking measures to freight food to Petersburg. Of the 1000 shock troops who advanced on Gatchina, 700 surrendered on November 4 and the rest fled; they are being pursued in the hope of stopping and disarming them. From Dvinsk, it is reported: barriers have been set up on the roads to Petersburg: Rezhitsa, Sokol'niki, and communication is established as far as Smolensk. The Fifth Army stopped three cossack regiments, 16 armoured cars and one armoured train with

---

* See pp. 141 - 142 of the present edition.
** See pp. 140 - 141 of the present edition.

definitely hostile intentions. If Petersburg needs help, then 24 hours after a radio message, Fifth Army detachments will be at Petersburg, Smolensk and in Velikie Luki.

The session of the *TsIK* of the Soviet of Workers' and Soldiers' Deputies adopted the Bolshevik group's resolution. The closure of the bourgeois newspapers was not only a response to purely military requirements during the insurrection and suppression of counter-revolutionary moves, but was also a transitional measure needed to establish a new regime in press matters, a regime under which capitalists with their own printing press and paper could not become autocratic manufacturers of public opinion. The next measure must be to confiscate private printing presses and stocks of paper and make them the property of the Soviet authorities in the centre and the localities so that parties and groups can use the technical printing resources according to their real ideological strength, i.e. in proportion to how many followers they have. To restore the so-called 'freedom of the press', i.e. simply to return the presses and paper to the capitalists, to the people who poison the consciousness of the people, would be to capitulate quite inadmissibly to what capitalists want and to surrender one of the most important positions gained by the workers' and peasants' revolution, i.e. it would undoubtedly be a counter-revolutionary measure. Therefore, the CC proposes that the Bolshevik group in the *TsIK* should categorically reject any proposals which tend towards the restoration of the old regime in press matters and should unreservedly support the Council of People's Commissars on this question against claims and importunities dictated by petty-bourgeoisie prejudices or by direct subservience to the interests of the counter-revolutionary bourgeoisie.

November 5 1917.

BULLETIN OF THE CC RSDLP(bolsheviks) No.8

Officers under the leadership of Purishkevich have been organising a new officer and junker conspiracy and setting up joint operations with Kaledin against the revolutionary soldiers, sailors and workers, simultaneously suggesting to the people through their aides that they should stop the terror against the bourgeoisie and give the counter-revolutionaries 'freedom' of action against the revolution Purishkevich was arrested on Sunday night. A letter to Kaledin was found on him. The CC has issued an appeal to all Party members and to all the working classes of Russia*, printed in yester-

---

* See p.144 of the present edition.

day's *Pravda* of November 6. The appeal says that in organising a Bolshevik government, the Party only executed the will of the Second All-Russian Congress of Soviets.

An offer was made to the Left S Rs to come into the government but they refused. The Second All-Russian Congress of Soviets approved a purely Bolshevik government list. It goes on to give a proper assessment of the resignation of Kamenev, Zinoviev, Nogin, Rykov and Miliutin from the CC and points out that their conduct is inadmissible for Party members and that they must either submit to the majority or promote their line outside Party ranks. The masses do not waver. All the proposals made by the conciliators only further Kornilovite subversion, as represented by Purishkevich and his officers' plot. The CC takes a firm stand on the principle of Soviet power, that is the power of the majority of the Soviets, and remains agreeable to sharing power with the minority provided that the minority loyally and honestly binds itself to submit to the majority and carry out the programme *approved by the whole* Second All-Russian Congress of Soviets. In conclusion, the CC appeals to the workers to be calm and steadfast because our Party, the Party of the Soviet majority, stands together and united in defence of their interests.

The troops in Finland and the Baltic fleet have all recognised the new government. During the revolution, order was not disturbed at all. Everywhere, agents of Kerensky's government were removed. Every institution has a commissar from the Finnish revolutionary organisations. Soon there is to be an all-Finland congress of the troops and workers to finally consolidate the gains of the revolution. The movement of the Finnish proletariat had our support in its strike.

The question of the food supply is extremely acute.

In Kiev, the junkers have surrendered. Power is held by the Soviets. In Kharkov and Belgrad [Belgorod], everything is quiet. The Kharkov producers' committee states that it is well supplied with mineral fuel. In Pskov, everything is quiet. A Military Revolutionary Committee has been formed. The garrison is on the side of the Soviets. It is decided that no troop formations are to be allowed into Pskov. Formations of cossacks have been sent back. Polish regiments in Belgorod, Tula province and at the Karavan station are on the side of the Military Revolutionary Committee. The Tenth Army welcomes the Military Revolutionary Committee. The first battery of the 129th artillery brigade welcomes the Military Revolutionary Committee and the Soviets and expresses its readiness to support them. Delegates from the 12th Army report that the vast majority of the Army is on the side of the Soviets. The Rights broke away at the All-Army Congress on October 28 and the Lefts united with the Military Revolutionary Committee. The Rights are threatening to send reinforcements to Kerensky if the Military Revolutionary Committee calls troop units out. A decision has been made to wait until the next All-Army Congress on November 15 and to send no forces without an order from the Military Revolutionary Committee.

Delegates from the Donets basin report that there are 600 cossacks in Makeevka and Dmitrovka and a hundred in the Chumkov mine. In the Kal'mius region, the military post has been removed under pressure from the workers. The workers are demanding the withdrawal of the cossacks by November 10 and are threatening to strike.

November 7 1917.

Published in the journal *Proletarskaia revoliutsiia* No.1,
1921 and No.4, 1922.
Printed from the originals kept in the archives of the IML,
f.17, *op*.1, *ed.khr*.91, *ll*.10-20.

Notes

The notes prepared by the Institute of Marxism-Leninism for the second Russian edition, Moscow, 1958, appear in roman type.

The additional notes prepared by Tony Cliff for the current edition appear in italic type.

1. The Moscow State Conference was called by the Provisional Government to mobilise the forces of the counter-revolution. The Conference was held on August 12-15 [25-28] 1917. The counter-revolutionary character of the Moscow State Conference was determined by its composition. According to data published in *Izvestiia TsI K i Petrogradskogo Soveta* of August 15 [28] 1917, 488 people attended the Conference from the State Duma of all four convocations; 129 from the Soviets and committees of public organisations; city dumas were given 147 seats; co-operatives 313; the army and navy 117; commercial and industrial circles and banks 150; trade unions 176; *zemstva* 118; peasants 100; scientific organisations 99; national organisations 58; the clergy 24, etc. The delegation from the Soviets consisted of Mensheviks and SRs. The Bolsheviks were barred from the Conference by the Central Executive Committee of the Soviets. Generals Kornilov, Alekseev, Kaledin and others presented a programme at the Conference for the suppression of the revolution. In his speech, the SR Kerensky threatened to crush the revolutionary movement by armed force and to stop attempts by the peasants to seize landed estates.

    The question of the attitude to take to the Moscow Conference was discussed by the Bolshevik Party Central Committee at the CC plenum of August 5 [18] and the sessions of August 6 and 20 [August 19 and September 2] 1917 (see pp. 12-13, 18, 19, 32).

2. The pre-Congress CC was the Party Central Committee elected at the Seventh All-Russian Conference of the RSDLP(b) in April 1917.

3. Rumours were already circulating at the beginning of August 1917 that Kamenev was a collaborator of the Kiev division of the Tsarist secret political police. On August 10 [23], this accusation against Kame-

nev appeared in bourgeois newspapers as an 'Announcement of the Ministry of Justice' of the Provisional Government. The *TsIK*, of which Kamenev was a member, set up a special commission consisting of Liber, Dan and Gots to investigate the matter. P.A.Dzhaparidze was delegated to the commission from the Party CC. The decision of the commission rehabilitating Kamenev after investigation was published by the praesidium of the *TsIK* in the newspaper *Rabochii* No.9 on August 31 [September 13] 1917. The Party did not hold an enquiry on this question. The Kamenev affair was discussed at the CC plenum of August 5 [18] and at the sessions of August 6 and 23 [August 19 and September 5] 1917 (see pp.12, 19, 35).

The insinuation regarding Kamenev is clear and nasty. Actually, on August 31 the VTsIK *accepted the conclusion of the commission of inquiry (published in* Rabochii*) restoring Kamenev to his former position. There was no Party inquiry as it was not thought necessary. Kamenev continued to be one of the most prominent Party leaders so long as Lenin was alive. He was a member of the Central Committee of the Party and its Political Bureau, deputy to Lenin as chairman of the Council of People's Commissars and chairman of the Moscow Soviet.*

4.   At the Sixth Congress of the RSDLP(b) (July 26-August 3) [August 8-16] 1917, a Central Committee of the RSDLP(b) of 21 members and 10 candidates was elected. Because the Congress took place in semi-legal circumstances and the Party was subjected to persecution by Kerensky's government, elections to the CC were held by a secret vote and the results were not made public at the Congress. Only the names of the four members who received the most votes were announced. The members of the Central Committee elected at the Sixth Congress included V.I.Lenin, Artem (F.A.Sergeev), Ia.A.Berzin, A.S.Bubnov, F.E. Dzerzhinsky, A.M.Kollontai, M.K.Muranov, V.P.Nogin, Ia.M.Sverdlov, I.V.Stalin, M.S.Uritsky, S.G.Shaumian and others. Elected as candidates were: P.A.Dzhaparidze, A.S.Kiselev, G.I.Lomov, N.A.Skrypnik, E.D.Stasova and others.

The four who received the highest vote to the Central Committee were the following: Lenin, 133 out of a possible 134; Zinoviev, 132; Trotsky, 131; Kamenev, 131.

5.   The inner membership of the CC was elected at the CC plenum of August 5 [18] 1917 (see p.12).

6.   The newspaper *Rabochii i soldat,* which came out instead of *Sol-datskaia pravda* as an organ of the Military Organisation under the CC RSDLP(b), replaced *Pravda,* which was banned by the Provisional Government and broken up during the July days of 1917. After this decision was passed, *Rabochii i soldat* was published as an organ of the CC RSDLP(b), the Petersburg Committee and the Military Organisation under the CC. The newspaper came out from July 23 to August 9 [August 5 to 22] 1917. Fifteen issues came out in all; it was closed by the Provisional Government on August 10 [23].

7.   The Military Organisation of the RSDLP(b) was formed under the Petersburg Committee in March 1917 for work among the troops in the Petrograd garrison. During April and May, military organisations were formed in military units at the front and at the rear. Once the Military Organisation had established contact with the provinces and the front and operated on the scale of the whole of Russia, the question arose at the CC session of April 10 [23] 1917 of transforming it into a military organisation attached to the CC RSDLP(b). From then on, the direction of its activity was under the control of the Central Committee. An All-Russian Conference of the Military Organisations was held in June and 26,000 Party members were represented. The Conference elected the All-Russian Central Bureau of the Military Organisations, which included: M.S.Kedrov, N.V.Krylenko, K.A.Mekhonoshin, V.I.Nevsky, N.I.Podvoisky and others.

8.   The journal *Vpered* was the organ of the Petrograd Inter-District Committee of the United Social Democrats.

The Inter-District Committee started in Petersburg in 1913 under the name 'the Inter-District Commission of the RSDLP'. At the end of 1914, the Commission was renamed 'the Inter-District Committee'. The organisation included supporters of Trotsky, the *Vpered* people, some of the Mensheviks and former Bolshevik appeasers who had broken away from the Party. The Inter-District Committee set itself the objective of forming a 'united RSDLP' through conciliation and the unification of different political currents inside the social democrats and splinter groups.

During the years of the imperialist war, the Inter-District Committee took a centrist position, proclaiming internationalist slogans in words while at the same time continuing to insist on unification, meaning in practice capitulation to social chauvinism. After the February revolution in 1917, the *Mezhraiontsy* declared that they agreed with the Bolshevik Party line and said they wanted to join the Party. At the Sixth Congress, the *Mezhraiontsy* were accepted into the Party ranks. *Mezhraiontsy* who joined the Party included M.M.Volodarsky, M.S.Uritsky, D.Z. Manuilsky and others, who had genuinely become Bolsheviks. Trotsky temporarily concealed his differences with the Bolsheviks and joined the Party in the hope of 'debolshevising' the Party from within. Trotsky and his supporters inside the Party continued the struggle against Lenin's line and were later driven out of the Party ranks for active anti-Party and anti-Soviet activity.

The journal *Vpered* came out once as an organ of the CC RSDLP(b) after this decision was approved – No.9 of September 2 [15] 1917. There was also discussion on the subject of the journal *Vpered* at the CC sessions of August 8 and 20 [August 21 and September 2]. After a decision by the CC on September 6 [19], the journal *Vpered* was closed (see pp.21, 32, 49).

A note in the first edition of Lenin's Collected Works *(vol.14, p.488) characterised the* Mezhraiontsy *in this way 'On the war question, the* Mezhraiontsy *held an internationalist position and in their tactics they were close to the Bolsheviks.'*

Among the leaders of the Mezhraiontsy *there were a number of people destined to play a central role in the October revolution and the Soviet regime following it: Trotsky, Lunacharsky, Ioffe, Uritsky, Iurenev, Riazanov, Karakhan, Manuilsky and others.*

9. *Rabotnitsa* was a journal of the CC RSDLP(b) devoted to issues of work among women. The journal appeared first in 1914; it was closed at the beginning of the imperialist war. Publication of the journal was resumed in 1917 (No.1-2 came out on May 10 [23]) and 12 issues came out in all for that year. The journal came out intermittently up to 1923. Since 1923, *Rabotnitsa* has been published regularly.

10. Elected to the editorial board were: Ko[ba] – Stalin, Kov – Sokolnikov, Min – Miliutin. The collegium of contributors under the editorial board of the Party's central organ was organised in such a way that each of its members was in charge of a particular section of the newspaper. The membership of the collegium of contributors and the allocation to sections were confirmed at the CC session of August 20 [September 2] 1917 (see pp.31-32).

11.   The question of Bolshevik participation in an international conference of socialist parties arose in April 1917. The Danish social chauvinist Borgbjerg, who was pro-German, came to Petrograd and on behalf of the United Committee of Labour Parties of Denmark, Sweden and Norway invited the Russian socialist parties to attend a so-called 'peace conference' of socialists to be held in Stockholm. The Mensheviks and S Rs accepted Borgbjerg's offer. The Seventh (April) All-Russian Conference of Bolsheviks, at Lenin's proposal, declared itself definitely against participation in the Stockholm Conference and exposed Borgbjerg as an agent of German imperialism. The Conference stated in its resolution that 'the Conference considers that it is inadmissible on principle for our Party to attend a Conference where Borgbjerg and Scheidemann are taking part for it is not our task to unify the direct or indirect agents of the various imperialist governments but the workers of all countries who, even in wartime, are carrying on the revolutionary fight with their own imperialist governments' (see *KPSS v rezoliutsiiakh i resheniiakh s'ezdov, konferentsii i plenumov TsK*, 7th ed., part 1, p.342). The Stockholm Conference was postponed several times and in the end was not held.

The subject of the Stockholm Conference was also raised at the C C sessions of August 8 and 16 [21 and 29] 1917 (see pp.22, 27).

12.   The Conference on the Defence of the Country was organised by the *TsI K* elected at the First Congress of Soviets and took place in Petrograd on August 7-8 [20-21] 1917. Calling the Conference was an attempt by the defensist Mensheviks and S Rs to attract the support of mass democratic organisations for the Provisional Government's imperialist policy of continuing the war. More than 600 representatives attended the Conference: from Soviets, city dumas, trade unions, cooperatives and other organisations. As a result of the decision at this plenum and those passed at the C C sessions of August 6 and 8 [19 and 21] (see pp. 18, 21), the Bolsheviks made a declaration at the Conference denouncing the Mensheviks and S Rs for the direct help they were giving to the bourgeoisie in its effort to drag out the imperialist war. The declaration was made in the name of the CC RSDLP(b), the CCs of the Polish and Lithuanian Social Democrats, the CC of the Latvian Social Democrats and of the Bolshevik groups of: the *TsI K*, the Petrograd Soviet of Workers' and Soldiers' Deputies, the Moscow City Duma, the Moscow Regional Bureau of the Soviets of Workers', Soldiers' and Peasants' Deputies. The Central Council of the Trade Unions also associated itself

with the political section of the Bolshevik declaration. After the declaration had been read out, the representatives of the organisations which had signed it walked out of the Conference.

13. The Sixth Congress of the RSDLP(b) decided that a manifesto should be issued 'To all working people, to all the workers, soldiers and peasants of Russia' and instructed the Central Committee to draw it up and publish it in the name of the Congress. The draft manifesto was considered at the CC plenum of August 5 [18] 1917 (see p.12). The manifesto was published in the Party's central organ, the newspaper *Proletarii* No. 1, August 13 [26] 1917 (see also *KPSS v rezoliutsiiakh i resheniiakh s'ezdov, konferentsii i plenumov TsK*, 7th ed., part 1, pp.389-394).

14. The CC usually allocated its members to the regions in which they had worked before. Special attention was given to strengthening workers' centres and regions. According to information given by representatives of Party organisations at the Sixth Congress of the RSDLP(b), in 1917 the Moscow Regional Bureau of the RSDLP(b) covered 13 provinces of the Central-Industrial region. In 1917, there were up to 58,000 Party members in organisations in this region. The Urals Regional Committee of the RSDLP(b) in 1917 brought together up to 25,000 Party members, chiefly workers. In July 1917, the Donetsk organisation had 16,000 Party members. In the Caucasus, large Bolshevik organisations existed in Baku, Groznyi, and Tiflis. The Baku and Grosnyi organisations consisted of workers, but soldiers predominated in the Tiflis organisation because of the large garrison. In Finland (the towns of Abo, Helsingfors, Vyborg), the Party organisation, which included a significant section of the sailors in the Baltic fleet in its membership, was one of the strongest in 1917; it had more than 5,000 members.

15. This refers to the manifesto of the Sixth Congress of the RSDLP (b).

16. The Bolsheviks were excluded from membership of the *TsIK* delegation to the Moscow State Conference. Signatories of the declaration drawn up by decision of the CC for reading out at the Conference were, in addition to the Bolsheviks not allowed in, Bolshevik delegates to the Moscow Conference from the city local government, the trade unions, workers' cooperatives, the union of city employees, the army and navy committees and others. The Bolsheviks gave their declaration to the Conference praesidium to be read out but it was not read out. Its text was published in the newspaper *Proletarii* No.4, August 17 [30] 1917.

17.   This evidently refers to the publication of the Party Central Committee's appeal on the State Conference in individual leaflets. The CC appeal was printed first on the opening day of the Conference – August 12 [25] in the newspaper *Proletarskoe delo* No.26, the organ of the RSDLP (b) group in the Kronstadt Soviet, and then in the Party Central Committee's newspaper *Proletarii* No.1, August 13 [26] 1917. The CC appeal used as its text the leading article 'Against the Moscow Conference' in the newspaper *Rabochii i soldat* No.14 of August 8 [21] 1917, written by I.V.Stalin (see *Sochineniia*, vol.3, pp.193 - 195), with a few changes.

18.   The resolution of the Central Committee of the RSDLP(b) on the Moscow Conference was passed at the CC session on August 6 [19] (see p.19) and printed in the newspaper *Rabochii i soldat* No.14, August 8 [21] 1917.

19.   The following articles and materials devoted to the Moscow Conference were published in the Party's central organ from August 8 to 17 [21 to 30] 1917; 'Against the Moscow Conference' – in the newspaper *Rabochii i soldat* No.14; 'Where the Moscow Conference will lead', 'Moscow on strike', 'The Petrograd proletariat and the Moscow Conference' (the resolution of the Second All-City Conference of Factory Committees and the resolution of the Regional Soviet of Workers' and Soldiers' Deputies of the Petrograd area), 'Two paths', 'The truth will be told' and 'Results of the Moscow Conference' – in the newspaper *Proletarii*, Nos.1, 2, 4. The author of four of these articles was I.V.Stalin (see *Sochineniia*, vol.3, pp.193 - 195, 200 - 205, 210 - 213, 214 - 216).

20.   The biggest workers' protest action against the Moscow Conference occurred in Moscow. At the appeal of the Bolsheviks' Moscow Committee, Moscow workers greeted the opening of the State Conference on August 12 [25] 1917 with a mass strike of more than 400,000 people. It was not only the factories and workshops which did not work on that day but the trams stopped, too. Even the cooks serving the Conference delegates went on strike. The strike found an echo in other Russian towns, too.

21.   This refers to the Azerbaidzhan social-democratic group *Gummet* (Energy), which the Baku Committee of the RSDLP decided to form in 1904 and which was part of the Baku Bolshevik organisation and worked under its direction. At the Sixth Party Congress, the chairman of *Gummet* A.B.Iusif-zade and P.A.Dzhaparidze (Alesha) moved that it should

be given material help and other support from the Party Central Committee. The motion was passed unanimously.

In the summer of 1919 there was a split in the *Gummet* organisation. A small Menshevik group, which had slipped into positions hostile to the proletariat, left it. The *Gummet* Bolshevik group and the Baku organisation of the *RKP(b)* merged in 1920 and formed the Communist Party (bolsheviks) of Azerbaidzhan.

22.   Until this CC decision, the Kazan Bolshevik organisation, which numbered 650 members in July 1917, was included among the Volga organisations.

23.   As in the first edition of the collection, in all cases here and elsewhere in the minutes where there are gaps in the items on the agenda for a CC session, the editors have taken out of the minutes disputed matters (Ia.S.Ganetsky, M.Iu.Kozlovsky and others), which were discussed at eight sessions in all. The short, fragmentary minute notes on these matters do not contain enough material to bring out the essence of the questions under discussion.

24.   The Party Central Committee rejected the proposal to boycott the Moscow Conference called by the Provisional Government for August 12 1917 (see p.12 of this edition). The minutes of the Petersburg Committee meeting of August 5 [18] mentioned here have not been found.

25.   The Second Conference of Petrograd Factory Committees was held on August 7-12 [20-25] 1917. About 400 delegates attended, including representatives from Novgorod and other provincial factory committees. Delegates took an active part in discussing reports on the current situation, control over production, unemployment and the other questions on the agenda. In their speeches, the factory workers declared their readiness to join forces and repulse the capitalists who were trying to crush the revolutionary struggle of the working class by the skeletal hand of starvation. The Conference took its lead from the Bolsheviks and passed the resolution 'The current situation and workers' control' moved by CC RSDLP(b) representatives in the spirit of the decisions made by the Sixth Bolshevik Party Congress.

26.   The Second Petrograd All-City Insurance Conference, which took place on August 21-23 [September 3-5] 1917. 162 delegates with a

deliberative vote and 40 delegates with a consultative vote took part in the Conference. There were reports at the Conference on the current situation and social insurance, dealing with such questions as unemployment insurance, changes in the insurance laws, etc. The Conference took place under Bolshevik influence. In its resolution on the report on the current situation, the Conference stressed that social insurance for the benefit of the workers could only be achieved if power was transferred into the hands of the proletariat and the poor peasantry.

27. A reference to the decision of the CC plenum of August 4 [17] 1917 on the membership of the editorial board of the CC organ – the newspaper *Rabochii i soldat* (see p.10).

28. This is about reviving publication of the monthly social and political Bolshevik journal *Prosveshchenie* which appeared in Petersburg from 1911 and was banned by the Tsar's government in 1914. Only one double number of the journal came out in 1917 (September-October). The question of the journal comes up in later CC sessions as well (see pp.21, 32, 50, 76).

29. The Orgburo gives information about the organisation of the group to work in the trade unions in its report at the CC session of August 31 [September 13] 1917 (see p.44).

30. The Electoral Commission for the Constituent Assembly selected a list of candidates the Party CC recommended for the Constituent Assembly and made preparations for the elections. Decisions on the commission's reports were taken by the CC at sessions on September 23 and 29 [October 6 and 12] 1917 (see pp.70, 75).

31. A representative of the Party CC was sent to Helsingfors to direct the work of the Russian Party organisations in Finland – in the garrisons stationed there and in the Baltic fleet.

32. After the CC decision on August 6 [19] 1917 to renew publication of a Bolshevik theoretical journal (see p.18), the choice lay between two names – *Prosveshchenie* and *Kommunist*.

The only number of *Kommunist*, a double one, was published in Geneva by the editorial board of the newspaper *Sotsial-demokrat* and came out on August 29-30 [September 11-12] 1915. Lenin carried on a struggle within the *Kommunist* editorial board against the Bukharin-Piatakov anti-Party group (the so-called 'Beaugis group') who tried to use the journal for sectional purposes. At Lenin's suggestion, relations were broken off with this group and joint publication of the journal halted. After October 1916, the editorial board of the newspaper *Sotsial-demokrat* began to publish *Sbornik sotsial-demokrata* instead of *Kommunist*.

Bukharin and Piatakov had the same position on the national question as Rosa Luxemburg. They argued that to preach the right of national self-determination would weaken the international solidarity of the proletariat and would nurture illusions among the workers of separate nations that they could achieve their liberation under capitalism. Hence Bukharin spoke about 'self-determination for the workers'. This is not the place to juxtapose to this formulation Lenin's position regarding the right of self-determination of nations. However, it is clear that the editors of the note above completely distorted Bukharin's and Piatakov's position. Again, one must mention the fact that Bukharin and Piatakov were among the few Bolsheviks abroad who supported Lenin's position of 'revolutionary defeatism' during the war.

33. The list of candidates for the Petrograd Central City Duma put forward by the Party Central Committee, the Petersburg Committee, the Military Organisation under the CC RSDLP(b), and also by the CC of the Polish and Lithuanian Social-Democrats and the CC of the Latvian Social-Democrats was published in the newspaper *Proletarii* No.4 of August 17 [30] 1917. The election of the Petrograd Duma members was held on August 20 [September 2] 1917. The election showed the further growth of Bolshevik Party influence among the masses. 183,000 votes were cast for the Bolshevik list and they received 33 per cent of the places in the Duma.

34. The appeals from the Petersburg Committee of the RSDLP(b) to the workers, soldiers and women were issued as leaflets the day before the elections (see *Listovki petrogradskikh bol'shevikov. 1917-1920,* vol.3, Lenizdat, 1957, pp.64-71). Bolshevik Party appeals to workers, soldiers, women workers and soldiers' wives to vote for the Bolshevik list at the election of the Petrograd City Duma were also printed in the newspaper *Proletarii* No.7, August 20 [September 2] 1917.

35. In the July days of 1917, the ballerina Kshesinskaia's palace where the Petersburg Committee was located was raided by junkers. During the search, almost all the Petersburg Committee materials were taken away by the Provisional Government's security services.

36. M.M.Volodarsky was taken on to the editorial board of the Party's central organ from the Petersburg Committee of the RSDLP(b) as a result of the CC plenum decision of August 4 [17] [1917] (see p.10).

37. This refers to the question which was first raised by the CC of suspending S.Ia.Bagdat'ev from Party work for arranging a meeting on his own initiative at Kshesinskaia's palace in May 1917 and for other disorganising actions which violated Party decisions.

S.Ia.Bagdat'ev was secretary of the Bolshevik Party Committee in the Putilov factory, a leading member of the Petersburg Committee of the Party and a candidate for the Central Committee at the Seventh Party Conference (April 24-29 1917). He was credited with having prepared a leaflet over the signature of the Petersburg Committee appealing for the immediate overthrow of the Provisional Government and having it circulated on April 21 and he was largely responsible for the appearance among the demonstrators of the 'Down with the Provisional Government' banners. Lenin criticised Bagdat'ev's stand as ultra-left, but a special investigating commission set up by the Petersburg Committee exonerated him and he still played a very prominent role in the Party. He took a leading part in the July days, again showing ultra-left tendencies. In the days of reaction after the July days, Bagdat'ev found himself together with other leading Bolsheviks in Kresty prison.

38. Members of the Petersburg Committee were elected at regional Party meetings at the beginning of 1917; each region delegated one representative for 400 Party members. New elections to the Petersburg Committee were held in August. The Petrograd All-City Conference, which reorganised the Petersburg Committee, took place in October 1917.

39. Some of the Bolsheviks arrested by the Provisional Government after the July days of 1917 were held in the Petrograd prison of Kresty without charges being preferred. A hunger strike was declared in Kresty

on August 7 [20]. An appeal 'To the Petrograd workers' about organising a protest campaign against the behaviour of the authorities was printed in the newspaper *Rabochii i soldat* No.15, August 9 [22] 1917.

Among the leading Bolsheviks incarcerated in Kresty were Trotsky and Lunacharsky.

40.   This refers to the legal proceedings planned by the Provisional Government implicating the Bolsheviks in the July 1917 demonstration.

41.   In the discussion on the Stockholm Conference at the *TsIK* session of August 6 [19] 1917, Kamenev spoke in favour of participation in the Conference and demanded that the Bolshevik Party decisions on this question be reviewed. The Bolshevik group in the *TsIK* disassociated themselves from Kamenev's speech at the session. In his letter to the editorial board of the newspaper *Proletarii*, 'Kamenev's speech in the *TsIK* on the Stockholm Conference', published in No.3, August 16 [29] 1917, V.I.Lenin exposed and condemned Kamenev's anti-Party attack (see V.I.Lenin, *Sochineniia*, 4th ed., vol.25, pp.219-221).

42.   The leading article 'More about Stockholm' was published in *Rabochii i soldat* No.15 of August 9 [22] 1917; its author is I.V.Stalin (see *Sochineniia*, vol.3, pp.196-199).

43.   This refers to the fact that even before the Sixth Party Congress, Kamenev considered that it was necessary for Lenin to appear in court. The question of whether Lenin should attend a court of the counter-revolutionary Provisional Government was discussed at the Sixth Party Congress. The Congress was unanimous in expressing itself against Lenin's appearance in court, taking the view that this would not be a court but a reprisal.

Compare the above with the reminiscences of Krupskaia: 'On the 7th (July) Maria Ilyinishna (Lenin's sister) and I went to visit Ilyich at Alliluev's house. This was just the moment when Ilyich wavered. He argued that he ought to surrender to the authorities and appear in court. Maria Ilyinishna objected violently. "Gregory and I have decided to appear, go and tell Kamenev", Ilyich said to me. At that time Kamenev was staying nearby at another flat. I hastily made ready to go. "Let us say goodbye," Vladimir Ilyich said, stopping me – "We may not see each other again." We embraced. I went to Kamenev and delivered Vladimir Ilyich's message.' (N.Krupskaia, Memories of Lenin, *London, 1970, pp.310-11)*

44. This is the Party printing press *Trud* which was bought in the spring of 1917 with the proceeds of collections among the workers. On July 6 [19], a detachment of junkers raided the printing press and also the editorial offices of the newspaper *Pravda,* and the press was destroyed.

Priboi was a Bolshevik legal publication which was founded in 1912 and after a break (1914-1917) took up its activity again in March 1917.

45. This CC decision on *Soldat* was reviewed at the session of August 16 [29] (see p.28). The newspaper *Soldat* came out from August 13 [26] until October 26 [November 8] 1917 as the organ of the Military Organisation under the CC RSDLP(b).

Proletarii – the central organ of the Party which replaced *Rabochii i soldat,* banned by the Provisional Government, began to come out from August 13 [26]. Ten numbers came out in all. On August 24 [September 6] 1917, the newspaper *Proletarii* was closed by the Provisional Government.

46. This evidently refers to a financial statement to be made by the Military Organisation which organised the publication of *Rabochii i soldat* up to the time when the newspaper began to fulfil the functions of a central organ. The Military Organisation's financial report was presented to the CC for the session of August 23 [September 5] 1917 (see p.35).

47. On the eve of the Moscow State Conference, August 8-10 [21-23] 1917, a so-called 'private conference of public figures' was held in Moscow. A 'bureau for the organisation of social forces' was elected at the conference and in August 1917 it was the legal centre for the counter-revolution. Because of possible counter-revolutionary action, a secret revolutionary committee of the Moscow Soviet was also formed in Moscow and worked to get armed forces ready for a struggle against the counter-revolution. As we know, Kornilov's attack occurred two weeks later.

48. Most of the *TsIK* members were in Moscow for the State Conference at this time. The *TsIK* members who were still in Petrograd selected an information bureau from among themselves because of the rumours of an imminent counter-revolutionary attack.

49.   A resolution by the Bolshevik group in the Petrograd Soviet under the title 'On the Stockholm Conference' was published in the newspaper *Proletarii* No.6 of August 19 [September 1] 1917. This, in all probability, is the resolution which this CC decision talks of drawing up.

50.   The conference of Zimmerwaldists – the third Zimmerwald Conference – was held on August 23 - 30 [September 5 - 12] 1917. A resolution favouring Bolshevik participation was adopted at the Seventh (April) Party Conference. V.I.Lenin disagreed with this decision since he considered that by remaining in the Zimmerwald Union, the Bolshevik Party was helping to postpone the creation of a Third International. He accepted Bolshevik participation in the conference of Zimmerwaldists as possible only for information purposes and wrote about the subject again in his booklet, 'The tasks of the proletariat in our revolution' and in a postscript to the booklet written in May 1917 (see *Sochineniia,* 4th ed., vol.24, pp.60, 66 - 67). Lenin noted that the mistake made by the April Conference on taking part in Zimmerwald had been half corrected by the CC decision published on May 12 [25] 1917. At Lenin's suggestion, the Party CC resolved 'to send a delegate to the Zimmerwald Conference which is being called and instruct him to walk out of this Conference immediately and withdraw from the Zimmerwald Union if the Conference expresses itself in favour of any kind of rapprochement or joint discussion of affairs with social-chauvinists' (see *ibid.,* p.353). The representatives of the CC RSDLP(b) at the Conference were V.V.Vorovsky and N.A.Semashko. They introduced a motion for a discussion of the situation in Russia and Kerensky's bonapartist policy and the adoption of a resolution giving 'a guarantee that preconditions must be satisfied for any kind of joint work'. This motion was rejected. The membership of the parties and groups taking part in the Conference was characterised by V.I.Lenin in an outline for an article, 'The tasks of our Party in the International. (Apropos of the Third Zimmerwald Conference)' (see *Sochineniia,* 4th ed., vol.26, pp.189 - 191).

51.   This refers to the Second Petrograd All-City Insurance Conference (see also p.18 of the present edition).

52.   Some of the leaders of the Central Bureau of the Military Organisations (Nevsky, Podvoisky and others) showed a tendency in 1917 to evade Central Committee direction. The Party CC confirmed this decision at the session of August 23 [September 5] 1917 (see p.35) and took a

series of organisational measures to strengthen CC direction over all the activity of the Military Organisation.

53. This warning to D.B.Riazanov is because he aligned himself during the imperialist war with the centrists, Kautsky, Trotsky, Martov and others, who justified and defended the overt social-chauvinists. Riazanov spoke against the line followed by the Zimmerwald Left group, which was formed on V.I.Lenin's initiative in early September 1915 at the first conference of Internationalists at Zimmerwald.

When the war broke out, Trotsky published a sharp anti-war pamphlet in German called War and the International, *for which he was condemned to imprisonment in his absence. Then he was deported from France for anti-war activity, arrested in Spain and deported to the United States. He carried on internationalist work in New York, participating with Bolsheviks in the editing of the newspaper* Novyi mir.

On 1st October 1914 Lenin said about Golos, *the paper Trotsky edited in Paris, that it was '... now the best socialist paper in Europe' (Lenin,* Collected Works, *translated from the Russian 4th edition, vol.36, p.300).*

Regarding D.B.Riazanov, we have only to mention that he was one of the greatest scholars of Marx's works and a member of the Mezhraiontsy *(see note to Note 8).*

54. A reference to the Party printing press *Trud*. What had to be put in order at the printing works and dispatch has not been established.

55. The resolution on the Moscow Conference was moved by the Bolshevik group in the Petrograd Soviet at the Soviet's session of August 21 [September 3] 1917 and rejected by the Menshevik and SR bloc.

56. *Novaia zhizn'*, a Menshevik-inclined newspaper, came out first in April 1917. A group of 'internationalist' social-democrats and a number of isolated intellectuals from among the writers and others gathered round it. The *Novaia zhizn'* group constantly vacillated between the conciliators and the Bolsheviks. The *Novozhiznentsy* were opposed to the establishment of a dictatorship of the proletariat and the poor peasantry, and to the introduction of workers' control over production; although they called themselves Internationalists, they did not break with the Menshevik defensists and advanced schemes for a reconciliation between

the imperialist and the revolutionary internationalist elements. After the October socialist revolution, the newspaper *Novaia zhizn'* took an anti-Soviet position and was closed in July 1918.

In 1917, A.V.Lunacharsky, M.S.Uritsky and a number of other Bolshevik Party members contributed to *Novaia zhizn'*. As a result of the decision made at this session, Uritsky published a statement on August 26 [September 28] 1917 in the Party's central organ, the newspaper *Rabochii*, withdrawing his name from the list of contributors to *Novaia zhizn'*. Later, at the sessions of August 30 [September 12], September 6 [19] and October 5 [18], the Party's CC confirmed the decision which obliged Party members to give up contributing to *Novaia zhizn'* (see pp.38, 51, 77).

Novaia zhizn' was Maxim Gorky's daily anti-war paper. Between April and September 1917 it was the mouthpiece of the Menshevik internationalists led by Martov and the Right Bolsheviks. While the Menshevik and Socialist-Revolutionary press were untouched by the authorities, the Bolshevik Rabochii *and* Novaia zhizn' *were closed down.*

57.   The issue of the money collections arranged by the *TsIK* to mark the first six months of the February revolution was also considered at the CC session of August 23 [September 5] 1917 (see p.35).

58.   The statement referred to was made by Riazanov at the session of the Petrograd Soviet on August 19 [September 1] 1917. As was reported in the newspaper *Novaia zhizn'* No.106, August 20 [September 2], Riazanov declared during the discussion in the Soviet about the arrest of Bolsheviks that Lenin and Zinoviev 'will appear in court at their own time'.

59.   It has not been possible to discover what manifesto is referred to in the minutes.

60.   An allusion to the CC decision taken at the session of August 20 [September 2] 1917 (see pp.32-33).

61.   Because they wanted a cover for Kornilov's counter-revolutionary plot, the bourgeois press assiduously spread rumours in August 1917 that an armed rising was being prepared under the direction of the Bolsheviks.

In particular, the Kadet Party newspaper *Rech'* wrote that the Bolshevik group in the Petrograd Soviet was taking the initiative in such a move. Denying this libel, the Bolshevik group in the Soviet published a statement pointing out that the report by *Rech'* and other bourgeois newspapers was an attempt by the counter-revolution to provoke the broad masses of workers and soldiers into an active attack. 'The group', said the statement, 'recalls our Congress decisions that "the proletariat must not succumb to provocation by the counter-revolution, which *at this moment* would very much like to stir it into a premature fight" . . . , advises all comrades to close ranks tightly round the Central Committee of the Russian SDLP' (see *Rabochii* No.1, August 25 [September 7] 1917.)

62.   The CC decision on the functions and rights of the All-Russian Central Bureau of the Military Organisations was adopted at the session of August 16 [29] 1917 (see p.28).

63.   As is evident from the CC minutes preserved, it was not a plenum which was held on September 3 [16] but an ordinary session of the Central Committee. A session for the CC members at large took place on August 31 [September 13] 1917.

64.   The 'Committee for the People's Struggle against Counter-revolution' was organised by the *TsIK* of the Soviets at the session of August 27 [September 9] 1917 when the Kornilov revolt had begun. The Committee's membership included representatives of the praesidiums of the *TsIK* and the Executive Committee of the Soviet of Peasants' Deputies (5 each); representatives from the CCs of the Bolshevik Party and the Menshevik and SR Parties (3 each); the All-Russian Council of Trade Unions (2); the Petrograd Council of Trade Unions (1); the Petrograd Soviet of Workers' and Soldiers' Deputies (2) and others. The Bolsheviks joined the Committee for purposes of information, retaining full independence for their political line. Because conciliators predominated in it, the Committee's position in relation to the Kornilov plot was indecisive. In the days of Kornilov's mutiny, the Mensheviks and SRs did not so much fight against Kornilov as protect Kornilov's allies. They supported Kerensky when, having removed Kornilov from the post of Commander-in-chief, he put Alekseev, Ruzky, Dragomirov and other counter-revolutionary generals who supported Kornilov into leading posts in the army. The *TsIK*'s conciliating line prompted the question of a Bolshevik withdrawal from the Committee for Struggle against Counter-

revolution. But the proposal to leave the Committee was not adopted by the Party's CC, which considered that only if the *TsIK* moved over to the side of the counter-revolution on key issues – power and arming the workers – would it become necessary to break with it. The *TsIK* was forced to agree to the workers being armed for the fight against the Kornilov revolt. At the appeal of the Bolshevik Party CC, the workers took to arms and during the time of the Kornilov mutiny the number of Red Guard detachments grew several times over.

65.   The question of the political situation was discussed at the session of the Central Committee in its enlarged membership on August 31 [September 13] 1917, when a resolution on power was adopted (see p.42).

66.   The first session of the newly-elected Petrograd City Duma took place on September 1 [14] 1917. A.V.Lunacharsky read out the declaration on behalf of the Duma's Bolshevik group at this session.

67.   Out of a total number of 200 seats in the Petrograd City Duma, the most belonged to the Bolsheviks (67) and the SRs (75). The Kadet Party along with its allies the Trudoviks and representatives of the Plekhanov group 'Unity' had about 50 seats in all. The Bolshevik proposal to boycott the Kadets – to prevent their representatives being elected to the praesidium of the Duma and to the municipal administration (in charge of the Petrograd economy) – gave the SRs the choice: to support the boycott or vote for the Kadets. The SRs rejected the boycott and during the elections helped the Kadets to get their representatives into the Duma's executive organs.

The CC also discussed the question of the elections to the Petrograd city administration at the sessions of September 3 and 6 [16 and 19] 1917 (see pp.45-46, 51).

68.   The Bolshevik group in the Petrograd City Duma included such members of the Party's CC as Ia.M.Sverdlov, M.K.Muranov and M.S. Uritsky.

69.   A joint session of representatives of the Petrograd Council of Trade Unions, of the Central Council of Factory Committees, and also of the Executive Committee of the Petrograd Soviet was convened on the initiative of the *TsIK* on August 22 [September 4] 1917. The subject for discussion was the events on the Riga front, the danger created for

Petrograd and the protection of factories by the workers. The Bolsheviks made the demand for serious measures to be taken to combat the counter-revolution. In their resolution, the Bolsheviks suggested sending the counter-revolutionary generals away from Petrograd, putting the garrison under the control of the Petrograd Soviet, organising a workers' guard capable of protecting the city, etc. Riazanov came out with a statement that the session had been called with a special narrow purpose and should not take political decisions. As a result, the session closed without passing a resolution.

70.   The Bolsheviks read out the resolution 'On power' at the session of the *TsIK* of the Soviets on August 31 [September 13] 1917 but it was rejected by the SR-Menshevik bloc. On the very same day, the Bolshevik group in the Petrograd Soviet proposed the resolution 'On power' at a joint session of the Petrograd Soviet of Workers' and Soldiers' Deputies. On the night of September 1 [14], the Soviet passed the Bolshevik resolution by 279 votes to 115 (with 50 abstaining). On September 5 [18], the Moscow Soviet also passed the Bolshevik resolution 'On power' (by 354 to 252).

71.   *Rabochii* was the Bolshevik Party central organ which came out from August 25 [September 7] to September 2 [15] 1917 instead of the Bolshevik newspaper *Proletarii*, closed by the Provisional Government. 12 numbers came out in all.
     This reference to the newspaper in the minutes apparently means that it was planned to publish the text of the resolution 'On power' in *Rabochii* after the CC session. The resolution was printed in the newspaper *Rabochii* No.10, September 1 [14] 1917.

72.   A CC decision of August 23 [September 5] 1917 fixed the plenum of the Party Central Committee for September 3 [16] (see p.35). No information that it took place has been found.
     V.I.Lenin, in hiding in Finland at that time, took part in the preparation for the CC plenum. The 'Draft resolution on the current political situation' and the letter 'On the Zimmerwald issue' were written by V.I.Lenin for the plenum (see *Sochineniia*, 4th ed., vol.25, pp.288-294, 280).

73.   The municipal group under the CC RSDLP(b) was organised in September 1917 to direct the municipal work of all the Party organisa-

tions in Russia. The work of forming the group was headed by Ia.M. Sverdlov. The Party CC confirmed the membership of the municipal group and took other decisions about its activity at the session of September 20 [October 3] (see p.66).

The Petrograd municipal group was organised then, too. A meeting of Bolshevik councillors of the central and district dumas of Petrograd took place in the City Duma on September 10 [23] 1917. Following Ia.M.Sverdlov's report and suggestions, the meeting passed decisions to institute a permanent conference of central and district duma councillors as a directing organ for municipal work in Petrograd and to form a Petrograd Bolshevik municipal committee.

74.   CC members were not chosen for the North-West and Southern regions and the Volga area in the allocation of CC members to regions by the plenum of August 5 [18] 1917. No materials have been found on the group of travelling CC agents.

75.   The All-Russian Democratic Conference called by the Mensheviks and SRs in the name of the *TsIK* of the Soviets was held in Petrograd from September 14 to 22 [September 27 to October 5] 1917. More than 1500 people attended the Conference. The Mensheviks and SRs selected the composition of the Democratic Conference in such a way as to assure themselves of an overwhelming majority. Thus, extra representation was given to city governments (300 seats), *zemstva* (200 seats), cooperatives under the control of the Mensheviks and SRs (120 seats) and the cossacks (33 seats). Meanwhile, organisations where the Bolshevik Party had the majority in September had their representation cut: for example, the Soviets had 230 seats, the trade unions – 100, workers' cooperatives – 38, the navy – 15. The organisers of the Conference saw it as their aim to weaken the growing revolutionary upsurge. With the help of the Pre-Parliament (the Provisional Council of the Republic) chosen by the Democratic Conference, the Mensheviks and SRs meant to shift the country away from the path of Soviet revolution on to a course of bourgeois-constitutional development.

The Central Committee considered the subject of its attitude to the Democratic Conference and the Pre-Parliament later on at the sessions of September 6, 13, 21, 23, 29 [September 19, 26, October 4, 6 and 12] and October 5 [18] 1917 (see pp.50, 52, 67, 68-69, 75-76, 78).

76.   This telegram signed by the CC was sent to 37 local party organisa-

tions on September 3 [16] 1917 (see the collection *Perepiska Sekretariata TsK RSDRP(b) s mestnymi partiinymi organizatsiiami,* Moscow, 1957, part 1, p.34).

77.   At the time when elections to the executive organs of the Petrograd City Duma were being held, the Bolsheviks had to keep up a persistent struggle with the SRs, who had in practice formed an alliance with the Kadets and representatives of the Plekhanov group 'Unity'. The election of three Assistant (Deputy) Mayors was held at the Duma session of September 4 [17] 1917. From the Bolsheviks, A.V.Lunacharsky was elected a Deputy Mayor. With the support of the SRs, the Kadets succeeded in getting in their candidate, Knipovich. Artem'ev (a 'non-party socialist') was elected as the third. The election of members of the city administration was held at the Duma session of September 11 [24]. Under pressure from the Bolshevik group, which had been active in exposing the SRs' alliance with the Kadets, and in fear of the electors, the SRs were forced to change their position when they voted on Bolshevik candidates. Six people joined the city administration from the Bolsheviks, including: D.Z.Manuilsky, P.A.Kobozev and I.A.Teodorovich. There was also discussion about the City Duma regarding the election of members of the administration at the CC session of September 6 [19] (see p.51).

78.   In what connection the question of the Shluesselburg factory was raised has not been established.

79.   In September 1917, the central organ of the Bolshevik Party came out under the title of *Rabochii put'*. The newspaper *Rabochii put'* replaced the newspaper *Rabochii* closed by the Provisional Government and came out from September 3 [16] to October 26 [November 8] 1917.

80.   This refers to the journal *Vpered,* published by decision of the CC plenum of August 4 [17] 1917 (see p.10). The journal's only number came out on September 2 [15] 1917.

81.   This CC decision changed the membership of the editorial board of the journal *Prosveshchenie* confirmed at the session of August 20 [September 2] 1917 (see p.32).

82.   The Petrograd Soviet of Workers' and Soldiers' Deputies elected V.I.Lenin a delegate to the Democratic Conference on September 11 [24]

1917. Because the Provisional Government's Ministry of Internal Affairs issued an order for Lenin to be arrested as he entered the Aleksandrinskii Theatre building where the Democratic Conference was held, the Bolshevik group notified the Conference's organising committee that another representative of the Party was being delegated instead of Lenin.

83.   No materials have been found either of the CC plenum planned for September 12 [25] or of CC sessions between September 6 [19] and 13 [26] 1917.

84.   The resolution on the current situation and the declaration to be passed at meetings which are mentioned in these minutes have not been found.

85.   The Moscow Regional Bureau of the RSDLP(b) at its meeting on September 4 [17] 1917 resolved to send a telegram round the region suggesting that delegations from factories and military units, as well as resolutions making Bolshevik demands, be sent to the Democratic Conference and to put an appeal to this effect in the newspaper *Sotsial-demokrat* and send a letter to the Party CC about this suggestion.

In accordance with this CC decision, the Bolshevik group in the *TsIK* appealed on September 8 [21] through the central organ of the Party, the newspaper *Rabochii put'*, to all local organisations to send their delegations and demands to the Democratic Conference. Delegations of this sort from factories and military units in Petrograd, Moscow and other Russian towns were organised for the time the Conference was at work.

86.   The Inter-District Conference was a permanent conference of representatives from the Petrograd district Soviets; it began work in April 1917. The Conference discussed how measures and actions of common interest to all the district Soviets could be carried out (electing the City Duma, arming the workers, combating counter-revolution, etc.). Created as a department of the Petrograd Soviet's Executive Committee as a link with the districts and with the aim of securing Menshevik and SR influence over the district Soviets, the Inter-District Conference was turned into an independent organisation in practice after the July days of 1917, becoming increasingly opposed to the conciliatory line of the Petrograd Soviet's SR-Menshevik Executive Committee. As the work of the Soviets gathered pace and the Bolshevik influence in them grew in

August-September 1917, the Inter-District Conference also came under the leadership of Bolshevik Party representatives.

87.   After the Petrograd Soviet adopted the Bolshevik resolution 'On power' (on the night of September 1 [14] 1917), the Menshevik Dan stated that the praesidium of the Executive Committee was relinquishing its authority. The Mensheviks and SRs tried to retain control of the praesidium, however, and moved a motion of confidence at the session of the Soviet on September 9 [22]. The Petrograd Soviet rejected the motion with 519 votes (against 414, 67 abstaining) and expressed no-confidence in the SR-Menshevik praesidium. After the vote, the old praesidium of the Soviet (Chkheidze, Tsereteli, Skobelev, Chernov, Anisimov, Dan and Gots) handed in their resignation.

The election of a new praesidium for the Petrograd Soviet was held on September 25 [October 8] 1917. Four Bolsheviks, 2 SRs and 1 Menshevik were elected as members of the praesidium.

V.I.Lenin considered the CC decision that the Petrograd Soviet praesidium should consist of a coalition to be wrong. Lenin referred to the place given to the Mensheviks in the praesidium of the Soviet as a mistake in an addition to the article 'The crisis is ripe' written on September 29 [October 12] 1917 and intended for distribution to members of the CC, the Petrograd and Moscow Committees of the Party and to Bolshevik deputies in the Soviets (see *Sochineniia*, 4th ed., vol.26, p.61).

Trotsky was elected chairman of the Soviet.

88.   This refers to the CC decision of August 20 [September 2] 1917 obliging Bolshevik Party members to give up contributing to *Novaia zhizn'* (see p.32).

89.   The situation in the Petrograd City Duma was discussed at this session because the SRs allied with the Kadets in the election of the Duma's executive organs to try to prevent the election of the candidates put forward by the Bolshevik group in accordance with the CC decision of September 3 [16] 1917 (see pp. 45-46).

90.   The CC decision to form an Electoral Commission for the Constituent Assembly was passed at the session of August 6 [19] 1917 (see p.19). The list of candidates recommended by the CC for the Constituent Assembly was discussed and confirmed for publication at the Central

Committee sessions of September 23 and 29 [October 6 and 12] 1917 (see pp.70, 75).

91.   The holding of a Party Conference, the agenda and the results of the Conference were considered at the following CC sessions, too: September 20, 23 and 24 [October 3, 6 and 7] 1917 (see pp.66, 68, 71). The Party Conference took place on September 24 [October 7] 1917. Taking part were members of the CC, the Petersburg Committee and local Party workers who came to Petrograd as delegates to the Democratic Conference. According to a report in the newspaper *Rabochii put'* No.21 of September 27 [October 10], the Party Conference heard a report on the current situation and passed a resolution on the report. No other materials on the Party Conference have been found.

92.   There are no notes in the minutes of subsequent CC sessions about sending out V.I.Lenin's letters for consideration by the most important Party organisations.

93.   The idea that 'insurrection is an art' belongs to F.Engels who expounded it in the work 'Revolution and counter-revolution in Germany' (see K.Marx and F.Engels. *Sochineniia,* 2nd ed., vol.8, pp.100-101).

94.   The unionists were the so-called United Social-Democratic Internationalists who had formed a group round the Menshevik-inclined newspaper *Novaia zhizn'*. The *Novaia zhizn'* people took a semi-Menshevik position on key political issues, came out in favour of a 'dictatorship of the united democracy', etc. The question of giving them one seat on the Petrograd Soviet's Executive Committee arose because an election of the Executive Committee was imminent.

95.   The municipal group formed in Moscow in September 1917 was not attached to the Moscow Regional Bureau but to the Party's Moscow Committee.

96.   The journal *Gorod i zemstvo* was the CC RSDLP(b) organ for questions concerned with municipal work. One number of the journal came out, on October 15 [28] 1917.

97.   On this very day, September 20 [October 3], the municipal group under the Party CC held a special meeting at Smolny of the Bolshevik

members of town dumas who were in Petrograd as delegates to the Democratic Conference. Representatives from 30 towns took part in the meeting. After discussing the convocation of an all-Russian municipal congress of Bolsheviks, the meeting drew up a draft agenda and expressed the wish that the Party CC should send out theses on the planned reports to local municipal groups of the Party before the congress. It was decided that this congress should be timed to coincide with the town's union congress.

The All-Russian Towns' Union Congress was held from October 14 [27] to 17 [30] 1917. The all-Russian municipal congress of Bolsheviks planned for the same time did not take place.

98. This refers to the Third Conference of Zimmerwaldists which was held in Stockholm on August 23-30 [September 5-12] 1917.

99. The special congress of the RSDLP(b) was fixed for October 17 [30] 1917 with two items on the agenda: 1. The revision of the Party programme; 2. Organisational matters. A notice that the Congress was being called and a description of the scale of representation signed by the CC's Organisational Bureau was published in the newspaper *Rabochii put'* No.21 of September 27 [October 10] 1917.

After the CC decision to call a special Party congress, V.I.Lenin wrote from hiding the 'Theses for a report at the October 8 conference of the Petersburg organisation and also for a resolution and a mandate to those elected to the Party congress' and also published the articles 'Revision of the Party programme' in the journal *Prosveshchenie* Nos.1-2 (see *Sochineniia,* 4th ed., vol.26, pp.116-118, 123-150).

The Central Committee considered the question of calling a special Party congress again at its session of October 5 [18] 1917 and decided to postpone the congress for a short time. The CC took decisions on when to call the Party congress and on its agenda at the sessions of January 19 and 24 [February 1 and 6] 1918 (see pp.187, 199-200).

100. On September 19 [October 2] 1917, the Democratic Conference resolved to organise a Pre-Parliament (a Provisional Council of the Republic). There were two conflicting points of view in the Party CC on the attitude to take to the Pre-Parliament. V.I.Lenin considered it wrong for the Bolsheviks to take part in the Democratic Conference and the Pre-Parliament envisaged by it. In his article 'From a publicist's diary. Our Party's mistakes' written on September 22-24 [October 5-7], Lenin

proposed a total boycott of the Pre-Parliament and an appeal to the Soviets and the trade unions – to the broad masses – summoning them to an armed rising (see *Sochineniia,* 4th ed., vol.26, pp.32-37). Kamenev, Rykov and Nogin tried to get the Bolsheviks to go into the Pre-Parliament because they wanted to turn the Party away from preparing an armed rising.

The Bolshevik group in the Democratic Conference met on September 21 [October 4] 1917. At the meeting, I.V.Stalin took Lenin's position in support of a boycott of the Pre-Parliament. Kamenev and Rykov came out in favour of taking part in the Pre-Parliament. Trotsky, though he supported a boycott to begin with, in practice joined those who wanted an active boycott of the Pre-Parliament to be rejected. By his proposal to adjourn the question of what to do about the Pre-Parliament until the Second Congress of Soviets, Trotsky was trying, under the guise of compromise, to prevent the Party Central Committee passing a categorical decision that the Bolsheviks should not go into the Pre-Parliament.

After a few days, the CC reviewed this session's decision. On October 5 [18], a resolution was passed on a Bolshevik withdrawal from the Pre-Parliament (see p.78).

At the meeting of the Bolshevik group at the Democratic Conference, Trotsky gave a report for the boycott, Rykov against. 50 voted for the boycott, 77 against. Lenin commented: 'We should have boycotted the Democratic Conference ... We must boycott the Pre-Parliament.' When he learned of the decision to participate in the Pre-Parliament, he took it as a sign of serious weakness in the Party. He wrote, 'We cannot and must not reconcile ourselves to participation ... At the "top" of our party we note vacillations that may become ruinous.' *He singled Trotsky out for praise in defending the revolutionary course: 'Trotsky was for the boycott. Bravo, comrade Trotsky! ... Long live the boycott!' (Lenin,* Sochineniia, *3rd ed., vol.21, pp.218-9).*

101. This is the agenda of the Party conference the convocation of which was considered at the CC sessions of September 13 [26] and September 20 [October 3] 1917 (see pp.52, 66).

102. This refers to the meeting of the Bolshevik group at the Democratic Conference on September 21 [October 4] 1917 where the subject of the attitude to take towards the Pre-Parliament was discussed.

103. Before it closed, the Democratic Conference passed a resolution declaring that on the peace issue it associated itself with the Petrograd Soviet's appeal 'To the peoples of the whole world' (published by the SR-Menshevik Executive Committee on March 15 [28] 1917 in No.15 of *Izvestiia Petrogradskogo Soveta*). The resolution went on to say: 'the will of the All-Russian Democratic Conference must be expressed in a manifesto to the democrats of the whole world'. A commission from the Conference praesidium, supplemented by representatives from all groups, was charged with composing the manifesto.

104. This refers to the declaration made by the Bolshevik group at the Democratic Conference about the reasons for the Bolsheviks' withdrawal from the enlarged Conference praesidium. This declaration was read out on the evening of September 22 [October 5] 1917 at the last session of the Democratic Conference and published the next day in No.18 of the newspaper *Rabochii put'*.

105. The SR N.D.Avksent'ev was elected chairman of the Pre-Parliament.

106. The Democratic Conference, having failed to solve the government problem, passed it on to the Provisional Government to decide together with a delegation specially elected at the Conference. Joint sessions of the Provisional Government, the Democratic Conference delegation and representatives of bourgeois organisations were held under Kerensky's chairmanship on September 22 and 23 [October 5 and 6] 1917. Those taking part in the sessions were the Provisional Government Ministers Tereshchenko, Nikitin, Verkhovsky, Verderevsky and others; the industrialists Konovalov, Tret'iakov, Kishkin and Smirnov; members of the Kadet Party CC, Nabokov and Efremov; eight representatives from the Democratic Conference – the Menshevik and SR leaders Chkheidze, Tsereteli, Avksent'ev, Gots and others. The sessions resulted in the formation of a new coalition Provisional Government with the Kadets participating.

The statement made by the Bolsheviks about the new Provisional Government being formed with the participation of the Kadets was read out at the first session of the Pre-Parliament on September 23 [October 6] 1917.

107. A list of 40 Bolshevik candidates to the Constituent Assembly

drawn up by the Central Committee was published in the newspaper *Rabochii put'* No.22, September 28 [October 11] 1917. 25 people from this list were declared the official candidates of the CC RSDLP(b): V.I.Lenin, F.E.Dzerzhinsky, S.G.Shaumian, I.V.Stalin, A.V.Lunacharsky, V.P.Nogin, A.S.Bubnov, A.M.Kollontai, P.I.Stuchka, M.N.Pokrovsky and others.

Compare the above with Stalin's own words: 'Comrades, I propose as candidates to the Constituent Assembly, Comrades Lenin, Zinoviev, Kollontai, Trotsky and Lunacharsky'. (Quoted in L. Trotsky, Stalin, *London, 1947, p.242.)*

108. This refers to the conference of CC members and Bolshevik delegates to the Democratic Conference which took place before the CC session on the same day.

109. The railway workers and employees had presented a number of demands to the Provisional Government, including a wage rise. The Provisional Government procrastinated for several months in making a decision and the result was the railwaymen's strike. The strike began on the night of September 24 [October 7] and ended on September 27 [October 10] 1917 after the railwaymen's demands had been partly satisfied. The appeal by the Party CC 'Help the railwaymen' was published in the newspaper *Rabochii put'* No.20, September 26 [October 9] 1917.

110. The Second All-Russian Congress of Soviets of Workers' and Soldiers' Deputies was the one in view.

111. According to inquiries made later by the Institute of Party History, Karl Moor offered financial resources from a large inheritance he had unexpectedly received.

112. The list of candidates for the Constituent Assembly which the CC adopted at the session of September 23 [October 6] 1917 (see p.70) was printed for a second time in the newspaper *Rabochii put'* No. 26 of October 3 [16] with some small changes. For the 26 people declared as the official candidates of the CC RSDLP(b), the electoral districts where the corresponding Bolshevik organisations had to put them at the top of their Party lists were noted. Apart from this list, *Rabochii put'* No.28 of October 5 [18] printed 'a list of Party members the CC recommends local Party organisations to put forward for the Constituent Assembly'

containing 119 candidates, among them K.E.Voroshilov (Lugansk), P.A. Dzhaparidze (Baku), Ia.M.Sverdlov, M.I.Kalinin, N.I.Podvoisky, N.K. Krupskaia (Petrograd), V.V.Kuibyshev (Samara), Mikha Tskhakaia (Tiflis), A.F.Miasnikov (Minsk), M.S.Ol'minsky (Moscow), B.Z.Shumiatsky (Krasnoiarsk) and others. This list with 5 candidates added (124 in all) was printed in *Rabochii put'* No.31 of October 8 [21] 1917.

See our addition to Note 107.

113. V.I.Lenin was put forward as a candidate for the Constituent Assembly in the following electoral districts: Petrograd – capital, Petrograd province, Ufa, Baltic fleet, Northern front.

114. The appeal, signed by the CC RSDLP(b), was printed as a leading article under the title 'Before the Congress of Soviets' in the Party's central organ, the newspaper *Rabochii put'* No.24 of September 30 [October 13] 1917.

115. The Congress of Northern Region Soviets was initially fixed for October 8 [21] in Helsingfors and was then moved to October 10 [23] 1917 in Petrograd. A preliminary conference of Congress delegates held on that day elected a Mandate Commission and drew up procedure. The Congress was held on October 11 - 13 [24 - 26]. The Petrograd Soviet took an active part in organising the Congress and sent 30 representatives to it. More than 23 Soviets were represented at the Congress: Petrograd, Moscow, Kronstadt, Reval, Helsingfors and others. 51 out of 94 delegates were Bolsheviks. Items on the agenda were: 1. Reports from the localities; 2. The current situation; 3. The country's military and political position; 4. the land question; 5. the All-Russian Congress of Soviets; 6. the Constituent Assembly; 7. the question of organisation. The Congress elected a Northern Region Executive Committee of 17 people, including 11 Bolsheviks. In his 'Letter to the Bolshevik comrades attending the Regional Congress of Northern Region Soviets' addressed to the Congress, V.I.Lenin set the Bolshevik delegates the objective of organising an armed insurrection (see *Sochineniia*, 4th ed., vol.26, pp.154 - 159). The Congress decisions summoned the masses to armed insurrection and the Congress played a significant role through organisation and agitation in preparing for it.

116. The subject of the Congress of Northern Region Soviets was discussed at the CC session of October 5 [18] 1917 (see p.78).

117. V.I.Lenin returned from Vyborg to Petrograd illegally on October 7 [20] 1917.

118. At the CC session of September 20 [October 3] 1917, the idea of putting forward Iu.M.Steklov, a member of the *Novaia zhizn'* group, for the Executive Committee of the Petrograd Soviet on the Bolshevik list was rejected (see p.65). Steklov joined the Bolshevik group in the Petrograd Soviet and the *TsIK* after he had left the Menshevik group of the so-called United Social-Democrat Internationalists.

119. The Petrograd area (provincial) organisation of the RSDLP(b) was formed on the initiative of the CC and the Petersburg Committee to integrate the activities of Bolshevik organisations in the Petrograd province. A private meeting of representatives from Krondstadt, Peterhof, Sestroretsk and Gatchina devoted to the subject of creating an area Party organisation was held in Sestroretsk on September 24 [October 7].

A preliminary conference of representatives from Bolshevik organisations in the Petrograd province (representing more than 6000 Party members) organised by the CC and the Petersburg Committee at Smolny on September 27 [October 10] recognised that it was urgent to combine forces and extend Party work in the province and passed a decision to call a constituent area Party conference. The first conference of all the Petrograd province Bolshevik organisations, with representatives from 16 organisations covering 8400 Party members, took place on October 1 [14] 1917. The conference confirmed the formation of an area (provincial) Party organisation and elected a Petrograd Area Committee. The conference nominated V.I.Lenin as the Petrograd province candidate for the Constituent Assembly.

120. The newspaper for the South-West front did not materialise.

121. This alludes to the CC decision obliging members of the Bolshevik Party to refuse to contribute to the newspaper *Novaia zhizn'*. The CC passed this decision at the session of August 20 [September 2] and confirmed it at the sessions of August 30 [September 12] and September 6 [19] 1917 (see pp.32, 38, 51).

122. A meeting took place on October 6 [19] 1917 of women workers who had organised a group to take the initiative in getting the first conference of Petrograd women workers held. Women representatives came

to the meeting from the Putilov factory, the cable and pipe factories, the *Treugol'nik* works and other enterprises, from a number of Petrograd districts and from the editorial board of the journal *Rabotnitsa*. It was decided that an initiating group under the Petersburg Committee of the RSDLP(b) should call the conference. The intention was that women delegates from all the workers' organisations where there were women workers: factory committees, trade unions, district committees of the RSDLP(b), etc. should take part in the conference. The Conference of Women Workers was held on November 5 [18] 1917.

123. The question of a congress of Northern Region Soviets was first discussed at the CC session of September 29 [October 12] 1917 (see p.76).

124. Judging by his statement attached to these minutes, Kamenev voted against withdrawing from the Pre-Parliament.

125. The Bolshevik declaration on withdrawing from the Pre-Parliament (the Council of the Russian Republic) was read out at the session of the Pre-Parliament on October 7 [20] 1917. After the declaration was read, the Bolshevik group left the Pre-Parliament. The text of the declaration was printed in No.31 of *Rabochii put'* the next day.

126. A CC session took place on October 10 [23] (see p.85). It has not been established whether there was any other Party meeting on that day.

127. This refers to a special congress of the RSDLP(b) which the CC discussed calling at the session of September 20 [October 3] 1917 (see p.66).

128. It has not been established what platform the minutes have in mind.

129. The joint conference of social-democratic organisations on the Rumanian front was held from October 1 [14] to 3 [16], 1917. There were Menshevik defensists and Menshevik internationalists on the joint list of candidates the conference nominated to the Constituent Assembly as well as Bolsheviks.

The (unified) CC mentioned here is the central committee of Mensheviks elected at the unifying congress of Mensheviks in August 1917.

130. This alludes to the decision of the Sixth Congress of the RSDLP (b). In the resolution 'The electoral campaign for the Constituent Assembly', the Congress passed the following decision on the subject of pacts and agreements: 'Pacts are only allowed with parties taking an internationalist position who have broken with the defensists not only in words but in action.' *(see KPSS v rezoliutsiiakh i resheniiakh s'ezdov, konferentsii i plenumov TsK* part 1, 7th ed. p.380).

131. The conference of Lithuanians in Moscow, called the 'Moscow Conference of Organisations and Cells of Lithuania's Social-Democrat Internationalists Operating in Russia', took place on August 12-14 [25-27] 1917. The Conference was called without the knowledge of the CC and Moscow Committee of the RSDLP(b). Along with Lithuanian Bolsheviks, Menshevik defensists also attended. The Conference aimed at creating a unified organisation out of the Lithuanian social-democratic groups which existed in a number of Russian towns in 1917. Lithuanian Bolsheviks from Petrograd, supported by Lithuanian Bolsheviks from other towns (Khar'kov, Irkutsk, Bogorodsk and others), attacked the opportunist policy of the organisers of the Moscow Conference and their attempts to make a pact with the Mensheviks in the pages of the Lithuanian Bolshevik newspaper *Tiesa* ('Truth') published in Petrograd.

A Provisional Bureau (the Provisional Central Bureau of Lithuanian Sections of the RSDLP(b)) was formed in Petrograd with V.S. Mitskiavichius-Kapsukas, Z.I.Aleksa-Angaretis and others as members.

An announcement that this directing centre of Lithuanian Bolsheviks had been created was published in the Bureau's organ, the newspaper *Tiesa* No.25 of October 14 [27] 1917. The Provisional Bureau worked hard to expose the Menshevik elements among Lithuanian social-democrats and to unite and rally Lithuanian Bolsheviks round the Bolshevik Party. On January 5-8 [18-21] 1917, the first conference of Lithuanian sections of the RSDLP(b) was held in Petrograd. A permanent Party centre for Lithuanian Bolsheviks – the Central Bureau of Lithuanian Sections of the RSDLP(b) – was elected at the conference.

132. Trying to do everything they could to prevent an armed rising of the workers and soldiers, Kerensky's Provisional Government and the counter-revolutionary generals, in league with the Anglo-French imperialists, made preparations at the beginning of October 1917 to surrender Petrograd to the Germans, seeing it as a way to suppress the revolution. In this connection, the Provisional Government planned a move

to Moscow at its session of October 4 [17]. The October armed rising intercepted the counter-revolution's schemes.

133. The position taken by the Bolsheviks' Moscow organisation on the question of an armed insurrection had been very clearly defined not long before this CC session when Lenin's 'Letter to the CC, the Moscow and Petrograd Committees and Bolshevik members of the Peter and Moscow Soviets' of October 1 [14] 1917 was discussed in Moscow. In this letter, V.I.Lenin stressed that it would be criminal to delay with the armed insurrection; he considered that the insurrection could begin in Moscow. 'The Bolsheviks have no right to wait for the Congress of Soviets, they must *take power right now,*' he wrote (see *Sochineniia,* 4th ed., vol.26, pp.114-115). Lenin's letter was considered first at a meeting of leading Moscow Party workers and then in the Party's Moscow Committee. Lenin's letter received full support from the Moscow Bolshevik organisation. Those at the meetings decided to direct work in the district Party organisations towards an insurrection. However, there were quite a few opportunist elements in the leadership of the Moscow organisation at that time. Both the Rights in the Moscow Committee (Rykov, etc.) and the 'Lefts' in the Moscow Regional Bureau (Bukharin, Sapronov, Osinsky, etc.) who did not believe that victory was possible for a socialist revolution in Russia without direct support from the West, tried to prevent Lenin's line from being pursued. Thus, when the question of whether the insurrection could be started in Moscow was being discussed at a session of the Moscow Committee, the opportunists came out with a statement that Moscow could not take the initiative for a rising and they were skilful enough to get the support of the majority at the meeting. This attitude of some of the leaders harmed the Party's cause and had an effect later, during the insurrection, on the power of the Soviets in Moscow.

This note is a mixture of half-truths. It is true that Moscow lagged far behind Petersburg in October-November 1917. It is a fact that after *the victory of the Bolsheviks in St. Petersburg on October 25, it still took eight long days for the Bolsheviks to wrest power in Moscow, going through a very bloody battle. (These facts in themselves, by the way, throw doubts on the soundness of Lenin's advice to start the insurrection in Moscow instead of Petersburg.)*

For various reasons, Moscow before October was more difficult to win over to Bolshevism than Petersburg. It was more isolated from the front, it did not have Petersburg's rebellious soldiers and sailors, it suffered much less from food supply difficulties. The Moscow proletariat was dispersed round smaller factories compared with the St. Petersburg giants (G.S.Ignat'iev, Oktiabr' 1917 goda v Moskve, Moscow, 1964, p.4). In the years when Bolshevism became a mass workers' party – 1912-1914 – Moscow lagged far behind Petersburg. As late as October 1917, the Social-Revolutionaries had a mass influence among the workers of Moscow, while their influence among the workers of St. Petersburg was practically non-existent.

Added to this were subjective factors. The most brilliant leaders of Bolshevism, including Lenin, Trotsky, Lunacharsky, were in Petersburg. The Moscow leadership was split (as was that of Petersburg). Bukharin took the same line as Lenin and Trotsky while Nogin and Rykov hesitated and vacillated. It was only on October 25 that a Military Revolutionary Committee was established in Moscow.

134.   The revolt in the German military marine occurred in September 1917. Sailors of five of the largest ships in the fleet rebelled. The sailors on the cruiser *Westphalia* threw the commander overboard and put ashore. On the cruiser *Nuernburg,* the sailors arrested the officers and tried to make for Norway, returning to Germany only under the threat that the cruiser would be sunk by submarines.

135.   An allusion to the elections to the district dumas in Moscow held on September 24 [October 7] 1917. The results of these elections showed especially clearly the growth of Bolshevik Party influence among the masses. For all 17 Moscow district dumas, Bolshevik candidates received about 200,000 votes or more than 51 per cent (five times more than at the elections in the summer of 1917), while the Kadets received 20 per cent, the SRs 15 per cent and the Mensheviks hardly more than 4 per cent of the total number of votes. Among the soldiers, the Bolsheviks gained 14,467 votes out a total of 17,819 votes cast by soldiers. As a result of the elections, the Bolsheviks won a majority in 11 Moscow district dumas.

136.   The resolution on an armed insurrection was moved at the CC session by V.I.Lenin. Kamenev and Zinoviev spoke and voted against the resolution and made a statement to the CC the day after the session continuing to defend their point of view (for the statement, see pp.89-95 of this edition).

137. An allusion to the All-Russian Executive Committee of the Railwaymen's Union (*Vikzhel'*).

138. The Cheremisov conference was a conference fixed by the Commander-in-Chief of the Northern front, General Cheremisov, for headquarters' officers, representatives from army organisations on the front and units of the Petrograd garrison. The conference was called with the aim of getting the agreement of the regiment and brigade committees to the withdrawal of troop units from Petrograd and their dispatch to the front under the pretext of urgent military needs. The headquarters of the Commander-in-Chief of the Northern front began preparations for the conference in the first half of October 1917. On October 14 [27], the Chief-of-Staff of the Petrograd military district, General Bagratuni, sent a telegram to commanders and committees of units of the Petrograd garrison suggesting that one representative be elected from each regiment and brigade committee to go to the front headquarters in Pskov on October 15 [28]. A joint meeting of the Petrograd regiment and brigade committees on the morning of October 15 [28] passed a resolution 'to adjourn the question of the journey to headquarters for the time being since it has been referred to the Executive Committee of the Petrograd Soviet of Workers' and Soldiers' Deputies for decision.' On October 16 [29], a plenum of the Executive Committee of the Petrograd Soviet decided in favour of sending a delegation to Pskov but noted at the same time that the delegation was going purely for information purposes. The conference opened in Pskov on October 17 [30]. The speeches by Cheremisov, the Commissar of the front Voitinsky and others tried to prove that it was necessary to submit to Cheremisov's order to withdraw the troops from the Petrograd garrison, but they did not succeed. During a break, the Petrograd delegation held a conference with the representatives of the army committees, and afterwards, a declaration was read out on behalf of the delegation expressing a Bolshevik view of the events (the declaration was written by Ia.M.Sverdlov – see *Proletarskaia revoliutsiia*, 1922, No.10, p.74) and stating that the question was being referred to the Petrograd Soviet for a final decision. On this, the Cheremisov conference ended work. In the end, the Petrograd Soviet refused to sanction the withdrawal of troops. The attempt by the Provisional Government and the generals to take the revolutionary troops out of Petrograd on the eve of the October armed insurrection was foiled.

† *This Centre of five members was designed to supplement the staff of the Military Revolutionary Committee created by the Petrograd Soviet and headed by Trotsky. 'The center never func-*

tioned as a separate group, but the decision establishing it did serve as the textual basis for the legend proclaimed in the official history later on that Stalin was the man in charge of the uprising.' (R.V. Daniels, The Conscience of the Revolution, *Cambridge, Mass. 1965, p.61.)*

139. The statement referred to here has not been found.

140. As well as the 'Letter to the Central Committee of the RSDLP' which V.I.Lenin addressed directly to the Party Central Committee on October 19 [November 1] 1917 and which was read out at this CC session, Lenin wrote a 'Letter to Bolshevik Party members' on October 18 [31] about the strike-breaking by Kamenev and Zinoviev (see annexed to the minutes, pp.114-116). These letters by V.I.Lenin are very important Party documents showing Lenin's relentless struggle against Kamenev's and Zinoviev's efforts to block the October armed rising and their open statements after the CC session of October 16 [29] in the semi-Menshevik newspaper *Novaia zhizn'* against the unpublished decision of the Central Committee (see p.121 of this edition).

    Interestingly, at the time, Stalin equivocated with regard to the stand taken by Zinoviev and Kamenev. See the statement by the editorial board of Rabochii put' *(p. 120 of the present volume) written by Stalin (see p. 112)*

141. In his speech at the session of the Petrograd Soviet on October 18 [31] 1917, Trotsky dealt with the question of an armed insurrection, saying that it had not yet been fixed but that 'at the first attempt of the counter-revolution to disrupt the congress our response will be a ruthless counter-offensive, pursued to the end'. This statement was endorsed by Kamenev, who spoke at the same session. The speech was printed the next day in *Izvestiia TsIK i Petrogradskogo Soveta* and other newspapers.

    Trotsky's statement 'was juridically screening a policy of attack with a speciously defensive formula.' (L.Trotsky, History of the Russian Revolution, *London, 1934, p.1011). On the same day, in a speech to the All-Russian Conference of Factory and Shop Committees, Trotsky said: 'A civil war is inevitable. We have only to organise it as painlessly as possible. We can achieve this not by wavering and vacillation, but only by a stubborn and courageous struggle for power.' All understood that those words about waver-*

ings were directed against Zinoviev, Kamenev and their colleagues. (ibid., pp. 1011-2) Trotsky's position can in no way be equated with that of Kamenev. See also Document 2. p.116.

142. The statement from the *Voenka* (the Central Bureau of the Military Organisations under the CC RSDLP(b)) has not been found.

143. After the CC sessions of October 10 [23] and 16 [29], when Kamenev and Zinoviev spoke and voted against Lenin's resolution to make an armed insurrection a practical objective, and as an answer to their statement 'The current situation' (see pp.89-95 of this edition), V.I.Lenin published the article 'Letter to comrades' (see *Sochineniia*, 4th ed., vol.26, pp.166-184) in the Party's central organ, the newspaper *Rabochii put'* Nos.40, 41 and 42. In this article, Lenin took the 'arguments' of those who had given the revolution away and who had tried to show that an armed insurrection was hopeless and, analysing them one after the other, utterly crushed them.

144. Zinoviev's letter to the central organ which Lenin mentions did not appear in the newspapers. The text of the letter has not been found.

145. A reference to V.I.Lenin's article 'Letter to comrades' published in the newspaper *Rabochii put'* of October 19, 20 and 21 [November 1, 2 and 3] 1917.

146. The Second Congress of Soviets planned earlier for October 20 [November 2] 1917 was changed to October 25 [November 7]. The resolution to postpone the Congress of Soviets was passed at a meeting of the SR-Menshevik Bureau of the *TsIK* on October 17 [30] 1917.

147. V.I.Lenin was not at this CC session nor at the two preceding sessions (see minutes Nos.27 and 28) because he was being sought by the Provisional Government and had to hide in the Lesnoi district of Petrograd. Lenin's letter to Ia.M.Sverdlov, written not later than October 23 [November 5] 1917, makes a direct reference to this situation. 'It seems I will not be able to come to the plenum', writes Vladimir Il'ich, 'because they are "hunting" me' (see the collection *Oktiabr'skoe vooruzhennoe vosstanie v Petrograd*, USSR Academy of Sciences, Moscow, 1957, p.66).

Since he could not attend the CC session, Lenin sent the same day,

October 24 [November 6], the famous letter to CC members giving instructions to start a decisive attack and carry out an armed insurrection on the night of October 25 (see V.I.Lenin 'Letter to CC members' *Sochineniia*, 4th ed., vol.26, pp.203-204). A few hours later, Lenin arrived at Smolny to direct the armed insurrection.

It is well known that the organiser of the October insurrection was none other than Trotsky. To quote only two witnesses: Stalin, in an article called 'The role of the most eminent Party leaders' written on November 6 1918, had this to say: 'All the work of practical organisation of the insurrection was conducted under the immediate leadership of the chairman of the Petrograd Soviet, Trotsky. It is possible to declare with certainty that the swift passing of the garrison to the side of the Soviet and the bold execution of the work of the Military Revolutionary Committee, the Party owes principally and above all to comrade Trotsky'; and a footnote in Lenin's Collected Works *(1st ed., vol.14, p.482): 'After the majority in the Petrograd Soviet passed into the hands of the Bolsheviks, [Trotsky] was elected its chairman and in that position organised and led the insurrection of October 25'.*

148.   This refers to talks between the Military Revolutionary Committee of the Petrograd Soviet and representatives from the headquarters of the Petrograd military district. They had begun on October 22 [November 3] 1917 after the Military Revolutionary Committee had directed that units of the Petrograd garrison should only execute orders which were supported by the signature of the Military Revolutionary Committee and had decided to appoint its commissars to military units, especially-important points in the capital and to the headquarters of the Petrograd military district.

149.   The Provisional Government made attempts to close the Bolshevik newspapers on October 24 [November 6] 1917. At dawn that day, a detachment of junkers appeared at the printers of the central organ with an order from the commander of the forces of the Petrograd military district to close down the printing press and suppress the newspapers *Rabochii put'* and *Soldat*. The junkers managed to seize part of the issue of the newspaper *Rabochii put'* which had already been printed, to break the plates and seal up the printing press. At the order of the Military Revolutionary Committee, Red Guards and revolutionary soldiers drove out the junkers and the printing press was opened. When the Bolshevik group met, I.V.Stalin reported to the delegates to the Second Congress

of Soviets that *Rabochii put'* was being published. Soldiers from the Lithuanian regiment and the 6th reserve sapper battalion undertook to guard the printers. The next issue of *Rabochii put'* came out at 11 o'clock in the morning of October 24 [November 6] with a leading article by I.V.Stalin 'What we need' and was distributed among workers and soldiers. At 6 o'clock that evening, a second attempt was made to close the Bolshevik newspapers. A fresh detachment of junkers headed by Lieutenant-Colonel Germanovich arrived at the printers of *Rabochii put'* with orders from the Chief-of-Staff of the military district, Bagratuni, to close *Rabochii put'*. Worker-members of the Red Guard and soldiers disarmed the detachment of junkers and dispatched it to the Peter-Paul fortress.

'A worker and a working-girl from the Bolshevik printing plant ran panting to Smolny and there found Podvoisky and Trotsky. If the Committee would give them a guard against the junkers, the workers would bring out the paper. A form was soon found for the first answer to the government offensive. An order was issued to the Litovsky regiment to send a company immediately to the defence of the workers' press. The messengers from the printing plant insisted that the 6th battalion of sappers be also ordered out: these were near neighbours and loyal friends. Telephonograms were immediately sent to the two addresses. The Litovsky and the sappers came out without delay. The seals were torn from the building, the moulds again poured, and the work went on. With a few hours' delay the newspaper suppressed by the government came out under protection of the troops of a committee which was itself liable to arrest. That was insurrection. That is how it developed.' (L. Trotsky, History of the Russian Revolution, London, 1934, pp.1054-5).

150. The Bureau of the *TsIK* of the first Convocation had a majority of Mensheviks and SRs and supported the Provisional Government during the October days, sabotaging the convocation of the Second Congress of Soviets. The conciliationist *TsIK* Bureau had no influence among the broad masses of the workers at that time, though it had some support based on the upper reaches of such organisations as *Vikzhel'*.

151. The Peter-Paul fortress with its huge arsenal was an important strategic point in Petrograd. On October 24 [November 6] 1917, the garrison of the Peter-Paul fortress went over to the side of the Military Revolutionary Committee altogether, declaring itself for transfer of power to the Soviets.

152. At an evening session on October 26 [November 8] 1917, the Second All-Russian Congress of Soviets elected a *VTsIK* of 101 members, which included 62 Bolsheviks and 29 Left SRs. The Congress formed a worker and peasant government. The government confirmed by the Congress consisted only of Bolsheviks. V.I.Lenin was elected chairman of the Council of People's Commissars. When the Soviet government was being formed, Lenin and the CC of the Bolshevik Party accepted the possibility that representatives of the Left SRs might be included in the government. The Left SRs refused the Bolshevik offer, however, because they could not make up their minds to break with the Right SRs who had left the Congress.

In the days following the Second Congress of Soviets, while the struggle was still going on to establish Soviet power in Moscow and other centres of the country and detachments of the Red Guard and revolutionary units of troops were suppressing the revolt of junkers in Petrograd and waging a battle against Kerensky's and Krasnov's troops, the counter-revolution used the SR-Menshevik *Vikzhel'* (the All-Russian Executive Committee of the Railway Union) in its struggle against Soviet power. On October 29 [November 11], *Vikzhel'* made a statement to the *VTsIK* about the government and sent round a telegram 'To everyone, everyone, everyone', saying: 'The country is not being governed . . . the Council of People's Commissars formed in Petrograd rests on only one party and so cannot get recognition and support from the country as a whole. A new government must be formed . . .' (see *Izvestiia TsIK i Petrogradskogo Soveta* No.212, October 31 [November 13] 1917, p.7.) *Vikzhel'* tried to get a so-called homogenous socialist government formed, to include all the socialist parties – from the Bolsheviks to the so-called Popular Socialists; *Vikzhel'* also demanded an end to the fight against the counter-revolution, threatening to bring the railways to a halt, and it was planning to hold a strike.

The Central Committee of the Bolshevik Party decided to widen the base of the government, as the first point of these minutes records, but at the same time, as the voting by name on the fifth point shows, it rejected a proposal pressed by Kamenev, Rykov, Miliutin and Sokolnikov that representatives of the Mensheviks, the Right SRs and other parties and groups should be included in a Soviet government.

The inviolability of the decrees of the Second Congress of Soviets and the government's accountability to the All-Russian Central Executive Committee (*VTsIK*) elected at the Congress were asserted by points three and four of the CC decision. In this way, the CC rejected the second S R and Menshevik demand, that the government be responsible to a so-called 'Popular Council' which the conciliators intended to create on the pattern of the Pre-Parliament (with a majority consisting of members of the first *TsI K*, the city dumas, etc.). The Bolshevik C C felt the *V TsI K* could be enlarged by adding representatives from the parties who had left the Second Congress of Soviets and from certain organisations not represented in it, as is shown by the seventh and eighth points of the adopted resolution.

153. The proposal referred to in this point has not been found.

154. This refers to the conference on the question of state power held at *Vikzhel'*. After the Central Committee had passed a resolution to take part in the talks, the *V TsI K* also decided to send five delegates to the conference. Among them were Sverdlov, Riazanov, Zaks (Left S R) and others.

Lenin's view was that the negotiations at the *Vikzhel'* conference 'should serve as a diplomatic cover for military operations' (see p.132 of this collection). *Vikzhel'* then still controlled the administrative apparatus of the railways and could exert an influence on some sections of railwaymen who were still wavering. It had to be exposed and rendered harmless to prevent Kerensky's troops being given transport and to ensure that revolutionary detachments could move to Moscow and other centres where the armed struggle to assert the power of the Soviets was still going on.

The question of negotiations was discussed at the expanded C C session of November 1 [14] and the C C session of November 2 [15] 1917 (see pp.129 - 135, 136 - 139).

155. This C C session evidently took place in the evening and night of November 1 [14] and 2 [15] 1917 simultaneously with a session of the *V TsI K* called at the same time. This appears from a note in the minutes that the *V TsI K* was waiting for a reply from the Party C C on the subject of talks with *Vikzhel'* (see p.131).

156. The conference at *Vikzhel'* began work on October 29 [November 11] 1917. About 30 representatives of the parties, *Vikzhel'* and other organisations took part in the conference. The Mensheviks and SRs sent the leaders of all their groups and elements: the Menshevik defensists Dan and Erlich, the Menshevik internationalists Martov and Martynov,

the Right SRs Gendel'man and Iakobin, the Left SRs Kolegaev and Malkin, the Menshevik Vainstein from the 'committee to save the country and the revolution', and others. Also represented were the All-Russian Soviet of Peasants' Deputies, the Union of Civil Servants and several other organisations. Kamenev and Sokolnikov attended the sessions on behalf of the Bolshevik CC and Riazanov was also there (from the *VTsIK*).

Banking on the successes of Kerensky's troops in the attack on Petrograd, the Mensheviks and SRs aimed to abolish the rule of the workers and peasants and everything the socialist revolution had achieved. At the first session on October 29 [November 11], the Menshevik Dan pressed for the Second Congress of Soviets to be regarded as null and void. This session resulted in a decision to appoint a commission to draw up proposals on the composition of state power and measures to stop the civil war. This commission, which was called the 'special commission to work out an agreement between parties and organisations' met on the morning of October 30 [November 12]. Dan, Vainstein, Kamenev, Riazanov and others were at the session. The Mensheviks demanded that the workers should be disarmed and resistance to Kerensky's troops ended. When Kamenev spoke in this commission, he kept silent about the decisions the Bolshevik CC had made on October 29 [November 11] about the talks. The commission decided on an 'immediate ceasefire and an appeal to the two hostile sides to stop military action'. Kamenev, Sokolnikov and Riazanov voted for this resolution. On that same day (at 11 o'clock in the morning and evening) two joint sessions were also held at *Vikzhel'*. Towards evening on October 30 [November 12], Kerensky's forces suffered a defeat at Pulkovo but the SRs and Mensheviks did not give up hope of getting rid of the Bolshevik government, with the help of the *Vikzhel'* people and the strike-breakers – Kamenev and his supporters. At the evening session, Kamenev repeated the statement he had made at the first session on the need to form a coalition government of parties from the Bolsheviks to the Popular Socialists. He ignored the decision on this subject approved by a majority of the CC.

A meeting of the *Vikzhel'* commission to work out an agreement was held on the night of November 1 [14] and there Kamenev, Sokolnikov and Riazanov assented to the formation of a so-called 'Popular Council', that is of a new pre-parliament in place of the *VTsIK*, violating the CC directive that one of the most important conditions in the *Vikzhel'* negotiations must be confirmation that the government should be responsible to the *VTsIK* elected at the Second Congress of Soviets.

When the commission went on to consider people as possible candidates for the government, Kamenev, Sokolnikov and Riazanov did not insist on Lenin remaining in the government. Having failed to stand up to the Mensheviks and SRs when they objected strongly to Lenin as a candidate, the strike-breakers had discussions with the leaders of the counter-revolution about Chernov and Avksent'ev as possible candidates for Premier.

As can be seen from the minutes, Kamenev, helped by Riazanov and Sokolnikov, tried to conceal from the CC his acts of treachery and the violation of the Central Committee directives.

The Socialist-Revolutionaries and Mensheviks opposed the candidature of Lenin and Trotsky as members of the government. Therefore, on November 1 1917, Lenin proposed an abandonment of the negotiations as futile. He encountered strong opposition from Zinoviev, Kamenev and Rykov. In the debate in the Party Central Committee, he received unequivocal support only from Trotsky. The majority voted for a resolution laying down conditions which would of necessity, however, lead to a breakdown of negotiations.

157. This decision is recorded in point 3 of the CC resolution passed at the session of October 29 [November 11] 1917 (see p.127).

158. The CC decision recalled by F.E.Dzerzhinsky here and in his second speech and also in A.S.Bubnov's speech (see p.132) is apparently the CC decision taken on October 29 [November 11] 1917.

159. M.S.Uritsky's objection is directed primarily against Trotsky who proposed representation for the City Dumas in the *VTsIK* in his speech. Trotsky's proposal on this matter was essentially a mark of support for Kamenev in the *Vikzhel'* negotiations and for a plot with the Mensheviks and SRs aimed at doing away with the *VTsIK* elected by the Second Congress of Soviets.

A completely phoney note. See our addition to note 156.

160. Two thousand Red Guards and sailors arrived in Moscow from Petrograd on November 1 [14] 1917 to take part in the final battles to establish Soviet power in Moscow. As well as the help from Petrograd, Moscow was also reinforced by detachments from Vladimir, Shua, Aleksandrov and Kovrov, which were commanded by M.V.Frunze.

161. The text of the resolution on *Vikzhel'* moved by V.I.Lenin has not been found.

162. A session of the *TsIK* was held on the evening of November 1 [14] 1917 and it also had the progress of the talks at the *Vikzhel'* conference on the agenda. The beginning of the session was postponed because many Bolshevik members of the *VTsIK* were engaged in the meeting of the Party CC. The *VTsIK* session opened late in the evening and continued into the night of November 1 [14] to 2 [15]. Bolshevik members of the *VTsIK* who attended it included: I.V.Stalin, Ia.M.Sverdlov, M.M. Volodarsky, F.E.Dzerzhinsky, M.K.Muranov, N.I.Podvoisky and M.S. Uritsky. A debate was held on Riazanov's report on the talks in the *Vikzhel'* commission. M.F.Krushinsky representing *Vikzhel'*, B.D.Kamkov from the Left SRs and V.A.Bazarov of the United Social-Democrat Internationalists made speeches. The conciliators proposed the formation of a so-called homogenous socialist government, a halt to the armed struggle against the counter-revolution, and they blamed the Bolsheviks for the bloodshed.

Volodarsky was the one to rebut the Mensheviks and SRs on behalf of the Bolshevik group. He proposed that the *VTsIK* approve a resolution about the talks, to be based on the Party CC's resolution on the ultimatum (see p.135). Bazarov came out with a statement against the Bolshevik resolution. In the statement he read out, it said in particular that the Bolshevik resolution 'completely breaks with the fundamental principles underlying the draft agreement drawn up by the inter-party conference, with the participation of Bolshevik delegates' (see *Protokoly zasedanii VTsIK Sovetov rabochikh, soldatskikh, krest'ianskikh i kazach-'ikh deputatov II sozyva.* Publ. *VTsIK*, Moscow, 1918, p.13) – i.e. with the concessions made by Kamenev, Sokolnikov and Riazanov at meetings of the *Vikzhel'* commission in defiance of the Party CC decision. Karelin read out the resolution from the Left SR group. Without formally refusing to recognise the decrees of the Second Congress of Soviets, the Left SRs proposed the creation of a 'convention', in which the City Dumas, etc., would take part, and calculated on replacing the *VTsIK* with this institution. When a vote was taken by name, the Bolshevik resolution got 38 votes. 29 people voted for the Left SRs' resolution. After an hour's break requested by the Left SRs, the Bolshevik resolution was voted on point by point. Since they feared that they would finally isolate themselves from the masses if they voted against the Bolshevik resolution, the Left SRs were forced to withdraw their own resolution. The Mensheviks left the *VTsIK* session. The *VTsIK* passed the resolution moved by the Bolshevik group unanimously (with one abstention).

163. This apparently refers to the leading article 'What a revolutionary power should be like' printed in *Izvestiia TsIK i Petrogradskogo Soveta* No.213, November 1 [14] 1917.

164. The resolution on the structure of power mentioned here has not been found.

165. After the counter-revolutionary troops had been defeated at Pulkovo and retreated from Tsarskoe Selo, Kerensky and Krasnov tried to consolidate their strength at Gatchina. They held a council of war at Gatchina on October 31 [November 13] 1917. To give them time to seek reinforcements, the leaders of the counter-revolution decided to propose peace talks. One offer was sent in Krasnov's name to the Gatchina front and the other in Kerensky's name to Petrograd. Kerensky asked the Bolsheviks to stop the armed struggle and to submit to a new government which would be constituted through an agreement between the Provisional Government and representatives of all the political parties and the 'committee to save the country and the revolution'. By sending Stankevich, the commissar under the supreme commander, to Petrograd to represent him in negotiations, Kerensky hoped, with the help of the SRs and Mensheviks, to bring the regiments of the Petrograd garrison over to his side. Kerensky's agents were unsuccessful in their efforts, however. Delegates from the Lithuanian, Semenovsky, Keksholm, Grenadier and other regiments and representatives from the soldiers at the front met at Smolny on the evening of October 31 [November 13] and had a talk with the Bolshevik CC member, I.V.Stalin. A decision was made to send a deputation to Kerensky's troops and to talk to the ordinary soldiers and cossacks, putting it to them that the *VTsIK* and the decisions of the Second Congress of Soviets should be recognised, resistance halted and Kerensky, Krasnov and Savinkov arrested. Soon Petrograd Red Guards workers, soldiers and sailors had talked with the soldiers in Gatchina itself. The soldiers agreed to stop military operations and sent a guard to Kerensky's quarters but he had managed to escape. The revolutionary forces occupied Gatchina on the day of November 1 [14] and arrested the headquarters staff of the Third Cossack Corps headed by General Krasnov.

166. What 'Obukhovo delegation' is referred to is not known.

At the time the counter-revolution, helped by *Vikzhel'*, was trying to overthrow Soviet power, the workers in the Obukhovo factory joined with all the Petrograd workers in defending the conquests of the October revolution with weapons in their hands. Only a small group of Obukhovo SRs was on the side of the counter-revolution. On October 29 [November 11] 1917, the SRs sent a telegram to *Vikzhel'* in the name of the Obukhovo factory committee with the assurance that the intention of *Vikzhel'* to form a government from representatives of all the socialist parties would be supported by the Obukhovo factory.

167. The All-Russian Executive Committee of the Railway Union (*Vikzhel'*) was elected at a founding congress in July 1917 and was initially in Moscow. It had a membership of 14 SRs, 6 Mensheviks, 3 Popular Socialists and 11 non-party. *Vikzhel'* was not supported by a wide section of ordinary railwaymen. The stand made by *Vikzhel'* against Soviet power and its connections and negotiations with Kerensky in October and November 1917 demonstrated its counter-revolutionary role to the workers. The Bolsheviks carried on a great deal of agitation among the broad masses of the railwaymen, revealing how much help *Vikzhel'* was giving to Kerensky, Kornilov, Kaledin and other enemies of the revolution. The workers at Khar'kov railway junction and meetings of railwaymen in other places, too, passed resolutions of no confidence in the current membership of *Vikzhel'* at the beginning of November and demanded new elections. A special All-Russian Congress of Railway and Depot Workers, which opened on December 12 [25] in Petrograd, fully endorsed the platform of the Second All-Russian Congress of Soviets. V.I.Lenin made a speech at this Congress. The Congress passed a resolution of no confidence in *Vikzhel'*. A special All-Russian Railway Congress which took place on January 5-30 [January 18-February 12] 1918 elected a new central organ of the railway union instead of *Vikzhel'* — the All-Russian Executive Committee of Railwaymen (*Vikzhedor*).

168. This obviously refers to the Second Congress of Soviets. When the Second Congress of Soviets opened, 649 delegates were registered. While the congress was at work, the number was increased by the attendance of several dozens more delegates. The Bolsheviks constituted the absolute majority of the Second Congress — 390. The SRs numbered 193 (and after the Right SRs had left, about 179 Left SRs remained in the Congress). Mensheviks of all tendencies, the Bundists included, had about

80 seats. An insignificant number of delegates represented the Polish Socialist Party, the Ukrainian socialists and others.

169. This resolution has not been found.

170. This refers to the 'CC Resolution' voted on a part at a time (see the document on p.135).

171. The ultimatum was given to the Left SR group in the *VTsIK*. Drawn up by the CC and voted on point by point, this resolution on the ultimatum was used as a basis for the resolution moved by Volodarsky on behalf of the Bolshevik group at the *VTsIK* session on the night of November 1 [14] to 2 [15] 1917. The *VTsIK* approved the Bolshevik group's resolution in the following form:

'Considering an agreement between the socialist parties desirable, the *TsIK* states that an agreement can only be arrived at on the following conditions:

1. Recognition of the Soviet government's programme expressed in the decrees on land and peace and both drafts on workers' control.

2. Recognition of the need for a ruthless struggle against the counter-revolution (Kerensky, Kornilov and Kaledin).

3. Recognition of the Second All-Russian Congress as the sole source of power.

4. A government responsible to the *VTsIK*.

5. The enlargement of the *TsIK* to include, apart from organisations which do not come within the Soviets, representatives of the Soviets of Workers', Soldiers' and Peasants' Deputies not already represented in it; proportional representation of those who left the Congress of Soviets of Workers' and Soldiers' Deputies and of all-Russian trade union organisations such as: the Council of Trade Unions, the Union of Factory Committees, *Vikzhel'*, the Union of Post and Telegraph Workers and Employees, on the condition that new elections are held and only after new elections are held for the All-Russian Soviet of Peasants' Deputies and those soldiers' organisations which have not had elections in the last three months.' (see *Protokoly zasedanii VTsIK Sovetov R., S., Kr. i Kaz. deputatov II sozyva*. Publ. *VTsIK*, Moscow 1918, pp. 15-16).

172. The fair copy of this resolution attached to the minutes is in Ia.M. Sverdlov's writing.

173. This CC session was, it seems, entirely devoted to discussing and adopting Lenin's 'Resolution by the CC RSDLP(b) on the opposition within the CC', as the introductory part of the resolution testifies. Minute notes have not been found for this session. Lenin's manuscript of the resolution has notes in the margin in Lenin's writing giving the results of the voting item by item. It is evident from the first note that a special vote was taken on the subject of the first, second and third items as to whether they should be put to the vote, after which Lenin wrote: 'Not to vote: voting 8, 5, 1' (that is they voted 8 for, 5 against, 1 abstained). The result of the voting on the fourth point was: '+8, −5, 0 1'. Point five was put to the vote three times: the first vote '+6, −6, 0 2'; the second '+7, −7, 0 1'; the third '+8, −7'. The results of point six: '+11, −0, 0 4'; point seven: '+10, −4, 0'; point eight: '+9, −1, 0 3'; point nine: '+9, −4, 0 2'. At the end of the manuscript, there is a note on the results of the vote on the whole resolution: 'As a whole: +10, −5, 0' (see the archives of the IML, *f*.2, *op*.1, *ed.khr*.4661). The resolution was published in *Pravda* No.180, November 4 [17] 1917 without the first three points.

174. The minutes of the CC session mentioned in the text have not been found.

175. In the interests of preserving and consolidating the dictatorship of the proletariat, Lenin considered that immediate measures should be taken to destroy the opposition represented by Kamenev, Zinoviev and others, who had tried to undermine the unity of the Party and prevent the fulfilment of CC decisions. On November 3 [16], according to CC member Bubnov, after Lenin had drawn up the 'Ultimatum from the majority of the CC RSDLP(b) to the minority', he invited each Central Committee member who was in Petrograd at the time separately to his room, acquainted them with the text of the document and suggested that they sign it. The ultimatum was read out at the CC session of November 4 [17] 1917 (the minutes of that meeting have not been found).

176. The *VTsIK* session began on November 2 [15] and ended early in the morning of November 3 [16] 1917. Not many people were at the session. Out of a total of 101 members of the *VTsIK*, fewer than 40 members attended. The Left SRs, counting on Kamenev's and Zinoviev's support, demanded as an ultimatum that the *VTsIK* resolution of November 1 [14] on the platform for an agreement between the socialist

parties be revised. As the *VTsIK* minutes show, when Malkin had read out the statement of the Left SR group, Zinoviev spoke at the meeting, reading the CC RSDLP(b) resolution (evidently the CC resolution of November 2 [15] without the first three points – that is in the form in which it was sent to *Pravda* for publication). Immediately after that, Zinoviev stated that the Bolshevik group had not discussed the CC resolution and suggested an hour's break. Kamenev and Zinoviev took the path of a split, putting the *VTsIK* group in opposition to the whole Party and its Central Committee. After the break, Kamenev moved another resolution on behalf of the group, directed at frustrating the CC decisions. This resolution demanded that negotiations on state power should continue with all the parties included in the Soviets. It envisaged giving half the places in the government to SRs and Mensheviks, expanding the *VTsIK* to 150 people and adding another 245 representatives to it: 75 people from provincial peasants' Soviets, 80 from committees of military units and the navy, 40 from the trade unions (including 25 from the All-Russian Trade Associations, proportionally to the number of their organisations, 10 from *Vikzhel'*, 5 from the post and telegraph employees), 50 from the Petrograd City Duma. There was no mention in all this of the requirement of new elections in the peasants' Soviets, the army committees and the City Dumas. Reference was also made to the allocation of ministries and the people who would represent the parties in the government. Kamenev's resolution suited the Left SRs perfectly and their representative Karelin stated that 'the Bolshevik resolution is a step towards an agreement. That is why we are voting for this resolution, reserving the right to change some details . . .' (see *Protokoly zasedanii VTsIK Sovetov R., S., Kr. i Kaz. deputatov II sozyva*. Publ. *VTsIK*, Moscow 1918, p.22). The resolution was passed (with 6 against and 1 abstaining). The session set up a commission composed of Kamenev, Riazanov, Zinoviev, the Left SRs Karelin and Prosh'ian which was instructed to continue the negotiations to form a government.

177. An allusion to the resolution which Kamenev, Zinoviev and their supporters put through with the Left SRs at the *VTsIK* meeting held on the night of November 2 [15] to 3 [16] 1917 (see preceding note).

178. The Central Committee of the Party, with Lenin at its head, emphatically rejected the policy of conciliation on the question of power and condemned the opposition's anti-Party actions. After this, Kamenev, Zinoviev, Rykov, Miliutin and Nogin declared on November 4 [17] 1917

that they were leaving the CC (see pp.140-141 of this edition). On the same day, Nogin read out a statement in the *VTsIK* on his own behalf and on behalf of members of the Council of People's Commissars Rykov, Miliutin and Teodorovich, in which Larin and others also joined, saying that they were leaving *Sovnarkom* (see p.141 of the present edition). This CC resolution passed on November 5 or 6 [18 or 19] 1917 addresses a second ultimatum to the Right capitulators as they continued their subversive activity against the Party. Internal and external enemies of the October revolution who calculated on a split in the Bolshevik Party and a weakening of Soviet power were confounded. The Party CC replaced the deserters in the Council of People's Commissars with new people and took other necessary measures to strengthen the governmental bodies.

179. It has not been established what meeting of Petrograd workers this refers to.

180. The armed attack on Petrograd made by the junkers on Sunday, October 29 [November 11] 1917 was organised by the 'committee to save the country and the revolution', which included the SRs Avksent'ev, Gots and Broun. The junkers' counter-revolutionary revolt was suppressed on the same day by detachments of worker Red Guards, revolutionary soldiers and sailors.

181. This refers to a conference at *Vikzhel'* on November 3 [16] 1917. Apart from Abramovich and Martov, other leaders of the Mensheviks: Ermansky, Martynov and Rosental' were also at the conference, as well as the Left SRs – Karelin, Schreider, Prosh'ian and others. I.V.Stalin was sent to the conference from the Bolshevik CC.

182. This letter from Zinoviev shows that after their plans for capitulation had failed, the opportunists decided to lay down arms temporarily and claimed that they were giving up the struggle against the Party's Leninist policy. Shortly afterwards, Kamenev, Rykov and Miliutin made a similar statement to the CC. It was considered at the CC session of November 29 [December 12] 1917 (see p.160-161).

From the notes referring to Zinoviev and Kamenev, one could not have guessed that these continued to play central roles in the leadership of the Party and government so long as Lenin was alive. Zinoviev was a member of the Political Bureau of the Party, chairman of the Soviet of Petrograd, chairman of the Praesidium of the Communist International. Kamenev was a member of the Political Bureau, chairman of the Soviet of Moscow, and deputy to Lenin, chairman of the Council of People's Commissars.

183. The All-Russian Central Executive Committee released Kamenev from his responsibilities as chairman of the *VTsIK* at a session held on November 8 [21] 1917 in the second half of the day. The following note on this matter appears in the *VTsIK* minutes, No.8: 'Comrade Kamenev relinquishes the title of Chairman of the *TsIK*. The Left SR group expresses its regret' (see *Protokoly zasedanii VTsIK Sovetov R., S., Kr. i Kaz. deputatov II sozyva*. Publ. *VTsIK*, Moscow 1918, p.40).

At the same session, Ia.M.Sverdlov was chosen as chairman of the *VTsIK*.

184. The resolution on the financial means to put the food supply right was introduced at a *VTsIK* session on the same day, November 8 [21] 1917, after a report by the Commissar of Finance V.R.Menzhinsky about sabotage by senior officials in the Ministry of Finance and the State Bank. The resolution adopted by the *VTsIK* was published under the title 'On sabotage' in *Pravda* No.185, November 10 [23] 1917.

The last paragraph of these CC minutes and the note about the *VTsIK* unanimously approving the resolution on financial means and the newspapers publishing it was added in pencil in Ia.M.Sverdlov's handwriting, as can be seen from the original of the minutes.

185. This refers to the 'Decree on the arrest of the leaders of the civil war against the revolution' proposed by Lenin and approved by the Council of People's Commissars on November 28 [December 11] 1917, the evening before this session of the Party CC. The decree, together with a governmental announcement issued by the *Sovnarkom* 'To all the workers and the exploited' declaring the Kadets enemies of the people, was published in *Izvestiia TsIK* No.239, November 29 [December 12] 1917 (see attached to the minutes, pp.164-166).

This proposal by Sverdlov, chairman of the *VTsIK*, at the CC session apparently also raised the question of whether *sovnarkom's* decree on the Kadets should also be sanctioned by the All-Russian Central Executive Committee.

The need for the decree to be sanctioned came about because the Left SR members of the *VTsIK* made protests against it. The decree on the Kadets issued by the Council of People's Commissars was discussed at a session of the *VTsIK* on December 1 [14]. Lenin made a speech at this session explaining the need for the measures taken to combat the Kadet counter-revolution, which had tried to use the convocation of the Constituent Assembly to launch an armed offensive against the Soviets. Lenin stressed that the 'Kadet Central Committee is the political head-quarters of the bourgeois class' (see *Sochineniia*, 4th ed., vol.26, p.316). The *VTsIK* passed a resolution, 'The decree concerning the Kadet Party', written by Lenin:

'After hearing representatives of the Council of Peoples' Com-missars explain the decree declaring the Kadets to be a Party of enemies of the people and ordering the arrest of members of the Party's governing bodies and surveillance over the Party as a whole by the Soviets, the *TsIK* confirms the need for a very determined fight against the bour-geois counter-revolution led by the Kadet Party, which has started a bitter civil war aimed at the very foundations of the workers' and peas-ants' revolution.

'The *TsIK* assures the Council of People's Commissars of its continued support for this course and rejects the protests made by politi-cal groups whose vacillations are undermining the dictatorship of the proletariat and the poor peasants' (see *ibid*, p.319).

The Left SRs continued to play the role of protectors of the Kadet Party later, too. Thus, at the *VTsIK* session of December 22 1917 [January 4 1918], the Left SR group moved a resolution demanding the cancellation of measures being taken with regard to the leaders of the Kadet counter-revolution in accordance with the *Sovnarkom's* decree. This SR resolution was rejected by the *VTsIK*.

186.   This refers to the 'All-Russian commission for matters concerning the Constituent Assembly elections' which was used by the bourgeois and landowner counter-revolution in the struggle against Soviet power. This commission had already been created before the October socialist revo-lution and consisted mostly of Kadets, with some SRs and Mensheviks, too. To ensure that all the preparatory work for convening the Constitu-ent Assembly was carried out properly, the Council of People's Commis-sars appointed Uritsky as Commissar of the Commission on November 23 [December 6] 1917, and also directed other workers to its apparatus. Later, *Sovnarkom* passed a special decision establishing the procedure for calling the Constituent Assembly. This decision said:

'1. The first session of the Constituent Assembly assembles at the invitation of the Commissar presiding over the All-Russian Commission for Matters Concerning the Constituent Assembly Elections when more than four hundred members of the Constituent Assembly are present in Petrograd.

'2. The session is opened by an official authorised by the Council of People's Commissars when no fewer than four hundred members of the Constituent Assembly are present in the hall'. (see *Izvestiia TsIK* No.237, November 27 [December 10] 1917).

Members of the old commission refused to recognise the Commissar appointed by the Soviet government, completely sabotaging *Sovnarkom*'s measures to prepare for the convocation of the Constituent Assembly. Counter-revolutionary elements, helped by the old membership of the commission, intended to declare the Constituent Assembly open on their own initiative, with any number of Deputies. An attempt of this sort was made on November 28 [December 11]. An anti-Soviet demonstration was organised at the same time. The Kadets, SRs and Mensheviks intended to accomplish an armed insurrection on that day and overthrow Soviet rule. Thanks to measures taken by the Party CC and the Council of People's Commissars, the plans of the counter-revolution were foiled.

The All-Russian Commission for matters concerning the Constituent Assembly elections was dissolved on November 29 [December 12]. A commissariat set up by the *Sovnarkom* took over the direction of everything to do with calling the Constituent Assembly.

187. By insisting on postponing the struggle with the Kadets until the opening of the Constituent Assembly and creating a 'revolutionary convention' out of it, Bukharin was essentially proposing the non-implementation of the decree on the Kadet Party approved by the *Sovnarkom* on November 28 [December 11] and of other measures to combat the counter-revolution which had begun an open armed attack against Soviet rule under the slogan 'all power to the Constituent Assembly'. In doing so, Bukharin misrepresented the facts about the composition of the Constituent Assembly. The elections to the Constituent Assembly, as is well-known, were held according to old lists compiled before the October socialist revolution and the election results did not reflect the will of the working masses. In spite of the fact that in industrial regions and the largest proletarian centres, the Bolshevik Party received 50 per cent and more of the votes cast, the result overall was that the Bolsheviks received 25 per cent of the votes, the SR and Menshevik bloc – 62 per cent, the Kadets – 13 per cent (see V.I.Lenin. 'The elections to the Constituent

Assembly and the dictatorship of the proletariat'. *Sochineniia*, 4th ed., vol.30, pp.230-233). As a result, the Bolsheviks, even with the Left SRs, had fewer than half the seats in the Constituent Assembly.

One could not have guessed from the note that Lenin's wish to postpone the elections to the Constituent Assembly was overruled by a majority of the Central Committee whose main spokesman on the subject was Sverdlov. For months prior to the October Revolution, Lenin put forward again and again the demand for the immediate convocation of the Constituent Assembly. The decree of October 26 [November 8], which established the Council of People's Commissars, described it as a 'provisional workers' and peasants' government' exercising authority 'until the convocation of the Constituent Assembly'. The decree on land opened with a statement that 'the land question in all its magnitude can be settled only by the nationwide Constituent Assembly'. However, when the results of the elections to the Constituent Assembly in December 1917 and January 1918 showed that the Bolsheviks made up only a quarter of the body of the Assembly, it became clear that the Constituent Assembly would serve as a rallying point for opposition to the Soviet regime. Now Lenin changed his tack, and on December 13 [December 26] he published 'Theses on the Constituent Assembly' which were a declaration of war on this Assembly. Alas, not all Bolshevik leaders were as quick to change their tactics and attitudes to the Constituent Assembly. Zinoviev, Riazanov and Lozovsky were for preservation of this institution. Bukharin proposed the expulsion of the Kadets while letting the Left wing of the Assembly continue to function.

Lenin, writing in retrospect in 1920, stated that the participation of the Bolsheviks in the elections to the Constituent Assembly had helped to 'prove to the backward masses why such parliaments deserve to be broken up.' (Sochineniia, vol.25, p.202).

188. As can be seen from these minutes, Trotsky took the same position as Bukharin about creating a 'convention' out of the Constituent Assembly. Trotsky spoke against the resolution by the Council of People's Commissars about opening the Constituent Assembly when not less than 400 of its members were present in Petrograd and suggested speeding up the convocation of the Constituent Assembly by summoning all the delegates by telegraph.

189. The evening edition of *Pravda* was published in Petrograd as an

organ of the Party CC from November 2 [15] 1917 to March 20 1918. *Krasnaia gazeta* came out from January 25 1918 to February 28 1939 and was the organ of the Leningrad City Committee of the *VKP(b)* and the Leningrad Soviet. On March 1 1939, *Krasnaia gazeta* merged with *Leningradskaia Pravda*.

190. The text of the statement by Rykov, Kamenev, Miliutin and Nogin, who had left the CC on November 4 [17] 1917, asking to be taken back into the Party CC has not been found.

191. The CC's reply, written by Lenin to the statement made by Rykov, Kamenev, Miliutin and Nogin has not come to light. Subsequent Central Committee minutes contain no reference to the return to the CC of the people who issued the statement.

192. The provisional bureau of the group, which included Kamenev, Rykov, Riazanov, Larin, Miliutin and Nogin, came out against the CC line on the issue of the Constituent Assembly. The Right capitulators regarded the convocation of the Constituent Assembly as the final stage of the revolution and suggested that control over its convocation be renounced, along with other measures taken by the Party CC and the *Sovnarkom* while preparing for its opening. The group's bureau carried a decision at one of its sessions to demand that a Party congress or conference be called 'to clarify' the question of the attitude to take to the Constituent Assembly. The group's bureau tried to use the Bolshevik group in the Constituent Assembly in their struggle against the CC.

193. The following draft resolution written by Lenin and dealing with the removal of the provisional bureau of the Bolshevik group in the Constituent Assembly has been preserved:

'Taking note of the fact that the provisional bureau of the social-democratic Bolshevik group in the Constituent Assembly has neglected its chief task, to work out a statement of principles on our Party's attitude to the Constituent Assembly;

That numerous statements, proposals and votes on a series of separate occasions have shown that the attitude of the majority of (or all?) the members of the provisional bureau towards the Constituent Assembly is not in the least social-democratic and displays a bourgeois-democratic point of view which ignores the real conditions of the class struggle and the civil war;

The group resolves to remove the provisional bureau and elect a new one' (see *Sochineniia*, 4th ed., vol.26, p.339).

194. Implementing the decision of this CC session, Lenin wrote 'Theses on the Constituent Assembly'. The Bolshevik group in the Constituent Assembly discussed Lenin's theses on December 12 [25] 1917. After the members of the Bolshevik group had discussed them at length, Lenin's theses were approved unanimously. The next day, December 13 [26], the 'Theses on the Constituent Assembly' were published in the newspaper *Pravda* No.213 (see V.I.Lenin. *Sochineniia*, 4th ed., vol.26, pp. 340-344).

195. This refers to the second point in the CC resolution on the question of the Constituent Assembly adopted at the session of November 29 [December 12] 1917 (see p.162).

196. *Petrogradskaia pravda* is a daily newspaper; it came out first on April 2 1918 as the organ of the Central and Petrograd Committees of the *RKP(b)*. After June 1918, *Petrogradskaia pravda* became the organ of the Central Committee, the Northern Regional and City Committees of the *RKP(b)*. Later, the newspaper was published as the organ of the North-West Regional Bureau of the CC, the Party committee of Petrograd province, the provincial trade union council and the regional economic conference. In January 30 1924, the newspaper was renamed *Leningradskaia pravda*. It now comes out as the organ of the Leningrad Regional and City Committees of the CPSU and of the regional and City Soviets of Workers' Deputies .

197. The first All-Russian Congress of Trade Unions took place on January 7-14 [20-27] 1918 in Petrograd. The Congress was attended by 416 voting delegates, divided into 273 Bolsheviks, 66 Mensheviks, 21 Left SRs, 10 Right SRs, 6 Maximalists, 6 Anarcho-Syndicalists and 34 nonparty delegates. Reports heard and discussed by the Congress were: accounting by the All-Russian Central Council of Trade Unions; the current situation and the tasks of the trade unions; the regulation of industry and workers' control and other questions.

When fundamental issues were discussed by the Congress, there was sharp conflict between the Bolsheviks and the Mensheviks and SRs, who advocated the 'independence' of the trade union movement from political parties. The Congress approved the resolution, 'The tasks of the trade union movement' moved by the Bolshevik group, and a statute for the All-Russian Central Council of Trade Unions. An election was held for the All-Russian Central Council of Trade Unions.

198. An armistice agreement was concluded on December 2 [15] 1917 between the Soviet government and the alliance of the four powers (Germany, Austro-Hungary, Bulgaria and Turkey). Peace negotiations began at Brest-Litovsk on December 9 [22]. At the very first session of the conference, the Soviet delegation proposed the following conditions as the basis for peace negotiations: 1. territories seized during the war not to be incorporated under duress; forces occupying these territories to leave them very shortly; 2. political independence to be restored to nations deprived of it during the war; 3. national groups which did not enjoy political independence before the war to be guaranteed the opportunity to decide by referendum whether to belong to one state or another, or to be an independent state; 4. the rights of national minorities to be protected by a special law; 5. no reparations of any kind to be permitted and reparations already exacted to be returned; losses of private individuals to be compensated out of a special fund formed by proportional payments by the belligerent states; 6. questions concerning colonies must be decided in accordance with the first four points of the proposals put forward.

The delegation from the Austro-German bloc found itself in a very difficult position. To refuse to accept the Russian demands would mean that the annexationist, imperialist aims of the war would be exposed in front of the whole world. At the session of the peace conference on December 12 [25] 1917, the German delegation announced that the governments of the alliance powers were agreeing to the start of peace negotiations on the conditions proposed by the Soviet delegation. At the sessions of the political commission on December 14 and 15 [27 and 28], however, the German representatives read out their draft of an annexationist peace treaty. The Soviet delegation broke off negotiations and left for Petrograd.

At the first session of the second stage of the peace negotiations on December 27 1917 [January 9 1918], Kuehlmann, the head of the German delegation, stated that the conditions for the peace proposed by the Soviet delegation on December 9 [22] and recognised in principle by the four governments of the alliance, were no longer in force because the governments of the Entente countries had refused to take part in the negotiations.

Taking advantage of Soviet Russia's grim position and the support of representatives from the Central Ukrainian Rada, whose authority was recognised by Trotsky, the head of the Soviet delegation, the German imperialists cast aside their peace-loving facade and went over to a policy of threats and ultimatums. The Soviet delegation was presented with the demand to recognise Poland, Lithuania, part of Latvia, Estonia and Belorussia as German territory, an area of more than 150,000 square kilometres. The Russian delegation was informed that the acceptance of these demands was an absolutely necessary condition for the conclusion of a peace.

In spite of an express directive from the Party CC and the Soviet government to conclude a peace, Trotsky stated at a session of the political commission on January 28 [February 10] 1918 that Soviet Russia was not signing the peace, was halting the war and demobilising the army. Trotsky's defiance of the instructions from the Party and the Soviet government played into the hands of the German imperialists, who broke off negotiations and began to prepare for an attack on the Russian front. Germany, having grossly violated the conditions of the armistice agreement, informed the Soviet delegation on February 16 that as from noon on February 18 Germany considered itself in a state of war with Russia. The protest by the Soviet government on February 17 that the Germans had breached the armistice conditions received no reply from the German imperialists. On February 18, German forces went into the attack along the whole front.

The war and the peace were considered at the Central Committee sessions of January 11 [24], January 19 [February 1], January 21 [February 3], February 18, 22, 23, and 24 1918. There was no consensus in the CC on the subject of the war and the peace. CC members V.I.Lenin, I.V.Stalin, Ia.M.Sverdlov and others, putting the interests of the development and consolidation of the socialist revolution first, considered it necessary to sign a peace with Germany. They were counterweighed by: Trotsky, advocating the position of 'neither war nor peace' and a group of 'Left' supporters of a revolutionary war – Bukharin, Lomov and others, who did everything they could to drag out and wreck the conclusion of a peace treaty. At the CC session of February 23, V.I.Lenin pressed the question of accepting the new conditions for a peace treaty, which were more severe for Russia. V.I.Lenin's proposal was adopted by a majority of votes and at the CC session of February 24 the composition of the peace delegation was confirmed; it left for Brest-Litovsk on the very same day. Peace negotiations were resumed on March 1; on March 3

1918, the last session of the peace conference was held. The peace treaty was signed.

Lenin's suggested tactics in the peace negotiations in Brest-Litovsk proved in practice to be correct. This, however, does not mean to say that Trotsky's position was bound to be wrong at the time. It was on the cards that the tactic suggested by Trotsky of 'neither war nor peace' would work. From the memoirs of Ludendorff and various statements made by German representatives at Brest-Litovsk, it is clear that the Austrian and German leaders hesitated before launching their offensive against Russia. Chancellor von Hertling and Baron von Kuehlmann had stated their opinion that the situation on the home front did not allow of an offensive. But at the end of the discussion, the generals – Hindenburg and Ludendorff – carried the day, thanks to the Kaiser's backing.

A testimonial from the other side of the German front, from Karl Liebknecht, writing from prison, also gives some support to Trotsky's tactics at Brest-Litovsk: 'In no sense can it be said that the present solution of the problem is not as favourable for future development as a surrender at Brest-Litovsk would have been at the beginning of February. Quite the contrary. A surrender like that would have thrown the worst light on all preceding resistance and would have made the subsequent submission to force appear as 'vis haud ingrata'. The cynicism that cries to heaven and the brutal character of the ultimate German action have driven all suspicions into the background.' 'The result of Brest-Litovsk is not nil, even if it comes to a peace of forced capitulation. Thanks to the Russian delegates, Brest-Litovsk has become a revolutionary tribunal whose decrees are heard far and wide. It has brought about the exposé of the Central Powers; it has exposed German avidity, its cunning lies and hypocrisy. It has passed an annihilating verdict upon the peace policy of the German [Social Democratic] majority – a policy which is not so much a pious hypocrisy as it is cynicism. It has proved powerful enough to bring forth numerous mass movements in various countries.' (Karl Liebknecht, Politische Aufzeichnungen, aus seinem Nachlass, Verlag Die Aktion, 1921, page 51.)

In the event, Lenin's tactics proved right, but the differences between him and Trotsky at Brest-Litovsk were purely tactical. That Lenin understood it in this way is clear from his address to the Seventh Congress of the Party (March 8 1918), when he said: 'Now I must say something about comrade Trotsky's position. There are two aspects to his activities; when he began the negotiations at Brest and made splendid use of them for agitation, we all agreed with comrade Trotsky ... Trotsky's tactics were correct as long as they were aimed at delaying matters; they became incorrect when it was announced that the state of war had been terminated but peace had not been concluded. I proposed quite definitely that peace be concluded. We could not have got anything better than the Brest peace.' (Lenin, Collected Works, vol. 27, p.113).

The note speaks about 'Trotsky's recognition of the authority of the Ukrainian Rada.' Actually the Bolshevik government as a whole recognised the Rada, and E.H.Carr explained 'the reluctant recognition of the credentials of the Rada's delegation at the peace conference of Brest-Litovsk, which could not have been withheld without throwing doubt on the sincerity of Bolshevik protestations of devotion to the cause of national self-determination.' (E.H.Carr, The Bolshevik Revolution, vol.I, London, 1950, pp.297-8).

The above remark refers also to notes 199 and 216.

199. This refers to the theses V.I.Lenin presented at a meeting of prominent Party workers in Petrograd on January 8 [21] 1918. V.I.Lenin spoke in favour of concluding a peace with Germany and her allies immediately. The majority of the people taking part in the conference, however, supported a revolutionary war. This was a deeply mistaken policy which would have brought the young Soviet Russia, as yet without an army, into a war with Germany. The minutes of the conference have not been found. V.I.Lenin's motion that it was necessary to sign a peace treaty was adopted by the Central Committee at its session of February 23 1918 (for Lenin's theses and a postcript to them, see Sochineniia, 4th ed., vol.26, pp.401-410).

200. V.I.Lenin evidently has in view the unsigned article printed in the newspaper Novaia zhizn' No.7, January 11 [24] 1918 under the heading 'The Bolsheviks and the German social-democrats'.

201. During the peace negotiations in Brest-Litovsk, Germany's representatives tried to use the slogan of the right of nations to self-determina-

tion proclaimed by the Soviet government exclusively for their own imperialist ends. Germany's representatives read out a draft peace treaty at a meeting of the political commission on December 14 [27] 1917, demanding that Poland, Lithuania, Courland and parts of Estonia and Latvia be detached from Russia and their explanation was that their peoples desired full state independence. This was a manoeuvre. The nationality policy of the Soviet government was cited because they wanted a cover for the German occupation of Poland and the Baltic region.

202. This is an allusion to the disagreements between the Bolsheviks and the *Nashe slovo* group headed by Trotsky in 1915-1916. Trotsky and his supporters denied Lenin's theory that it was possible for the socialist revolution to be successful in a few countries first or even in one country taken on its own. They saw the Russian revolution as dependent on the success of proletarian revolution in other capitalist countries and reproached Lenin for national exclusiveness.

Until Lenin's death, no one in the Bolshevik Party suggested that Russia could build socialism by her own unaided efforts. Lenin himself repeatedly emphasised the opposite. 'The Russian revolution,' he wrote on June 4 1918, '... was due not to the special merits of the Russian proletariat, but to the course of historic events, and this proletariat was placed temporarily in the leading position by the will of history and for a time made the vanguard of the world revolution ...' (Lenin, Sochineniia, 4th ed., vol.27, p. 387).

'We always staked our play upon an international revolution and this was unconditionally right ... we always emphasised ... the fact that in one country it is impossible to accomplish such a work as a socialist revolution ...' (November 6 1920. Lenin, Sochineniia, 3rd ed., vol.25, pp.473-4. Emphasis added. The emphasised sentence is struck out of the fourth edition of Lenin's Sochineniia. See Volume 31, p.370).

Even after Lenin's death, Stalin, who later propounded the idea of 'socialism in one country', said: '... But to overthrow the power of the bourgeoisie and establish that of the proletariat in a single country is still not to assure the complete victory of socialism. The chief task, the organisation of socialist production, is still to be accomplished. Can we succeed and secure the definitive victory of socialism in one country without the combined efforts of the proletarians of several advanced countries? Most certainly not. The efforts of a single country are enough to overthrow the bourgeoisie: this is what the history of our revolution proves. But for the definitive triumph of socialism, the organisation of socialist production, the efforts of one country alone are not enough, particularly of an essentially rural country like Russia; the efforts of the proletarians of several advanced countries are needed . . .' (J.V.Stalin, The Theory and Practice of Leninism, *published by the Communist Party of Great Britain, London, 1925, pp.45-6.) In the second Russian edition of this book, which appeared in December 1924, the above section is omitted, and instead one reads: 'Having consolidated its power, and taking the lead of the peasantry, the proletariat of the victorious country can and must build a socialist society . . . Such in general are the characteristic features of the Leninist theory of the proletarian revolution.'* (I.V.Stalin, Sochineniia, *vol.6, pp.107-8; also* J.V.Stalin, Problems of Leninism, *pp.27-8).*

203. While the Party was battling for the Brest peace, the Petersburg Committee put its weight against Lenin's peace policy, advocating a revolutionary war against German imperialism, demanding a halt to the peace negotiations and expressing no confidence in the Central Committee's political line.

For more detail on the Petersburg Committee's attitude to the issues of war and peace, see the 'Statement from the Executive Commission of the Petersburg Committee to the CC' and 'Theses by the Petersburg Committee of the RSDLP(b) on the current situation and the war' on pp.190-192 of this edition. See also the collection *Pervyi legal'nyi Peterburgskii komitet bol'shevikov v 1917 godu, GIZ,* 1927, pp.379-386.

204. Smilga's statement has not been found.

205. Between the CC RSDLP(b) sessions of January 11 and 19 [January 24 and February 1] 1918, a joint meeting of the Central Committees of the Bolsheviks and the Left SRs was held on the question of the war and the peace. The minutes of the meeting have not been found. The following report on its work in the newspaper *Sotsial-demokrat* (Moscow) No.9, January 14 [27] 1918 has been preserved:

January 13

WAR OR PEACE

Late yesterday evening, a joint session of the Central Committees of the Bolsheviks and the Left SRs was held on the question of the war and the peace. One section of those present put forward the slogan 'do not fight the war, do not sign a peace'. The champions of this slogan were moved by the view that the complete disorganisation on the front makes it impossible to continue the war any longer; and the Germans, too, for the very same reason, are in no position to fight an offensive war on our front. But if, contrary to all expectations, the Germans start to attack, it will produce a surge of patriotism not only among the Russian workers and soldiers but among the working classes of Western Europe. A considerable majority at the meeting were of the opinion that Russia cannot conduct a war of any kind now, not even a revolutionary war.

Some members of the Central Executive Committee, Left SRs and Bolsheviks, took the opposite point of view and, asserting that the German peace conditions were unacceptable, insisted on the declaration of a holy revolutionary war. Mstislavsky spoke for the view taken by this group. It was resolved by a majority of votes to propose the formula: 'do not fight the war, do not sign a peace' to the Congress of Soviets for consideration.

206. The Moscow Regional Bureau of the RSDLP(b), temporarily led by 'Left Communists', passed a resolution on December 28 1917 [January 10 1918] demanding a halt to the peace negotiations and continuation of the war with Germany. On January 15 [28], a group of 'Left Communists' headed by Bukharin and Lomov (Oppokov) presented a statement to the Central Committee asking for a Party conference to be called immediately to resolve the peace issue. V.I.Lenin spoke against this proposal at the CC session of January 19 [February 1] 1918. He did not want a conference called but a congress because he considered that only a congress had the power to express the will of the whole Party.

After the Central Committee accepted the new conditions of peace with Germany at its session of February 23 (see p.233), the inner membership of the Moscow Regional Bureau met on February 24 and passed a resolution (see p.195) declaring lack of confidence in the Central Committee and refusing to submit to CC decisions associated with implementing the conditions of the peace treaty.

In his article 'Strange and monstrous', V.I.Lenin sharply condemned the Moscow Regional Bureau's policy on the issues of the war and the peace (see *Sochineniia*, 4th ed., vol.27, pp.46-53). For more on the Moscow Regional Bureau's position on the question of the war and the peace, see also p.193.

207.   The Third All-Russian Congress of Soviets of Workers', Soldiers'
and Peasants' Deputies took place in Petrograd between January 10 and
18 [23 and 31] 1918. 317 Soviets and 110 army corps and division committees were represented at the Congress.

On January 13 [26] 1918, the Third All-Russian Congress of
Soviets of Peasants' Deputies opened, attended by representatives from
more than 250 peasant Soviets. The very first session of the Congress took
a unanimous decision to join with the Congress of Soviets of Workers'
and Soldiers' Deputies. The Congress continued its further work as a
Congress of Soviets of Workers', Soldiers' and Peasants' Deputies. While
the Congress was at work, the number of delegates grew steadily and by
the end of the Congress, 1587 delegates were present with the right to
vote.

Questions discussed by the Third Congress of Soviets were: the
activity of the *VTsIK* – report by Ia.M.Sverdlov; the activity of the
Sovnarkom – report by V.I.Lenin; the nationality question – report by
I.V.Stalin; the war and the peace, and other questions. On a motion by
the Bolshevik group, the Third All-Russian Congress of Soviets approved
the Soviet government's policy and expressed full confidence in it. On
the peace question, the Congress gave unlimited authority to the *Sovnarkom* in the matter of concluding a peace.

208.   This refers to the Seventh Congress of the *RKP(b)* which was
held in Petrograd on March 6-8 1918. The Congress was attended by 46
delegates with a deliberative vote and 58 with a consultative vote, representing 170,000 Party members. At the time the Congress was convened,
Party membership was about 300,000. A number of organisations did not
manage to send delegates because the Congress was called so hastily and
some had no chance to do so because of the temporary occupation of
some regions of Soviet Russia by the Germans.

The Seventh Party Congress was a special one called to decide
the peace question finally. The report on the war and the peace was
made by V.I.Lenin. Trotskyists and 'Left Communists' presented their
theses, putting up Bukharin to report. The Congress passed the resolution
on the peace proposed by V.I.Lenin by 30 votes to 12 with 4 abstaining.
The Congress recognised the necessity of confirming the peace treaty
signed by the Soviet government and proposed its ratification to the Congress of Soviets assembling in the next few days.

The Fourth Special All-Russian Congress of Soviets held on
March 14-16 1918 ratified the peace treaty.

209.   The *VTsIK* delegation abroad to establish close ties between

Soviet Russia and Left internationalists in European countries and to make preparations for the convocation of an international socialist conference on the subject of the struggle for peace was confirmed by the *VTsIK* at its session on February 2 [15] 1918. A.M.Kollontai and Ia.A. Berzin were the Bolshevik members of the delegation. The conference did not take place.

210.   Shlichter disagreed with the position taken by the *Sovnarkom* in using the old food specialists in the organs dealing with food supply. In February 1918, he was replaced as People's Commissar for the Food Supply by A.D.Tsiurupa.

211.   The All-Russian Special Railway Congress took place on January 5-30 [January 18-February 12] 1918. The Congress recognised all the decrees of Soviet rule, drew up a new wages scale for railway workers and employees and passed a statute for the administration of the railways. The Congress elected the All-Russian Executive Committee of Railwaymen – *Vikzhedor*. The overwhelming majority within *Vikzhedor* favoured the Bolsheviks (37 Bolsheviks, 17 from the Left SR group, 4 from the group of the social-democratic Left Internationalists).

By decision of the Congress and agreement with the *VTsIK*, *Vikzhedor* had the right to elect a collegium from its midst to administer the Russian network of railways. The Bolshevik A.G.Rogov initially headed the collegium and then V.I.Nevsky was appointed People's Commissar for Means of Communication.

212.   The meeting of the Central Committee held on January 21 [February 3] 1918 with spokesmen for different viewpoints was devoted to a single subject – the conclusion of a peace treaty with Germany. The minutes of the session have not been found.

The second phase of the peace negotiations had begun at Brest-Litovsk on December 27 1917 [January 9 1918]. The delegation from the Austro-German bloc was dragging out the negotiations with Russia and trying to conclude a separate peace to its advantage with the Ukrainian Rada so that it could then present an ultimatum to the Soviet delegation to accept the one-sided peace conditions it proposed immediately. The day of this meeting – January 21 [February 3] – the German delegation broke off the peace negotiations and its representatives left for Berlin to determine the line to be taken towards Russia in the last stage of the negotiations.

On January 27 [February 9], Germany and the Central Rada

signed a treaty on the occupation of the Ukraine by Austro-German forces and on the same day the Austro-German imperialist bloc presented an ultimatum to the Soviet republic.

213. V.I.Lenin raised the question of the need to revise the Party programme in the 'April theses' in 1917. The Seventh (April) Conference of the RSDLP(b), after examining this question, passed a decision that the programme needed to be revised and instructed the Central Committee to compose a draft programme within two months for confirmation at the next Party congress. Soon after the Conference, a brochure 'Materials for the revision of the Party programme' was published under the editorship and with a foreword by V.I.Lenin (see *Sochineniia*, 4th ed., vol.24, pp.417-442). The Sixth Congress of the RSDLP(b) (July-August 1917) did not settle the matter of the programme finally but confirmed the decision of the April Conference and charged the CC with organising a wide discussion on questions relevant to the programme.

The revision of the programme was discussed more than once at sessions of the CC RSDLP(b). On October 5 [18] 1917, a commission headed by V.I.Lenin was created by decision of the Central Committee. The commission's membership was reviewed at the session of January 24 [February 6] 1918. A new commission under Lenin's direction was entrusted to draw up the Party programme.

The subject of the programme came up again at the Seventh Party Congress (March 1918). A rough copy of a draft programme written by Lenin was distributed to delegates as material for discussion. The Seventh Party Congress did not, however, discuss the programme in detail. The Congress decided to set up a commission consisting of V.I. Lenin, I.V.Stalin and others to prepare a conclusive draft Party programme.

The Party programme was adopted at the Eighth Party Congress held in March 1919.

The Seventh Party Congress (March 1918) elected a programme commission to revise the Party programme: Lenin (37 votes), Trotsky (37 votes), Bukharin (36), Smirnov (32), Zinoviev (30), Sokolnikov (25), Stalin (21) (Sed'moi s'ezd rossiiskoi kommunisticheskoi partii, *Moscow-Petrograd, 1923, pp.185-6).

214. This session of the Central Committee met after the German military command had stated on February 16 1918 that the armistice was to end and that the Austro-German forces were to resume military opera-

tions against Russia from 12 noon on February 18. The conditions of the armistice agreement concluded on December 2 [15] 1917 in Brest-Litovsk provided that the parties to the agreement were obliged to give warning of any abrogation of the agreement to the opposing sides seven days before the start of war. By declaring a state of war in two days, the German command flagrantly and treacherously violated one of the armistice conditions. On February 18, forces of the Austro-German bloc began to invade the territory of the Soviet republic.

215. The Central Committee session was held in the evening of the same day (see p.206).

216. Having violated the armistice agreement adopted on December 2 [15] 1917, the German forces began to attack Soviet Russia on all fronts during the day of February 18 1918. After receiving news that Dvinsk had been attacked and occupied by the Germans, the Party Central Committee met again in the evening. Trotsky, wanting to prevent a peace being concluded whatever happened, proposed not to demand an armistice but to ask Berlin and Vienna what demands they were making of the Soviet republic. In practice, this proposal clearly meant a delay, allowing the Germans to advance into the heart of Russia.

At the Central Committee session, V.I.Lenin very emphatically put the point that peace negotiations should be resumed and a peace treaty with Germany signed. I.V.Stalin, Ia.M.Sverdlov and other CC members supported V.I.Lenin. The Central Committee approved the decision to send the Soviet government's agreement to conclude a peace treaty to the German government.

217. This refers to the result of the vote when the issue of the peace was considered at the sessions of the CC RSDLP(b) on January 11 [24] and February 17 1918. At the first session, only two CC members voted for a revolutionary war, against – 11 (see p.179); at the second session, no one voted for a revolutionary war; Bukharin, Lomov and Ioffe refused to vote (see p.202).

218. The Ukraine was represented at the peace negotiations in Brest-Litovsk by a delegation from the bourgeois-nationalist Ukrainian Central Rada, which shamefully betrayed the national interests of the people, the cause of the revolution and a democratic peace. At the session of the peace conference on December 28 1917 [January 10 1918], the leader of

the Ukrainian SRs, Golubovich, read out a note from the Central Rada stating that it did not recognise the Soviet government and had decided to take part in the negotiations on an equal footing with other powers.

Trotsky, then spokesman for the Russian delegation in Brest, stated that it was agreed to regard the Central Rada representatives as an independent delegation. In this way, Trotsky gave support to the Ukrainian bourgeois nationalists and freed the hands of the imperialists in the Austro-German bloc to struggle further against the Soviet peace conditions.

See my comment on note 198 – T.C.

219. The draft wireless message to the government of the German empire was written straight away by V.I.Lenin (see *Sochineniia*, 4th ed., vol.26, p.479). The radiogram was sent in the name of the Council of People's Commissars to the German command on the night of February 18 to 19 1918. In the message, the Soviet government made a protest against Germany's deceitful offensive and stated that the Soviet government was forced, in the situation that had arisen, to sign a peace on the terms presented by the German government. To secure for themselves the most profitable peace conditions, the Germans continued the attack and occupied a considerable portion of the territory of Soviet Russia.

220. This refers to the joint session of the CC RSDLP(b) and the CC of the Left SRs, where the peace question was discussed. The minute notes of this session have not been found. The newspaper *Sotsial-demokrat* (Moscow) No.28, February 20 1918, published a report on the session, which we reproduce in full:

WAR OR PEACE

During the night, there was a session of the Central Committee of the Bolsheviks and the Central Committee of the Left SRs. To begin with, the sessions were held separately and then a joint session was organised. Two points of view were articulated: one said that Russia was unable to fight and that a peace had to be signed on the conditions dictated to us, but this current of thought turned out to be in the minority.

The majority took the view that the Russian revolution would withstand this new test; it was decided to resist as long as possible.

221. The German government's reply to the Soviet government's note of February 19 1918 was received in Petrograd on February 23 at ten-thirty in the morning. The new peace terms presented to Russia by the

German empire were even more burdensome than the previous terms Trotsky rejected at Brest-Litovsk on January 28 [February 10] 1918.

According to the new terms, Soviet Russia lost all the Baltic territory, part of Belorussia and it was proposed that the towns of Kars, Batum and Ardagan be surrendered to Turkey. Under the conditions of the ultimatum, Russia would have to completely demobilise the army immediately, withdraw forces from Finland and the Ukraine and conclude peace with the Ukrainian People's Republic, i.e. with the bourgeois-nationalist Central Rada. The German government proposed that the terms it had set out be adopted within 48 hours, that plenipotentiaries be dispatched immediately to Brest-Litovsk and that a peace be signed in three days. About the acceptance of these peace terms, V.I.Lenin wrote: 'Let everyone know: he who is against an immediate peace, even though it is extremely severe, is endangering Soviet power' (See *Sochineniia*, 4th ed., vol.27, p.22).

222. This refers to the session of the CC RSDLP(b) on February 22 1918 where the question of acquiring weapons and food from the Entente powers to help with defence against the German imperialists was discussed. (CC session, see pp.212-215).

223. The *VTsIK* session took place in the night of February 24 1918. The *VTsIK* heard and considered a report by V.I.Lenin on the German conditions for a peace treaty. The signature of a peace was opposed by the Mensheviks, the Right and Left SRs and the anarchist-communists. The resolution moved by the Bolsheviks approving the signature of a peace treaty was adopted by 116 votes against 85, with 26 abstaining. The majority of 'Left Communists' took no part in the voting.

The decision to accept the peace terms was transmitted to the German government on the morning of February 24 1918.

224. A delegation consisting of G.Ia.Sokolnikov, G.I.Petrovsky, G.V. Chicherin and L.M.Karakhan with full powers to sign a peace treaty left for Brest-Litovsk on February 24 1918. The session of the peace conference began on March 1 and the peace treaty was signed on March 3 1918.

225. *Nash vek* was one of the titles of the newspaper *Rech'*, the central organ of the Kadets. The results of the voting in the CC are given in issue No.33 (57), February 24 1918.

226. Trotsky's written statement has not been found. For Trotsky's oral statement at the CC session of February 22 1918, see p.214 of the present edition.

227. Lenin has in mind the inquiry telegraphed to all provincial and district Soviets and all provincial, district and *volost* land committees on their attitude to the new peace terms. The enquiry was sent by the *Sovnarkom* and also by the *VTsIK* on February 25 1918 as a result of a resolution by the CC RSDLP(b) proposed by Lenin and adopted on February 23 1918. Replies to the inquiry already began to arrive on the following day; they were published in *Izvestiia VTsIK* up to March 9. The replies to the questionnaire showed that the majority of the local Soviets supported the position that it was necessary to sign a peace.

228. The bulletins were published by the CC secretariat after a decision by the CC RSDLP(b). Ia.M.Sverdlov was in overall charge. Comrades E.D.Stasova, K.T.Novgorodtseva and G.K.Sukhanova were directly involved in publishing them. The bulletins were distributed to Party organisations by post and at times passed on by hand. They were very important in informing Party organisations about the progress of the October socialist revolution.

229. *Rumcherod* was the Central Executive Committee of the Soviets of the Rumanian front, the Black Sea fleet and the Odessa region elected in May 1917. The Mensheviks and SRs headed it and pursued a conciliation policy. The majority of *Rumcherod's* members greeted the October socialist revolution with hostility, fought against the Bolshevik organisations and opposed the Bolshevisation of the Soviets.

In the second half of December 1917, a congress of representatives from the Rumanian front, the Soviets of Workers' and Soldiers' Deputies and representatives from the peasants elected a new *Rumcherod* and the Bolsheviks came to lead it.

230. The announcement that power had passed to the Soviets in Moscow and Mogilev on October 29 was not accurate. Power was established in Moscow on November 2 [15] and in Mogilev on November 18 [December 1] 1917. Information about the position in Moscow is given in more detail in the following bulletins.

231. Evidently, a slip in the document. Kerensky advanced on Petrograd with General Krasnov, not Kornilov.

232. The decree on the press was passed on October 27 [November 9] 1917 after the closure of bourgeois newspapers on the day of the revolution. At the *VTsIK* session on November 4 [17], Iu.Larin moved a proposal to abolish this decree. By a majority of votes, the Bolshevik group's proposal approving the closure of the bourgeois newspapers was adopted. The decree played a large part in the struggle against the counter-revolutionary press in the country as a whole.

233. A letter from the Kyshtym Committee of the RSDLP(b) on November 12 [25] 1917 reports that this bulletin No.7 does not correspond with the real position in Cheliabinsk, since there was no fighting in Cheliabinsk at that time. See *Perepiska Sekretariata TsK RSDRP(b) s mestnymi partiinymi organizatsiiami*, Moscow 1957, part 11, p.258.

Index to the Minutes and Documents

Subjects

Index to the Minutes and Documents

Names

Bureaucracy and Revolution in Eastern Europe

Chris Harman

Chris Harman analyses the self-styled 'socialist' societies
established in Eastern Europe after the second world war. He
shows how the post-war division of the world into rival spheres of
influence allowed local Communist Parties to set up monolithic
political systems under Russian protection; how the Parties were
forged into weapons of totalitarian domination by internal purges
and by repressing every competing organisation, especially those
rooted in the working class.

The workers resisted – in East Germany, in Poland, in Hungary,
in Czechoslovakia. Chris Harman shows why and how they resisted
in each case; how they rejected bureaucratic 'planning' and
refused to bear the cost of the regimes' crises.

The book ends with an analysis of the economic reforms, and
shows how they only intensify the contradictions of Eastern
Europe's class societies. There is no reformist road to socialism in
these countries – workers themselves need to take power and
exercise it in their name.

£1.50 paperback   £4.30 hardback

Pluto  Press

Pluto Press, Unit 10 Spencer Court
7 Chalcot Road, London NW1 8LH

Lenin
Volume 1: Building the Party

Tony Cliff

In this first volume of his three-volume study, Cliff traces Lenin's life from birth through political obscurity to prominence as the leader of a mass working class party.

It shows Lenin fighting hard for doctrinal purity against competing organisations; but even harder for the proletarian content of his own organisation. It shows how he learnt from even the most fleeting contact with workers and how he instilled into his organisation the conclusions he drew. Above all it shows Lenin's maturing as a practitioner of revolution in the period before revolution.

The story breaks off in 1914, on the eve of war, when Lenin and the party he created were poised for taking power.

£1.20 paperback   £5.40 hardback

Pluto  Press

**Pluto Press, Unit 10 Spencer Court
7 Chalcot Road, London NW1 8LH**